ADAMS
Streetwise

Hiring
Top Performers

*600 ready-to-ask interview questions
and everything else you need to hire right*

by Bob Adams and Peter Veruki

ADAMS MEDIA CORPORATION
HOLBROOK, MASSACHUSETTS

Published by Adams Media Corporation
260 Center Street, Holbrook, Massachusetts 02343

ISBN: 1-55850-684-5

Printed in the United States of America.

J   I   H   G   F   E   D   C   B

Library of Congress Cataloging-in-Publication Data
Adams, Bob
Adams Streetwise hiring top performers / Bob Adams, Peter Veruki
p.   cm.
ISBN: 1-55850-684-5 (pb)
1. Employees—Recruiting—United States.   2. Employee selection—United States
3. Employment interviewing—United States.
I. Veruki, Peter.   II. Title.
HF5549.5.R44A25   1997
658.3'11—dc21   96-48008
CIP

Inside photos: Photodisc™ Images ©1996, PhotoDisc, Inc.
Cover photo ©1996, Comstock. Cover background photo UPI/Corbis-Bettmann

This publications is designed to provide accurate and authoritative information with regard to the subject matter covered.
It is sold with the understanding that the publisher is not engaged in rendering legal, accounting, or other professional advice.
If legal advice or other expert assistance is required, the services of a competent professional person should be sought.
—From a *Declaration of Principles* jointly adopted by a Committe of the American Bar Association and a Committee of Publishers and Associations.

*This book is available at quantity discounts for bulk purchases. Multi-media versions of this text are available in CD-ROM form for Windows.
For further information, check your local retailer or contact Adams Media at 1-800-872-5627 (in Massachusetts call 781-767-8100).*

Visit our home page at http://www.careercity.com

Book design by Amy C. Thompson

Table of Contents

Table of Contents

Table of Contents

With increasing demands to juggle multiple responsibilities, it is no wonder that today's managers in organizations of all sizes find little time to devote to the hiring process. Yet these very demands are what make hiring top performers a necessity for these managers. All too often, managers simply don't have the time or resources to carefully select top-notch applicants for open positions. In addition, managers can easily overlook the legal aspects of the hiring process, which can present problems for the manager or his company. Even if the manager is hiring only one employee per year, it is imperative that he or she understands all of the ramifications of finding, interviewing and hiring that one employee.

There are two ways to ensure that your company has the very best talent available. First, you can hire average workers and train them to be top performers. While this method can boost employee morale, it is often time-consuming and costly to the point that the company's overall productivity lags behind that of its competitors. The second, and more preferred method, is to hire top performers who can hit the ground running and make your company or division more profitable and productive immediately.

Even if you hire one employee per year, it is imperative that you understand all of the ramifications of finding, interviewing and hiring that one employee.

You might ask at this point, where can I find these top performers? How will I know that I am making the best hiring decision for my division or company? Hiring Top Performers was written with the idea that hiring managers are not born; they must constantly do their homework in preparing to interview and hire top talent. To be an effective hiring manager, you must know what questions to ask as well as which questions are most appropriate for any given opening or particular candidate (such as a recent college grad versus someone who has been laid off or is returning to the workforce after a leave of absence).

In Hiring Top Performers, we give you over 600 questions to choose from so that you can select the best candidate for your current and fu-ture openings. We also provide you with expert advice on each question and what to look for in a candidate's answer as well as sample answers to each question. In addition, we provide complete interviews in various industries or job functions such as Product Marketing Manager, Retail Buyer, and Systems Analyst so that if you have a candidate coming in for an interview in the next two minutes, you'll have a great, well-prepared set of questions ready to go.

In this hiring book we give you over 600 questions to choose from so that you can select the best candidate for your current and future openings.

We cannot emphasize enough the importance of legalities in hiring employees. We think it is so important that we have devoted an entire chapter to this topic and we encourage you to read it thoroughly before proceeding with your next interview.

Hiring employees for any level requires a lot of time and preparation and this book was written with that in mind. There is no faster way to drive your business forward and and increase overall productivity than by having the right people on board. With Hiring Top Performers, you've already taken the first step towards finding and hiring top talent for your organization.

Bob Adams and Peter Veruki

ACCOUNTING MANAGER

Growing auto repair shop seeking top-flight Accountant with aggressive, hands-on accounting management skills including AP/AR. Knowledge of auto repair industry and Quick-books a +. Fax resume and salary requirements to 508

Accountant: Accounts Receivable

National automobile rental agency seeks organized, detail-oriented entry level individual to coordinate accounting for credit card transactions and associated receivables related to business in its busy Hartford aeroplex office. Motivated individual with demonstrated ability to juggle multi-tasks must have BA in accounting. Interested applicants are invited to submit resumes to Car-4-A-Day, 120 Airport Way, West Hartford, CT 06107.

BANK TELLERS

IMMEDIATE OPENINGS!

Immediate openings in all branches of AtlantaBank for experienced Bank Tellers. Growth potential, for the motivated. Fax resume to Business Resources at 404-555-6778.

BOOKKEEPING/ ACCOUNTING

Small medical office requires the services of savvy bookkeeping/ accounting professional to oversee financial responsibilities for two busy family practice physicians. Experienced required in receivables, payables, and aggressive, but gracious, bill collections. 5+ years experience necessary with medical office background a definite +. Qualified applicants should fax resume and salary requirements to 514-555-3467.

Computer Technician

Chicago's largest electronic imaging service bureau is expanding rapidly with new branches opening in seven metro locations. Full-time experienced graphics output wiz with hands-on laser printer, digital printer, Iris Imaging, flatbed and drum scanning, Linotronic, Macintosh, and PC troubleshooting capabilities sought immediately to travel locations as required to keep us up and running and number one. Fax resume to 312-555-9999.

CUSTOMER SERVICE REPRESENTATIVE

Residential Interior Decorator pursuing creative individual with an avid interest in home decor to assist interior designers in servicing clientele. A background in design or demonstrated applied arts skills required. If you are also energetic, intuitive, wild about color and texture, eager to learn the trade, and flow with the trends, send us your resume today. TrendSetter Interiors, P.O. Box 950, Miami, FL 03111.

Electrical Engineer

Westerlund Ambitronics is searching for an electrical engineer with ten+ years in the home lighting system design and installation field. Excellent communication skills required to work closely with owners, architects and building contractors. management and marketing skills a definite plus. Excellent salary, company car and great benefits package. Please forward resume and salary expectations to N.K. Westerlund, Westerlund Ambitronics, 151 Razor Back Road, Rutland, Vermont 05701.

EVENT DIRECTOR

Centre Dome North desperately seeking a energetic, organized, multi-talented events coordinator to oversee planning and execution of sports, convention, trade show, fund-raising, and other events held at the dome. Must be able to prepare and target budgets, source and contract vendors, and manage time schedules. Outgoing, diplomatic personality required for close work with clients. Ten years experience corporate or facility events planning experience a must. Business background or education a +. Fax or send resume and salary requirements to Human Resources, Dept. C, Centre Dome North, 1045 Highland Street, Redlands, CA 00000, Fax: 804-555-5566. Equal Opportunity Employer

Field Recruiter

Fast paced personnel placement agency seeks well organized, charismatic communicator with strong networking skills to recruit and place professionals in high level positions at prestigious firms. Travel required. Fax resume to 617-555-8989.

Graphic Designer

Highly creative graphic designer sought to develop business communication, presentation, internet presence, and direct mail pieces for American Crafter's Catalogue Company..We represent internationally recognized artisans and require collateral and multimedia materials that reflect elegance and quality. The ideal candidate will be skilled in QuarkXpress, Director, Photoshop and Illustrator. He or she will have a minimum of five years retail/direct marketing design experience; will be capable of producing CD-ROM and Web Site graphics. If your portfolio is exceptional, your attitude dedicated, your imagination beyond limits—send three non-returnable samples, your resume and salary requirements to ACCC, P.O. Box 45, Charlotte, NC 28201. All submittals will be acknowledged. ACCC is an equal opportunity employer.

IMPORT CLERK

International freight forwarder has immediate opening for Ocean Import Clerk. One year experience required. Full time position with excellent benefits. EOE. Please call 212-555-5656 for appointment.

Legal Secretary

Part time legal secretary sought for busy law firm. Flexible hours—mother's, evenings, weekends OK with potential for full time in the future. Excellent Word Perfect 5.2 skills and experience required. Fax resume to 617-555-8900. EOE. .

LEGAL SECRETARY

Experienced legal secretary sought by Waltham firm. Top pay for top skills and credentials. Mr. Walters 617-555-9350..

Marketing Coordinator

Leading construction management company seeking organized, motivated individual with excellent administrative, interpersonal and communication skills to support marketing management team. Work includes PR implementation, media contact, event and presentation coordination and database management. WP and ACT! required. Writing and design skills a definite plus. Excellent entry position with advancement potential. Degree preferred. Fax resume 518-555-9900.

MARKETING DIRECTOR

West Coast Gourmet Coffee purveyor with chain of trendy coffee bars and catalog mail order service conducting a search for a savvy, proven marketing director to position our company for success along the Northeast Corridor—Maine to Florida. This is a start-up opportunity integrating West Coast marketing resources with your own team development. Your resume must demonstrate extensive knowledge of the gourmet food industry, proven market development and penetration skills and fast track results. If you think you can place our name on the public's palette in six months—you're the key player we're looking for. Forward resume in confidence to Dept. G, The Daily Hemisphere, P.O. Box 780, 99 Planet Drive, Portland, OR 97201

Medical Receptionist/Secretary

Full time medical receptionist/secretary sought for busy four physician office in Troy. Knowledge of managed care procedures, familiarity with national and local medical plans, computer billing using Medi-Bill 3.1, appointment scheduling, and diplomatic, caring attitude all necessary. References required. Salary negotiable dependent upon experience. Benefits. Equal Opportunity Employer. Send resume to 45 East Main Street, Troy, NY 12180.

NURSING SUPERVISOR Psychiatric Home Care

Home care organization seeks Master's prepared psychiatric nurse with seven years acute experience and a minimum of two years home care experience. Demonstrated management skills required to schedule and oversee activities of ten visiting nurses and associated staff. Must have excellent communication and organizational abilities. Full benefits package. Send resume in confidence to HCS, Department PY, Code 3456, P.O. Box 78, Omaha, NB 68112.

SUNDAY CLASSIFIEDS GET RESULTS!

More regional companies, large and small rely on the Sunday Sphere Classifieds to attract the top candidates for their job openings than any other search vehicle. Searching for the right applicant? Have your query in by Wednesday.

BUILDING AN INTERVIEW

GENERAL QUESTIONS

The following set of general questions has been divided into several different categories to allow you to pick specific questions for any type of interview. For example, you may want to measure a candidate's ability to complete tasks, or to motivate others to complete projects. Similarly, you may also want to know what the candidate's preferred management style is and if it matches your company's or department's management style. Questions that relate to these and other subject areas such as creativity, problem-solving ability, accomplishements, and passion for the business can be found on the following pages. These questions are not intended as a substitute for particular industry- or job-related issues and should ideally be used in combination with a career-specific interview.

Motivation and Purpose

When you are managing people, it doesn't take long to figure out that it's often a lot easier to teach workers new skills than to improve their motivation. This is why it's so important to hire well-motivated people at the outset. Often, the tendency during interviewing is to focus more on measuring skills and accomplishments—perhaps because it is more difficult to measure a candidate's motivation. One way to get a candidate to reveal his or her degree of motivation is to ask open-ended questions, such as the classic "Tell me about yourself." Another way is to ask questions that probe the candidate's purpose in seeking a job with you, such as "What do you really want out of your next job?"

1. Tell me about yourself.

Sample Answer: I'm the kind of person who thrives in an environment where I have to coordinate lots of different people and lots of ideas and agendas. I think that's what has earned me my success in brand management.

Advice: As a hiring manager, you are looking for the applicant to go beyond the resume and share something from his or her background that will give you an indication of whether he or she can handle the job. How organized is the applicant's thought process? What does the applicant value about him- or herself? You should not be looking for a programmed response—just something that will give you a sign that the candidate is focused and can articulate his or her strengths in a concise manner.

Motivation and Purpose

2. *Tell me something about yourself that I wouldn't know by reading your resume.*

Sample Answer: Well, you wouldn't know that since age eighteen I've managed my own small portfolio. I've averaged 12 percent return over the last eight years.

Advice: You want the candidate to reveal some skill or ability that has been developed over time but does not necessarily translate into a typical resume accomplishment. Does the candidate have some special communication, technical, or other skill that is not readily apparent on the resume? What can the candidate offer your company other than what appears in the job description? You are looking for intangibles—qualities or experiences that will enhance or add value to the job opening and, ultimately, to the company.

• • •

3. *Why do you want to work here?*

Sample Answer: Your company's software caught my attention last year. I'm also intrigued by your internal incentive program that encourages employees to push new product ideas.

Advice: Try to determine why the applicant wants this job and what is driving him or her to this company and, in some cases, city. You want to see consistency and to get a sense for the total package. It is important for the applicant to have done some research on your company—but not the typical kind of research that includes annual reports or recruiting brochures. Ideally, the applicant has done some homework on his or her own time, digging out information on your products or services, and understands how your company fits into the broader industry spectrum. The candidate must be convincing and must sell you on his or her potential compatibility with your company, job, or industry.

Motivation and Purpose

4. What do you want out of your next job?

Sample Answer: I'm really interested in being given a territory where the company isn't very well positioned. I also hope to be offered an aggressive commission structure if I'm able to turn around that problem territory.

Advice: The candidate should convince you that he or she is seeking the responsibilities and challenges that you offer in your current opening. The job requirements should be consistent with the candidate's goals and interests. Get the candidate to give specific examples of past positions that were unfulfilling, and duties or tasks that were missing from, or could have enhanced, a prior position. Why does the candidate believe your position will satisfy his or her career aspirations at this time?

• • •

5. What are your salary goals or expectations?

Sample Answer: Because my background exceeds the minimum requirements for this position, I would hope that my salary would fall into the upper end of the salary range. What is the range for this position?

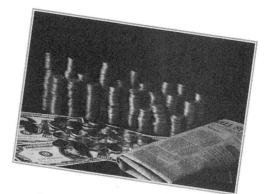

Advice: Ideally, you want to evaluate the candidate's range before you bring him or her in for a formal interview. You need to make sure the candidate has a realistic expectation of what the job will pay, both now and in the immediate future. Is this expectation in keeping with your idea of what to offer for the position? Do not deviate from your salary range unless the candidate is truly exceptional.

6. What new skills or ideas do you bring to the job that internal candidates might not offer?

Sample Answer: Well, because I have experience working with the oldest player in the industry, I'd be able to offer you some insights that would help you avoid some of the mistakes we made.

Advice: A candidate may feel the need to regurgitate job descriptions to sell him- or herself to the hiring manager. You need to probe into the candidate's background to discover any special skills or talents that could improve or impact your department and, by extension, your company. Can the candidate draw parallels between his or her past job experience and the one at hand and highlight unique skills or knowledge that significantly contributes to this job? Get the candidate to tell you how these special skills will translate to your open position.

• • •

7. What would you like to accomplish that you were not able to accomplish in your past job?

Sample Answer: I was hampered by a small budget that limited our marketing efforts to print advertisements and traditional resources. What I'd really like to do is try interactive media, because people eighteen to twenty-five years old respond to computer-based media.

Advice: The job applicant should demonstrate some idea of what he or she would like to do and where he or she would like to be in a new position. These aspirations should also dovetail with what you need the person to accomplish. Keep in mind what tasks must be executed in the job, and pay close attention to the candidate's expectations. Is the applicant looking to improve his or her writing output? Or looking for more budget responsibility? Does he or she want to bring new and innovative products to market? Whatever the goals, they should be in line with the job you are offering.

Motivation and Purpose

8. What have you learned about our company from employees, customers, or others?

Sample Answer: I actually called several of the key accounts listed in your company brochure. Two of the customers I spoke with gave your distribution operation high marks.

Advice: You will very quickly separate the serious candidate from one who is merely shopping by determining how thoroughly the candidate has researched your company. How well does he or she know your product or service? Whom has the candidate talked to, and what did he or she find out? You want to make sure the job seeker is not just providing you with information that has been public knowledge for some time. Does he or she know something unique about the company or industry that could be discovered only by talking to someone internally or to a customer or supplier?

• • •

9. Why should I hire you?

Sample Answer: My uncle had a company that was a small-scale manufacturer in this industry and, although he later sold the business, I worked there five summers doing all sorts of odd jobs. For that reason, I believe I know this business from the ground up, and you can be assured that I know what I'm getting into as a plant manager in this industry.

Advice: You want the candidate to present evidence that he or she stands apart from the crowd and will bring skills and talents to your company that other candidates do not possess. Or perhaps the candidate could give you compelling reasons why he or she is uniquely suited to the position and to your company. Maybe the candidate offers skills or abilities beyond those required by the position.

10. ## What brings you to this point in your career?

Sample Answer: I'm ready to manage my own department, and I just don't believe our current lab manager will ever vacate her position, so I need to move on. The three-month period when I ran the lab during her absence proved to me that I'm qualified.

Advice: You should be looking for the candidate to explain logically his or her career path and the reasons he or she is interviewing with you today. There should be clear evidence of upward career development, and the candidate's desire for your position should dovetail with his or her skills and prior experience. Are the candidate's career aspirations compatible with your expectations of the person who fills the position?

• • •

11. ## Why are you ready to leave your current job?

Sample Answer: My interest lies in returning to the banking industry. I can work in human resources management in many environments, but I really believe that my experience as a lender will help me recruit effectively for new lenders in the training program.

Advice: The candidate should give you ample evidence that he or she is looking for the new challenges that your position can provide. Probe the candidate's background to make sure there are no surprises with respect to job performance or any other negative issues that may require this job seeker to leave his or her current position. You don't want to hire someone who is going to bring similar problems to your company.

Motivation and Purpose

12. *What is your motivation to do this kind of work?*

Sample Answer: I have been fortunate in my own schooling; I had wonderful teachers. I want to be that same kind of teacher who motivates kids to learn but also sets an example that encourages some of them to consider teaching as a profession. In the long run that's our best chance of turning around the quality of education in this state.

Advice: Ask the candidate for concrete examples of daily tasks—such as working on budgets, writing press releases, or managing inventory—that demonstrate why the candidate enjoys doing this type of work and what drives him or her to excel in this type of position. The candidate should cite more than just those responsibilities found in the job description; the ideal applicant should be able to discuss at length specific examples of why this kind of work is challenging and stimulating and can hold his or her interest over the long haul.

• • •

13. *What interests you least about this job?*

Sample Answer: I wouldn't be as interested in this position if I thought you wanted to continue emphasizing the oil-based line, but my information indicates you want to move into the fat-free line.

Advice: Be prepared for the candidate to turn this question around in an effort to discuss some interesting aspect of the job rather than dwell on the less desirable qualities of the position. Press the candidate to tell you some of the duties he or she would least enjoy, to make sure the job applicant doesn't dislike anything you consider crucial to performing effectively in the position.

Motivation and Purpose

14. What interests you the most about this job?

Sample Answer: I would love the opportunity to work with John Smith, whom I watched build the financial services practice under bank deregulation. I look forward to meeting him.

Advice: The candidate should be prepared to discuss at length specific areas of the job that he or she finds motivating or exciting. What, in particular, has brought the candidate to you today to discuss this opening, and why would this position hold the candidate's interest for more than a year or two? You want to make sure the job seeker is not just a tire kicker out for another paycheck but has solid reasons for pursuing the position and your company.

• • •

15. What are your impressions of our company and its reputation?

Sample Answer: Cordon was one of our suppliers, so I'm sold on the quality of your product line and, more important, the quality of people you hire. Joe Johnson really encouraged me to apply.

Advice: You will quickly separate the serious applicant from those who are merely shopping by probing the depth of the candidate's research on your company. How well does the candidate know your product or service? Whom has he or she talked with, and what information was obtained? You want to make sure the candidate isn't providing you only with information that has been public knowledge for some time. For example, does he or she know something unique about the company or industry that could be discovered only by talking with someone internally, or with a customer or supplier?

Motivation and Purpose

16. *We have a number of applicants interviewing for this position. Why should we take a closer look at you?*

Sample Answer: I'm probably one of the few CPAs you will find who have worked in two Hispanic countries. With all the production that you are outsourcing to Mexico, I may be able to provide some assistance with your inventory planning.

Advice: Make sure the candidate gives you concrete examples that illustrate why he or she will bring more skills and greater ability to your company than other candidates applying for the position. What personal qualities or talents does the candidate offer that you have not seen in other applicants? Keep in mind the daily tasks and responsibilities of the position, and pay close attention to the candidate's expectations.

• • •

17. *Prove to me that your interest is sincere.*

Sample Answer: I actually tried to get an internship here last summer, but the contract with IBM hadn't been finalized. Now that you are starting implementation, I could really aid in the conversion to the new system. I have followed those developments carefully through my contacts from last year.

Advice: You want the candidate to give you tangible proof that he or she is genuinely excited about working for your company and in your industry. What is it about the job or your company that truly energizes the candidate? Look for concrete examples, such as information about your products, company culture, or people, that would not be readily available to the public at large and that prove the candidate has dug deep to identify particularly compelling, unique aspects of the job.

18. *How have your career motivations changed over the past few years?*

Sample Answer: When I started in sales, I didn't realize how much I would miss it if I left. Now I want to stay close to the field organization, even though I'm looking at marketing jobs. Your firm attracts me because the account-team concept would keep me in tune with the customers.

Advice: You want to see how the candidate has managed his or her career and what specific goals or objectives he or she has set for the future. What is motivating the candidate at this time to pursue the opening at your company? Does the candidate have a realistic assessment of his or her career path, and does it fit with the growth opportunities in your company? You must make sure the candidate's expectations for his or her career path will be satisfied by what your company has to offer.

Diligence and Professionalism

*T*he big difference between one candidate and another may not be evident until he or she is already on the job and confronted with a major challenge or obstacle. Will the candidate retreat or shy back from a roadblock? Or will he or she keep going regardless of how difficult the challenge may seem? And what will he or she be like to work with under stressful circumstances? How well does he or she take criticism and setbacks? Judging how candidates will respond during the most difficult times may be a very different issue from judging how well they will handle their work when everything is going smoothly.

1. Tell me about your most difficult work or personal experience.

Sample Answer: I had a coworker who went through rehab for six months after a bad car wreck. I picked up some slack to help him out, and I know that he would've done the same for me.

Advice: How did the candidate overcome frustration? Can he or she acknowledge failures and talk frankly about them and the methods used to deal with them? The example can come from either a work-related issue or an experience outside the workplace. You want the candidate to demonstrate that he or she was able to learn from the experience and grow as a person and as a professional. What lessons did the candidate learn as a result of this experience?

2. Give me an example of how you completed a project despite obstacles.

Sample Answer: I actually rotated off an account but remained involved as an adviser because the client threatened to pull the account if he wasn't dealing with me. Over time I gradually decreased my presence.

Advice: You must first get the candidate to outline the project, then describe the problems encountered once the project was under way. How did the candidate assess the situation and retrench and overcome the obstacle? What approach did the candidate use to deal with the problem? Could the obstacles have been predicted? What did the candidate learn from the experience?

• • •

3. Give me an example of your determination.

Sample Answer: I led an effort to change our production system over to dedicated lines. The biggest challenge was trying to get the factory workers to understand that it was a good idea. I persuaded management to increase the profit-sharing account using some of that savings. That got the employees on my side.

Advice: You want a concrete example from either a work or personal experience that shows how the candidate stuck to a project. You are not worried here about whether there was a successful conclusion to the situation; you simply want the candidate to give you an example indicating how he or she will tackle tough job assignments that involve a few minor obstacles or even a major problem.

Diligence and Professionalism

4. *Describe a time when you tackled a tough or unpopular assignment.*

Sample Answer: I had to determine which budgets would be cut within my division to lead to an overall 5 percent cost reduction. I tried to keep the department heads' personalities out of the equation so I could remain objective.

Advice: Every candidate has at least one story in his or her professional experience about a particularly difficult assignment. You are looking for initiative on the part of the candidate and a willingness to dive in and take charge of a project that is basically unappealing. What approach did the candidate take to make an unpleasant assignment more appealing? What was the methodology? What was the result of his or her efforts? Ask for a description of how the candidate persevered and overcame obstacles to achieve a positive result.

• • •

5. *Would your current boss describe you as the type of person who goes that extra mile?*

Sample Answer: Absolutely. In fact, in her annual report she writes that I am the most dependable and dedicated person on her staff. I think this is due to my ability to juggle and prioritize.

Advice: Here you want the candidate to assess his or her skills and abilities in light of what a current supervisor might say. How much does the candidate embellish, and how much is  believable? If you were to call the supervisor, what would that person say about the candidate? Ask for examples of how the individual goes the distance to add value to the company or department.

6. *Tell me about a time you didn't perform to expectations.*

Sample Answer: That would be the first time I had to give a presentation to the board. I didn't anticipate any of the questions. I was unprepared for anything other than what I wanted to report.

Advice: You are looking for the candidate to reveal a situation in which he or she failed to meet either personal goals or the expectations of a supervisor. The candidate should be able to talk frankly about how he or she failed to deliver the right solution to a problem, or to perform required duties satisfactorily. Look for reasons, not excuses. You want to see how the candidate has dealt with failure and what steps were taken to ensure that the mistake would not happen again.

• • •

7. *How have you handled criticism of your work?*

Sample Answer: The first time I had a complaint from a client, I found it very difficult to react objectively to criticism about personal service I had given the account. I learned that showing empathy can help calm a situation.

Advice: Criticism of one's output is a very sensitive, personal issue. You want to see evidence of how the candidate deals with critical comments about his or her work. Does the candidate revisit mistakes and try to rectify them on the next go-around? How does he or she respond to the boss in such a situation? You need to find out if this job seeker is likely to react professionally to your expressed dissatisfaction with his or her efforts.

Diligence and Professionalism

8. *People tend to be concept oriented or task oriented. How do you describe yourself?*

Sample Answer: It's important to me to have clear direction on each project. That's why I'm good in support roles, whereas most of our managers have very specific ideas. I'm thorough at carrying out tasks.

Advice: Determine whether the candidate has an orientation that will work effectively with the duties and problem solving that take place in your department. Can the candidate handle the responsibilities of the position if he or she is generally more comfortable with a concept than with a nuts-and-bolts task? This question tends to be black-and-white—you want either someone who deals well with facts and figures, or someone who theorizes and deals in the abstract.

• • •

9. *What would your colleagues tell me about your attention to detail?*

Sample Answer: My coworkers always count on me to discover what might have been overlooked. They would tell you that I'm the kind of person who thinks through a process from A to Z.

Advice: Does the candidate take the time to evaluate and assess all aspects of his or her work? This can be an important gauge in determining how the candidate values detail as opposed to the big picture. If the job you're seeking to fill requires even the smallest amount of detail work, you must be sure the candidate has an appreciation for the nuts and bolts of getting a job done. Get the candidate to give you examples of past projects, writing assignments, or production-oriented tasks that have demonstrated an ability to work well with details.

Diligence and Professionalism

10. How do you manage your work week and make realistic deadlines?

Sample Answer: I always try to reserve two hours within my day to handle the unanticipated setbacks. This gives me enough leeway to finish projects on schedule.

Advice: You need to make sure the candidate has a reasonable set of expectations about what it will take to get a job done in a specified period of time. How organized is this candidate? Does he or she set realistic goals, managing to get at least some tasks done at the beginning of the work week, or make it up as the week goes along? Skills such as organizing, planning, and coordinating look great on a resume, but you want proof that the candidate knows what it takes to meet deadlines and can appreciate your needs week in and week out.

• • •

11. Tell me about a time you had to extend a deadline.

Sample Answer: Two weeks into a project it was clear that our client wanted us to add more features as the project went along. I took time to renegotiate the deadline and produced an acceptable solution.

Advice: Everyone has had to extend a deadline at one time or another in his or her professional life. How did the candidate you are interviewing handle a late project? Did external factors or something the candidate overlooked cause the delay? How did the candidate manage the extension? What steps did he or she take to expedite the process and keep the deadline extension reasonable? You want to see here how the candidate might react to an unexpected set of circumstances.

Diligence and Professionalism

12. *What personal skill or work habit have you struggled to improve?*

Sample Answer: I had to learn to say no. I used to be helpful to the point that other staff abused my goodwill. Now I've learned to offer my help only after requesting that the favor be returned in the future. That kind of reciprocal interaction makes the job go easier for everyone.

Advice: The candidate should have at least one or two examples of how he or she has grappled with a skill that needed work, and took steps to improve it. What, specifically, has the candidate done to strengthen a personal skill or work habit that needed attention? Did the candidate recognize the weakness, or did his or her supervisor have to point out the weakness and suggest steps for improvement? You want to determine here how motivated the candidate is in trying to improve overall performance.

• • •

13. *How do you manage stress in your daily work?*

Sample Answer: I try to get out for lunch once during the middle of the week to clear my head. I also have a personal rule that stops me from reacting to any problem until I feel calm about it. I think, then act, but I had to learn to do that over time.

Advice: The candidate should give you at least two or three examples from a work-related project when he or she dealt with stress in a positive manner. What actions did the candidate take to deal with a stressful situation, and what was the outcome? Does the candidate demonstrate the ability to handle stress in such a way that it will not hamper productivity in your department? With more and more companies looking to squeeze additional productivity out of fewer employees, it is critical that you determine whether this candidate can deal with the day-to-day pressures of working at your company.

Diligence and Professionalism

14. How do you regroup when things have not gone as planned?

Sample Answer: I start by trying to identify the worst possible outcome; then I back up and try to identify precautions that will help avoid that scenario. In this way I usually end up with a result close to the original goal. The training example I described earlier is proof of that skill.

Advice: How does the candidate handle unexpected obstacles—internal or external forces that impede his or her progress in completing a project or task? What techniques does this candidate use to refocus and get back on track? You want to see evidence that the candidate has the emotional maturity and ability to overcome setbacks and to continue to produce high-quality work.

• • •

15. How have you prioritized or juggled your workload in your current job?

Sample Answer: I juggle by working only on my two major accounts early in the day. That way, if interruptions occur, my most critical customers are still taken care of.

 **Advice:** The candidate should give you a blueprint for how he or she organizes daily tasks such as writing business correspondence, scheduling meetings, or making phone calls to prospective customers. You should get a good feel for how this job seeker decides what is a top priority for that particular day and what tasks can wait until later in the day or week. This question is especially important if your department or organization is in a fast-growth mode and the person filling the position is expected to handle multiple assignments on an ongoing basis.

Diligence and Professionalism

16. *Describe a professional skill you have developed in your most recent job.*

Sample Answer: I am most proud of my new skills in applying database technology—for example, in our mailing services. What used to take us one day of manual sorting now takes fifteen minutes through a quick-search feature.

Advice: You want to find out here if the candidate takes the initiative to learn new skills that will enhance his or her professional credentials, as opposed to being satisfied with the same daily routine. In what context did the candidate develop the skill? Do you consider the skill to be important to the job in question? What new skills does the candidate look forward to acquiring while working for your company?

• • •

17. *When have your skills in diplomacy been put to the test?*

Sample Answer: A customer came in once and demanded money back for an evening dress that had apparently been worn. She claimed it was a different color after dry cleaning and that the cleaner said the source of the problem was faulty fabric. I quickly responded that we'd be happy to refund her money, even though I thought she wasn't being honest. I believed it was important to keep other customers from hearing her and perhaps doubting our high-quality merchandise.

Advice: The ability to remain objective, listen calmly, and respond to a customer or coworker is critical in any professional environment. You want to make sure the candidate communicates in a thoroughly professional manner with customers or coworkers no matter what the situation, be it a customer service complaint or a coworker unhappy about working on a project with the candidate. Does the candidate know how to keep his or her cool and remain tactful under such trying circumstances? How would the candidate deal with a difficult customer, or with a coworker who questions the candidate's ability to complete tasks in a professional manner?

Job Fit

W hat with inflated job titles, corporate downsizing, and the accompanying broadening of individual responsibilities, job fit has become a big issue recently. The candidate's view of what the job may entail is often very different from the realities at the hiring company. Testing a candidate's "fit" will help both the recruiter and the candidate test key job compatibility issues. Special emphasis needs to be given to avoiding a situation in which the candidate encounters the same major on-the-job concerns that prompted him or her to leave any prior positions.

1. What were the most rewarding aspects of your previous job?

Sample Answer: My favorite aspect of being a recruiter is the satisfaction I get knowing I've made a good match.

Advice: You, as the hiring manager, must focus on the candidate's job history and find out what the candidate considers the most appealing aspects of his or her last position. Will the candidate find the same rewards in your position? What does the candidate want to accomplish in his or her next job? Get the person to draw comparisons between his or her last job and your opening. Does the move make sense to you as a hiring manager? Do you see a logical progression?

Job Fit

2. ## What has frustrated you about your current or previous job?

Sample Answer: The most difficult thing was that our R-and-D facility was three states away. That made it really hard as a technical product manager to develop rapport with our design team.

Advice: This is the flip side of the most rewarding aspects of the candidate's previous job. You want to find out what frustrations the candidate has experienced at his or her last job—you do not want to hire someone who might experience the same frustrations in the job you're trying to fill. The more concrete the example, the better you will be able to determine whether the candidate is a good match with your position.

• • •

3. ## Describe your ideal job.

Sample Answer: My ideal job would combine a sales territory I managed with additional responsibility for sales training, so that I could use my teaching background.

Advice: You should be on the alert if the "dream job" the candidate describes is not in sync with past positions. There should be a close tie between what the candidate did in his or her last job and what he or she wants to do in the next job—including, of course, your current opening. You should be able to see some logical progression indicating that careful thought has been given to what the candidate wants to do, based on the skills and abilities he or she has to offer.

Job Fit

4. What are the limitations of your current job?

Sample Answer: My job is limited now because the industry that I'm in is not in a growth mode. I've tried to retain customers through customer satisfaction programs.

Advice: You are looking for responses here that would indicate the candidate is unhappy about professional growth opportunities in his or her current position. What does the candidate see as limiting factors in his or her current job? Are the candidate's career aspirations and timetable realistic? You don't want someone walking into the same unfulfilling situation at your company.

• • •

5. What do you wish to achieve or develop in your next position?

Sample Answer: I hope to be able to move into finance in a company's manufacturing group. I think that would be important to my overall understanding of the company's core business.

Advice: Look for concrete examples of accomplishments that the candidate wants to achieve in his or her next position. Are these goals reasonable, based on what the candidate has done in past positions? Does he or she provide real examples, rather than pie-in-the-sky rhetoric, that pertain to the responsibilities in your open position?

Job Fit

6. What interests you most about this job?

Sample Answer: I was really excited to learn about your recent corporate acquisitions in South America. My experience as an exchange student there could help in your marketing effort in Latin America.

Advice: The candidate should mention not only specific duties that attract him or her to the position, but also a solid desire to work for your company or your industry. The ideal answer should include mention of daily tasks the candidate finds particularly attractive, as well as a broad overview of the position. Do not get swayed by talk regarding job titles, salary expectations, or travel, unless travel is a required part of the job. The candidate must sell you on what excites him or her the most about the position.

• • •

7. What interests you least about this job?

Sample Answer: One thing I hope not to do is spend all of my time focusing on small accounts. In my last job I focused on several major accounts, which increased my key business by 20 percent.

Advice: Encourage the candidate to be honest about the least attractive aspects of the position you are offering. The candidate may or may not try to avoid or dance around this question—be persistent and try to probe his or her background to look for indications of a less than enthusiastic attitude about certain aspects of previous positions.

8. What concerns you the most about performing this job?

Sample Answer: I'm concerned that there isn't adequate staff to handle customer support. In my last job we were often shorthanded when introducing new products, and customers weren't given the service they should have been.

Advice: You must elicit from the candidate specific situations or duties that may cause concern. Are there certain responsibilities in the position you are offering that the candidate fears he or she cannot handle or would have difficulty adjusting to? Again, the candidate's background should provide some clues as to what he or she thinks might hamper effectiveness in the job you are offering.

• • •

9. Considering your own resume, what do you think your weaknesses are regarding this job?

Sample Answer: I believe that my skills and abilities are a great fit for this position. Do you have any particular concerns?

Advice: Get the candidate to address his or her own possible weaknesses. How will the candidate overcome these weaknesses? Does the answer here match your expectations based on the candidate's resume? Don't be swayed by programmed responses; make sure the candidate gives you enough detail about any lack of skills necessary to perform in your company and has a good answer about what might be done to overcome such weaknesses.

Job Fit

10. *How did the realities differ from your expectations in your previous job?*

Sample Answer: The hardest thing to predetermine was how other departments within the company viewed my market research department's work. Unfortunately, I discovered that many groups preferred to go outside for specialized research service.

Advice: It is important to probe the candidate's assessment of his or her skills in terms of the last job held and its day-to-day responsibilities. Was the candidate realistic in terms of what to expect on a daily basis? Does he or she have an understanding of what is called for in the position you're trying to fill? Ask the candidate to describe daily, or other regularly occurring, tasks. Were they consistent with what he or she had anticipated before taking the job?

• • •

11. *Would you be able to travel or to work extended hours necessary to perform the job?*

Sample Answer: If I have forty-eight hours' notice, I can stay as late as necessary to finish the work. Typically, however, I work until at least six o'clock because I get a lot of work done in that hour after the office closes. As far as travel's concerned, that's no problem.

Advice: What sort of commitment will the candidate make to the job? Try to determine if the candidate has a realistic expectation of what the job involves, and if he or she is prepared to make all necessary commitments.

12. *Do you prefer continuity or frequent change in your daily routine?*

Sample Answer: I enjoy a good challenge and change. That's why I typically ask for the tough assignments. The last two projects we discussed were assignments I specifically asked for.

Advice: Get the candidate to reveal his or her preferences for accomplishing daily tasks, and determine whether he or she is happiest when there is a routine and tasks are fairly mundane, or when diversity and challenge are part of the job. You will quickly learn if the candidate will bring a creative spark to the position, or if he or she is more interested in having everything laid out on the table from starting to quitting time.

• • •

13. *What aspects of the job give you the most confidence?*

Sample Answer: I believe I can effectively engage an audience. When I get up in front of the room to present a new idea, I can usually get people on my side in a short amount of time.

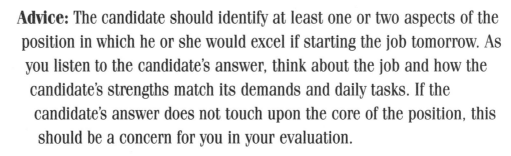

Advice: The candidate should identify at least one or two aspects of the position in which he or she would excel if starting the job tomorrow. As you listen to the candidate's answer, think about the job and how the candidate's strengths match its demands and daily tasks. If the candidate's answer does not touch upon the core of the position, this should be a concern for you in your evaluation.

Job Fit

14. What skills do you offer that are most relevant to this job?

Sample Answer: My engineering background gives me a logical problem-solving ability that I know will be useful in assessing client needs. That background will also help your consulting firm sell business to manufacturers who themselves employ many engineers.

Advice: Your responsibility, as hiring manager, should be to ensure that the candidate's skills do in fact fit well with your current opening. Ask for examples that clearly demonstrate an ability to function successfully in your department and to be an asset to your company. Why does the candidate believe that his or her skills are, in fact, relevant to this opening? Does the candidate's answer make sense with respect to the position's daily responsibilities?

• • •

15. How would you enrich your current or most recent job?

Sample Answer: If I decide to stay where I am, I'm going to volunteer to be on the communications task force, which is presently trying to get all of our offices linked to the Internet and other resources.

Advice: What you should be looking for in the candidate's answer has more to do with his or her career aspirations and development than with specific day-to-day tasks and responsibilities. The concern here is that if your position or company does not offer much more than what the candidate already has and the candidate accepts your position, he or she may decide to leave after a relatively short period of time, making your decision a costly one.

Job Fit

16. Why are you particularly well suited to this job?

Sample Answer: Based on what you have told me about the last person who excelled in the job, I'm confident that I have the same skills in spreadsheet analysis and statistics. I would also work well with your audit team because I come from that type of environment and know what a client can do to make the consulting relationship more productive.

Advice: The candidate should identify at least one or two areas that make him or her a strong candidate for your opening. It is next to impossible to find the perfect candidate for any position, so you should be concentrating on one or two aspects of the job as you listen to the candidate's answer, which should include mention of both skills and personal qualities. For instance, if you know that your company has a hardworking roll-up-your-sleeves attitude and the candidate indicates that he or she doesn't mind working eighty-plus hours a week, then you can rest assured this person will fit into your organization smoothly.

• • •

17. What is your most productive or ideal work setting?

Sample Answer: I like having at least one hour of uninterrupted time in the early morning to plan my day, so I usually start work around 7:15 a.m. Otherwise, I enjoy an office with open doors, constant feedback, and a lot of energy and activity. I can work more productively when I sense how busy everyone else is too.

Advice: No two companies have exactly the same type of work environment, so you should make sure the candidate gives you a frank response about the type of working situation he or she finds most productive. Specifically, does the candidate like to work alone or as part of a team? Will he or she be happy in an open-air cubicle, or does the candidate require an office with plush carpeting, fancy wallpaper, and windows?

18. *Tell me about two or three aspects of your last job that you would never want to repeat.*

Sample Answer: I'm glad that I have experience in credit collections, but it isn't something I want to do again. That background has enabled me to make better risk assessments, though.

Advice: You want the candidate to give you an honest assessment here of what he or she does not particularly enjoy doing so that you can weigh the negative aspects of the answer against the important criteria for success in your opening. For instance, if the candidate prefers not to do a lot of cold calling and you need someone to get on the phone every day, you should obviously be concerned. However, the candidate may have strong positive feelings about other aspects of the job that you believe are even more critical for overall success. In this case the positives may outweigh the negatives, and the candidate should still be considered for the position.

Accomplishments

he idea here is to sort out what the candidate personally, or as part of a group, actually got done, as opposed to what the job description was. Facts such as how many people reported to the candidate and how large a budget he or she was responsible for are interesting, but they don't tell you how well he or she performed the job. Did performance improve? Did sales go up? Did costs go down? Did he or she basically perform within reasonable expectations, or did he or she exceed expectations? Is the candidate's discussion of accomplishments focused on what he or she individually accomplished, or is it also balanced with his or her achievements as part of a group?

1. Tell me about a contribution you have made to a team effort.

Sample Answer: With my last team I helped put together more cohesive presentations for our client. I think our preparation indicated the attention to detail that we would give to systems installation.

Advice: The candidate should give a specific example of something he or she has accomplished within a team environment. This could be something outside of work, such as community service, or within the company, such as an instance when the candidate helped out others to increase the overall bottom line. The accomplishment must be specific and tied directly to the candidate's effort, such as sending work out for competitive bids.

Accomplishments

2. *Tell me about a special contribution you have made to an employer.*

Sample Answer: In my last job I ran the United Way campaign for three consecutive years. I think it's a good cause, and I know it's difficult for the company to find volunteers.

Advice: What does the candidate consider important in terms of contributing to the company's bottom line? Look for specific examples from previous positions. Was there something unusual or creative about the contribution or accomplishment? Get the candidate to break down the accomplishment in terms of people, things, resources, and ideas.

• • •

3. *Give me an example of a time you delivered more than was expected of you.*

Sample Answer: In my last job my boss asked me to take over uncollected accounts. I was able to collect more than the 20 percent he had hoped for.

Advice: You want the candidate to discuss an assignment whereby he or she was able to enhance and add value beyond what was expected. What motivated the candidate to push ahead and do more than was asked? Is he or she always this highly motivated, or was this a one-time situation? What would the candidate's boss say about his or her actions? Ask the candidate to define the end result clearly and simply, so that you can filter out any embellishment, a nearly inevitable result of this kind of question.

4. What accomplishment is your greatest source of pride?

Sample Answer: I'm very proud of how we turned a profit in our first year under private management. With that goal accomplished, I'm ready to do it for another hospital such as yours.

Advice: This accomplishment can be of a professional or a volunteer nature. It should reflect something close to the person's heart—look and listen for enthusiasm in the response. What was the nature of the accomplishment? How did it measure up over time? Is it an accomplishment that would draw attention in your company? Your definition of something truly exemplary may differ from the candidate's so you should prod the person to elaborate on his or her response. Use this question to encourage the candidate to clarify what truly makes him or her happy and fulfilled.

• • •

5. What situations do your colleagues rely on you to handle?

Sample Answer: People often rely on me to handle client confrontations. They know I'm the kind of person who never loses my temper in front of customers.

Advice: Try to elicit from the candidate an example that involves people and ideas, creativity, and a concern for the quality of the company's products and/or service. Encourage the candidate to describe a situation at work or within a volunteer capacity in which teammates or colleagues turned to him or her to resolve a problem or to develop a creative solution. Is the situation qualitative or quantitative? Why did the teammates or colleagues turn to the candidate instead of to someone else in the group?

Accomplishments

6. *Tell me about a corporate goal that you were able to support through one or more of your actions.*

Sample Answer: I helped to meet our goal of "value to stakeholders" by holding a fire sale to clean out our warehouse. The public was invited, and we netted $120,000.

Advice: Here you want the candidate to be precise about what he or she did to help an employer achieve an important goal or objective. Make sure the candidate offers specific actions and does not simply give a general, overall performance measurement, such as increasing shareholder value. What would the candidate's coworkers say about his or her participation and overall contribution to the corporate goal? Does the candidate know how to translate a corporate goal into one's own job responsibilities—then achieve some result or effect an action that contributes to the achievement of that goal?

• • •

7. *Tell me about a measurable outcome of one of your efforts.*

Sample Answer: I reorganized inventory planning and was able to automate the inventory reorder function. It reduced our costs by 35 percent.

Advice: The candidate should be prepared to give an answer that provides details in terms of numbers and/or specific accomplishments that can be measured. Here the candidate should give examples, such as reducing costs by 47 percent or increasing revenues by 60 percent. You should try to determine exactly how the candidate accomplished those results within his or her job.

8. *Describe an ongoing problem that you were able to overcome.*

Sample Answer: I was working once with three different groups, each of which had its own "homegrown" schedule, even though we had to rely on each other for our work and timing. I networked the computers and set up weekly brainstorming sessions to solve the problem.

Advice: Make sure the answer indicates a real problem, and encourage the candidate to identify or explain why there was a problem and what the consequences would have been if it had not been overcome. Try to uncover the candidate's thought process behind tackling the problem and the specific steps taken to resolve it. You want to assess the candidate's maturity level here, as well as his or her ability to see beyond immediate difficulties and formulate a solution.

• • •

9. *Tell me about a major accomplishment.*

Sample Answer: I'm really proud of the business I obtained with Fred's Wholesale Club. I believe these types of companies will continue to thrive in the next few years.

Advice: A lot of candidates will try to embellish when given the opportunity to talk about their accomplishments. You need to try to flesh out the substance of the accomplishments and determine whether they would draw attention in your company. Use this question to get the candidate to clarify what truly makes him or her happy and fulfilled.

Accomplishments

10. If I were to hire you today, what would you accomplish first?

Sample Answer: I would help you increase your business within the OEM market. As an OEM contractor for four years, I understand how to structure deals that will be profitable.

Advice: You want to see if the candidate understands the true nature of what is called for in your current opening and how quickly he or she can contribute to your department. Ask for three examples—such as improving the quality of direct mail lists, cutting operational costs, or improving efficiency in customer service response time—that indicate the candidate would jump in tomorrow and effect a positive result. Any answer that reflects a wait-and-see attitude should be a warning to you that the candidate may not have the personal initiative you seek for your opening.

• • •

11. Which of your accomplishments was the most difficult to achieve?

Sample Answer: I found it intimidating to work with the marketing research staff when first I started my job, mostly because I hadn't done well in statistics or market research in college. I decided to enroll in an executive seminar on market research, which really boosted my confidence. Now I don't feel at a disadvantage when I meet with the research group, and I know what questions to ask to get information that is meaningful to me.

Advice: Make sure that the accomplishment the candidate describes has some substance behind it, and ask the candidate to identify key factors that led to this accomplishment. Probe the candidate's thought process and try to discover any obstacles or problems that hampered his or her ability to achieve this accomplishment. You want to determine the candidate's maturity level in problem solving as well as his or her ability to see beyond the problem and to formulate a solution.

12. *Tell me about a time you saved money for an employer or an organization.*

Sample Answer: I was able to eliminate a middleman we had worked with for years when producing our employee magazine. We planned the issues, collected research, wrote the articles, did most of the editing, and handed the information to him, which he took to a designer and printer. After I managed this process twice, I decided to do the coordinating work myself. The additional time cost for me was eight hours, but we saved a 10 percent markup. Even better, the issues now get completed faster and with greater accuracy.

Advice: Go beyond the numbers to find out specifically how the candidate helped the company. What steps did the candidate take to arrive at a solution that ultimately saved the company money? Was it a one-time-only occurrence, or did the candidate effect other solutions that helped the organization reduce costs? This question measures the candidate's initiative and aggressiveness in discovering methods of producing more efficiently for his or her company.

• • •

13. *What is your greatest achievement to date?*

Sample Answer: I'm proud of the fact that I graduated on time with a solid GPA while working full-time at a television station for two years. A lot of my classmates who worked or had internships either took a reduced course load or let their grades suffer. I believe the reason I got through it all was sheer determination; I never even let myself visualize anything but finishing on time with good grades. So I firmly believe, as a professional counselor, in the importance of a positive outlook.

Advice: Encourage the candidate to expand on the achievement; as a hiring manager, you want to draw out the true nature of the achievement and determine why it was important to the candidate. Does the achievement carry any weight with you? How would it stack up against what you need the candidate to achieve? What does it say about the candidate's personal qualities, character, and initiative in tackling problems or overcoming obstacles?

• • •

14. *Tell me about something you accomplished that required discipline.*

Sample Answer: I had to work two jobs to put myself through graduate school. I interned at the newspaper while studying journalism during the week. Then, on weekends, I sold real estate. Juggling those three schedules was a challenge, but I did it because it was important to me to graduate without school loans.

Advice: The candidate should give you an example of how he or she was able to focus on a project or task that required intense concentration, or on a highly technical or complex project that involved multiple responsibilities. How was the candidate able to remain focused, avoid distractions or interference, and complete his or her task? What skills or abilities does the candidate rely on to stay on track from start to finish?

• • •

15. *Tell me about a project you completed ahead of schedule.*

Sample Answer: I was in charge of a new product rollout. In general, we completed each phase without a major setback—which was partially luck—but I also systematically called two days ahead of every deadline to check the status with all groups involved. I believe that made the difference. The launch took place two weeks ahead of plan; this is significant in our industry, where shelf life for products is less than one year.

Advice: This question goes to the heart of the candidate's ability to prioritize and use time efficiently. Can the candidate effectively manage multiple tasks, personnel, and resources so that a project is delivered ahead of schedule? What techniques or skills has the candidate employed to finish a project early? Determine if the candidate brought in a project in advance of a deadline or if colleagues and coworkers shared responsibility in helping the candidate to finish ahead of schedule.

• • •

16. *Tell me about a person or group you had to work with to achieve something important.*

Sample Answer: I joined a group of concerned citizens in my town to lobby for a recycling site. Our efforts paid off when the town council adopted a recycling measure to collect bottles, cans, and newspapers every week.

Advice: Ask the candidate to describe an experience in which he or she made a significant contribution to a team or organizational goal. What specifically did the group accomplish? Why did the candidate choose to work with these individuals in the first place?

Accomplishments

 Tell me about an organization outside of work that has benefited from your participation.

Sample Answer: I was involved in Junior Achievement as an economics undergrad. I believe I was able to make a difference for several high school kids in my group.

Advice: The type of organization mentioned here is not necessarily important; you should be more interested in what the candidate did to help that organization achieve an important goal or objective. What did the candidate take away from this experience that would benefit your company or department? Make sure not to discriminate against a candidate whose membership or participation in an organization indicates a particular race, color, national origin, religion, sex, physical handicap, age, or other characteristic protected by federal or local employment laws.

Corporate Fit

Today's leading recruiters often see corporate "fit" as the key factor in hiring decisions. However, today's professional worker is less willing to change his or her style to conform to that of a corporation or that of coworkers. At the same time, today's worker also expects to achieve higher levels of job satisfaction than in days past, and is often willing to go that extra mile if he or she is in a highly satisfying work situation. Don't assume that just because you are talking to a candidate from a similar-sized firm in the same industry that the corporate culture at his or her firm is similar to that of your firm. It may be very different! And it may even vary from one division or even one work group to the next within the same corporation.

1. What would your friends tell me about you?

Sample Answer: My friends would tell you that I move faster than most people, eat more than most people, work harder than most people, and still find time to spend with friends—despite my schedule.

Advice: How an individual sees his or her own personality from a friend's perspective can often reveal some important aspects of what the candidate is like to work with. A candidate will usually be very careful when describing him- or herself through a friend's eyes, revealing only those personality characteristics that are the strongest. Look for personality traits that will fit with your corporate culture and, more specifically, with the work group that this person would be a part of.

Corporate Fit

2. *Tell me about your relationships with your previous bosses.*

Sample Answer: My bosses would tell you that I've often been a sounding board for them. I've developed a close rapport with all three of my supervisors.

Advice: You should try to determine how the candidate has dealt with problems he or she may have had with a boss. What special problems did the candidate encounter when working with previous bosses, and how were they resolved? Would the solutions work in your corporate culture? You should find out as much as possible about how the candidate prefers to interact with a boss. Ask for specific examples of ways the candidate communicates with supervisors.

• • •

3. *Describe your working relationship with your colleagues.*

Sample Answer: They would probably tell you that nothing ever shocks me or sets me back too much and that I'm really an asset as an adviser when they're suffering a roadblock.

Advice: Encourage the candidate to describe specific interactions with colleagues. Does the candidate prefer a more formal, structured approach when interacting with others, or does he or she enjoy dropping by colleagues' offices unannounced? How well will the candidate fit into your company? How does he or she prefer to communicate with colleagues? By asking for specific instances of professional interaction, you should try to determine if the candidate can develop solid working relationships with people in your department.

4. *Tell me about a work environment that is ineffective for you.*

Sample Answer: I don't do terribly well when someone has a specific idea of how he or she wants a goal accomplished. It doesn't give me enough latitude to develop my own style.

Advice: Ask the candidate to describe, based on past experience, a work environment that he or she finds restrictive. You do not want to hire someone who will be unhappy in your company, so probe the candidate's background to determine what kind of environment he or she will thrive in, and what company cultures turn him or her off.

• • •

5. *What situations excite and motivate you?*

Sample Answer: What I really enjoy is working on a reengineering project whereby a true improvement results—for example, the Just in Time project, by which we slashed our inventory by $100,000.

Advice: Get the candidate to tell you about positive experiences with coworkers or managers. Carefully assess whether the candidate's answers satisfy you about whether he or she will fit into your group or department. Are the applicant's current or previous coworkers similar to the people in your company? Is there a crossover? Or are there great differences in corporate culture?

6. Tell me about a situation at work that frustrated you.

Sample Answer: I was frustrated once when one of my investment clients, who had insisted on a high-growth stock, called in a panic because the stock price had dropped more than 20 points in one day.

Advice: You want to measure here the candidate's ability to deal with setbacks or obstacles that get in the way of productivity on the job. How did the candidate initially cope with the problem, and how long did it take to resolve the situation satisfactorily? Would the candidate likely encounter similar situations at your company or within your department tomorrow? Are you satisfied with the way the candidate dealt with his or her frustration? How could the candidate have reduced the level of frustration or eliminated the source entirely?

• • •

7. Tell me about a problem you had with one of your work associates.

Sample Answer: We brought in a new associate who immediately offended one of the interns with his attitude. I took him aside and suggested that I often find it easier to ask people for help rather than just to give orders.

Advice: Evaluate how this person will fit in with your coworkers. What type of problem did he or she have with a coworker? How was it resolved? Is this sort of problem likely to come up in your division or group? You want to ensure that the problem is not an ongoing one and that the candidate had enough maturity and resolve to come to an amicable solution.

8. Can we check all of your references?

Sample Answer: I'd prefer that you call my current boss only after you've made me a firm offer of employment and I've had a chance to tell her myself that I'm considering changing jobs.

Advice: Included in the group of professional and academic references should be a reference for each full- or part-time position listed on the candidate's resume. What criteria did the candidate use to select these individuals as references? Does the list reflect a diverse group of people who can give you an overall assessment of the candidate and an idea of how he or she will perform for your department and company?

• • •

9. What would your last boss want to change about your work habits?

Sample Answer: He'd want me to be a morning person rather than a night owl. I like to work late at night; he likes to be at his desk by 7 a.m.

Advice: You are looking here for specific examples of how the candidate's previous supervisor might want to change some of the candidate's habits. This will give you clues as to what might be a problem in hiring this person into your group. Are the habits serious enough to cause a problem in your working relationship with this candidate? Do you consider the habits a potential problem for you or for members of your department? Will they hinder the candidate's overall effectiveness in relating to others in the company?

10. *Are you most productive working alone or in a group?*

Sample Answer: I need some private time for planning, but I like the activity of people around me and the ability to share ideas.

Advice: What is the candidate's preferred work environment? You need to determine how productive the candidate will be in your group or department, given the company culture and its demands on individuals. Does your department rely on teamwork to complete projects? If so, you must ensure that the candidate feels comfortable working in this sort of environment. Can you afford to bring into your group a candidate who is more independent-minded than other members of your department, even if the candidate is supertalented? How would such a hiring decision affect overall productivity?

• • •

11. *Tell me about a situation in which it was difficult to remain objective.*

Sample Answer: I had researched a new on-line service for our library, and my manager decided to pull funding at the last minute. It was frustrating for me because I was excited about the product and the vendor.

Advice: Does the candidate take work situations personally? In other words, will the candidate become offended if his or her ideas or concepts do not become reality? Were there any situations in the past in which the candidate had to defend a colleague or take a stand on an issue that had some emotional implications? You want to determine if the candidate can distinguish his or her feelings about how a project should proceed from what is best for the company.

Corporate Fit

12. ## What is your real personality beyond your professional image?

Sample Answer: I laugh a lot at my own shortcomings. I see irony in most things; I'm outspoken; but I also bring some humor and noise to any office. I think it provides a nice balance of warmth in a work setting.

Advice: Try to get the candidate to provide evidence of what he or she is like to work with on a daily basis. Look for personal characteristics, such as a sense of humor, tactfulness, and sensitivity, that add to the candidate's effectiveness in a variety of situations. You need to be careful with this type of question so as not to delve into someone's private life unless it relates directly to performing the job. Check the section on illegal questions on pages 428–429 if you have any concerns.

• • •

13. ## What environments allow you to be especially effective?

Sample Answer: I love environments where people are their own bosses—within reason. I like to have a goal but be able to draw my own map to get there. To accomplish goals, I rely on asking questions and finding people receptive, so cooperation and access are important to me in a work group.

Advice: Determine how productive the candidate will be in your group or department, given your company's culture and the demands placed on employees. Does your department rely on teamwork to complete projects? If so, you must ensure that the candidate feels comfortable in this type of working environment.

14. *How would your last employer describe your work habits and ethics?*

Sample Answer: I received an MVP award from my division for the extra efforts I put into one of our customer relationships. The customer had threatened to pull the account, so I stepped in and debugged the system, even though it required me to work through a holiday weekend.

Advice: If you were to call the candidate's supervisor, what would he or she say about the candidate's desire to dig in and get a job done? Does the candidate go the extra mile to help his or her company succeed in the marketplace? Is the candidate willing to come in on a weekend so that a project meets a deadline, or to make an extra effort to solve a customer problem, thus ensuring that customer's continuing patronage?

• • •

15. *Did your customers and primary constituencies enjoy working with you?*

Sample Answer: My client base changed very little, except that billings increased, so I think that's evidence the clients were satisfied enough to stay with me for more than three years. That's particularly unusual in the ad agency business. They simply knew they could count on me to treat their business as if it were my own.

Advice: Get the candidate to describe specific interactions with customers. Does the candidate prefer a more formal, structured approach when interacting with customers, or does he or she prefer to call on them at the drop of a hat? What would the candidate's customers say about this person if you decided to call one of them tomorrow? How do you think your customers will react to dealing with this candidate? You must feel entirely comfortable with the idea that if you hired the candidate today, he or she would interact and communicate effectively with your customers tomorrow.

16. ### Will you complement this department?

Sample Answer: I enjoy an environment where people bounce ideas off each other and have the flexibility to ask for help when they need it. I am usually a great troubleshooter for PC problems in my office, but I often ask for help proofreading important memos. I believe in give-and-take.

Advice: What skills and talents will the candidate bring to your department that others cannot offer? Ask the candidate for one or two examples—such as technical ability with computers or the ability to negotiate—that demonstrate how the candidate will improve your department's productivity and the productivity of others in the department. Does the candidate's work ethic and determination reflect the work ethic of your department?

• • •

17. ### Tell me something you learned recently from a book.

Sample Answer: I enjoy reading biographies, especially those of people who lived in a different era. I recently read Winston Churchill's biography, which taught me a lot about the value of leadership and good PR in times of stress.

Advice: Look for the candidate to draw parallels between literature that he or she enjoys on a regular basis and his or her professional life. What is it about the book that attracted the candidate in the first place? Did the candidate find lessons to apply to his or her current or future job? Would he or she recommend the book to a colleague or supervisor, and why?

18. Tell me about a work group you really enjoyed.

Sample Answer: My product management group in the marketing department really meshed. When one of us approached the final day before a launch, we all rolled up our sleeves and helped put together press packets or any other last items to be shipped to the sales force. Although it was an administrative task, it had to be done, and it was a good time for us all to speculate on the success of the product and any major concerns.

Advice: Get the candidate to describe in detail a work group situation in which he or she benefited from the experience of working with peers. What contribution did the candidate make to the team, and what did he or she learn from other team members? Implicit in this question is a test of the candidate's willingness to share information with colleagues and coworkers, as well as credit for accomplishments. You also want to see if the candidate really enjoys working as part of a group or would perhaps prefer to be an individual contributor to a department or organization.

• • •

19. Describe a time when you had to assist a coworker.

Sample Answer: I helped an associate understand survey methodology so he could write a report. He had never taken a research course and didn't know how to structure questions.

Advice: With this question your focus should be on whether the candidate sees him- or herself as a team player. Can the candidate put aside any personal agendas for the sake of the department or organization and help others achieve their goals and objectives? Or is the candidate motivated purely by personal gain and accomplishment? Keep in mind how individuals in your department prefer to interact with each other as you evaluate the candidate's response to this question.

Personal and Management Style

With tightened corporate policies and increased litigation making references from previous employers increasingly difficult to obtain, you often need to construct a picture of the candidate largely from the candidate alone. Ask open-ended questions to get the candidate to draw as full and complete a picture as possible. The questions in this section are designed to give you a feeling for how candidates approach their work, prioritize their time, and work with others. Weigh how important each of these issues may be in the new position. Will the person you hire interact with others frequently? Will prioritization of work be a crucial skill?

1. Tell me about your least favorite manager or professor.

Sample Answer: I worked with a manager who was inaccessible. If you walked in to ask him a question, you felt as though you were bothering him, so we all just learned to get help from each other.

Advice: The candidate should describe qualities, characteristics, or situations that illustrate why he or she was uncomfortable working with a former supervisor or teacher. What did the candidate least admire about this individual? You want to discover if there was a personality clash, or perhaps something more substantive about the manager's or teacher's shortcomings, that caused problems for the candidate. In either case you do not want to bring aboard someone who might very well find your personality or management style in conflict with his or her ability to be productive.

Personal and Management Style

2. **What type of management style do you think is particularly effective?**

Sample Answer: I've always learned well from people who are coaches rather than experts. When someone comes to me with a problem, I try to be supportive as well as analytical.

Advice: Get the candidate to describe the kinds of people, including coworkers and bosses, that he or she likes to work with. Does the candidate think his or her boss communicates effectively on a daily basis? Does the candidate prefer to micromanage, or does he or she prefer a hands-off approach? Is the candidate more effective in a highly structured, rigidly managed environment, or does he or she prefer a free-wheeling, take-the-initiative approach? Make sure the candidate's answers are consistent with your company's own approach to managing people.

• • •

3. **Tell me about your personal management style.**

Sample Answer: When people come to me with an issue or a problem, I repeat what they have told me, but I try to reorganize the ideas so that they're able to see the problem or answer for themselves.

Advice: Press the candidate for specific examples of how he or she motivates and leads employees through various situations. Does the candidate's style mesh with your style? How will other employees in your department respond to this candidate's management methods?

4. *What are some of the things your previous supervisor did that you disliked?*

Sample Answer: The only thing I really don't like is to get feedback in front of other people. I like to hear good or bad feedback in private, so I have time to think and react to the issue without other distractions.

Advice: How did the candidate deal with his or her previous boss? The response here should indicate whether the candidate will get along with you and work well under your management style. It should also tell you if you are going to be hiring someone who will likely clash with your approach and ideas and make your department less productive.

• • •

5. *How do you organize and plan for major projects?*

Sample Answer: I like to brainstorm a best, most likely, and worst scenario, then set a timetable that is realistic.

Advice: As a hiring manager, you are looking for the candidate to tell you how he or she handles major projects. The answer will indicate whether the candidate is more comfortable doing things on the fly, or working in a rigid, structured environment. Some people think and plan "organically"; others need structure and a step-by-step methodology for planning out a project. How does the candidate's approach fit with your company and department? How comfortable are you with the candidate's method of accomplishing tasks?

Personal and Management Style

6. *Tell me about a time you had to work under intense pressure.*

Sample Answer: I had to complete an end-of-quarter report while on a business trip. With the help of my secretary, I was able to locate and review files and complete the report on time.

Advice: Your definition of "intense pressure" may differ from the candidate's view of meeting a tight deadline. How does the candidate respond to an assignment delegated at four o'clock on a Friday afternoon? Does he or she prefer to work alone or require guidance and hand-holding? How does the candidate's temperament change with additional pressure? You need to feel totally comfortable with this person's ability to handle pressure on your terms, without any loss of quality.

• • •

7. *How do you handle tension with your boss?*

Sample Answer: The only tension I've ever felt was when we were both too busy to keep each other informed. Once my boss overcommitted me while I was busy with other deadlines.

Advice: How communicative is the candidate with respect to situations that produce a certain amount of tension? Ask for specific examples from the candidate's past in terms of prior relationships with the boss. Does the candidate become emotional, or does he or she internalize conflict? You also need to evaluate how you prefer to handle such tension. Does your method of dealing with subordinates complement the candidate's way of dealing with superiors?

Personal and Management Style

8. Tell me about a time you had to defend an idea to your boss.

Sample Answer: Once I had to convince my boss to change PR firms. I believed that our West Coast interests were not being handled properly by our Chicago-based PR firm.

Advice: Ask the candidate for an example of a time when he or she had to stand up and convince the boss that an idea was solid and should be implemented. What method or style did the candidate use to convince the supervisor that the idea was a sound one and would benefit the company? Are you convinced that the idea or concept was, indeed, worthwhile? Was the candidate creative in his or her approach and persuasive in argument? Did the boss ultimately agree 100 percent or present some type of compromise or alternative?

• • •

9. Tell me about a learning experience that affected your personal management style.

Sample Answer: Early on in my job at the bank I wrote a letter to a senior manager but failed to copy his two assistants. One of them was negatively impacted by the content of the memo.

Advice: You want the candidate to describe a situation in which his or her judgment or decision making yielded a poor result. What did the candidate take away from the experience, and what would he or she do differently if the situation presented itself again? Make sure the candidate convinces you that he or she is ready for new challenges and can be a more effective leader and manager as a result of prior mistakes.

Personal and Management Style

10. What personal characteristics add to your effectiveness?

Sample Answer: I always stay in touch with my network. If I see an article that I think might be of interest to someone I know, I clip it and send it to that person.

Advice: Have the candidate describe the kinds of people, including coworkers and supervisors, he or she likes to work with. What is the candidate's strongest personal asset or talent, and how will it help your company? How does the candidate like to communicate with superiors, coworkers, and subordinates? Listen for any characteristics that you know are similar to, or compatible with, other individuals in your group or department.

• • •

11. Tell me about an effective manager or professor you have known.

Sample Answer: The best professor I ever had always reviewed the most important points from our previous class before moving on to new material. He also watched our faces carefully and repeated information whenever he saw blank stares. Sometimes he would just ask for feedback by saying, "What are you having difficulty with?" He never assumed too much or made us feel stupid for not grasping a concept quickly.

Advice: Look for characteristics, qualities, and management styles that closely resemble your own in the candidate's answer. You want to bring someone aboard who will respond positively to your style, and if the candidate has had a positive experience with an individual either in an academic or professional environment who shares your leadership or management style, it's a safe bet you will have a productive professional relationship with the candidate.

12. What type of people do you work with most effectively?

Sample Answer: I tend to work well with people who are confident and straightforward. It is more difficult for me to be around timid people because I move quickly and am decisive.

Advice: Encourage the candidate to describe the kinds of people, including coworkers and bosses, that he or she likes to work with every day. Does the candidate think his or her boss communicates effectively on a daily basis? Does the candidate prefer to micromanage, or does he or she prefer a hands-off approach? Is the candidate more effective in a highly structured, rigidly managed environment, or does he or she prefer a free-wheeling, take-the-initiative approach? Make sure the candidate's answers are compatible with your company's approach to managing people.

• • •

13. In your last job, what projects did you give priority?

Sample Answer: I've always put work with established clients first because it offers a better risk/return value. The last thing I do is general correspondence, especially internal correspondence, which I take care of at the end of the day or week.

Advice: Don't look for details about any one particular project here; rather, focus on the candidate's ability to organize projects based on deadlines or importance to the company's bottom line. Does the candidate have the ability to recognize the value of a particular project to the department or company? What criteria does he or she use to determine the value and importance of projects?

14. *Describe a time when you acted on someone's suggestion.*

Sample Answer: I changed my open office hours because several of my employees found it difficult to drop by except in the early mornings.

Advice: How receptive is the candidate to assistance or advice from colleagues and coworkers? The answer to this question will help you determine the candidate's flexibility and willingness to listen to others. You should get a clear indication here of the candidate's ability to work in concert with other people and to use their knowledge and experience to contribute productively to your organization.

• • •

15. *What aspect of your management style would you like to change?*

Sample Answer: I've been working on resisting the urge to tell people the answers when they ask for advice. I think it is more important to teach people how to solve their own problems. I've gotten better at coaching and presenting supportive questions and feedback, without telling people what to do.

Advice: The candidate's answer should focus on some managerial skill that involves people or resources, and how he or she plans to improve in the short term. You should be concerned if the candidate discusses some aspect of his or her managerial ability that you believe is a key component to managing the people or resources in your department on a daily basis.

Personal and Management Style

16. *Have you ever felt defensive around your boss or peers?*

Sample Answer: Once I had to explain why I thought a black-and-white brochure was more suitable for the content of an insurance product brochure. No one in my office liked the idea initially because they were all used to color brochures and thought black and white just looked cheap. Eventually I convinced them a black-and-white brochure would work better, in a subtle way, to present information about a difficult topic—death benefits.

Advice: Some employees refuse to admit defeat or try to explain away a problem rather than owning up to the situation and taking responsibility. Depending upon your management style, you will want to find out how the candidate reacts to criticism of his or her work. Can this candidate deal with negative comments and harsh critiques and produce better, more dynamic output, or will he or she rebel and make life difficult for you and others in the department?

• • •

17. *Have you patterned your management style after someone in particular?*

Sample Answer: I've emulated my first boss in many ways. I keep a file on my desk for each of my staff members. They can throw notes, ideas, work they want me to review, or anything else in there, and I do the same. It's an extra form of communication whenever one of us gets an idea. Then when we sit down to talk, that file provides the framework for what we need to cover.

Advice: The answer here should describe a former supervisor, teacher, or someone else who had a profound influence on the candidate in either a work or an academic setting. What aspects of the individual's managerial style did the candidate find appealing or impressive? Encourage the candidate to give specific instances of how the individual managed groups or departments; then see if you can draw any parallels to your own managerial style.

• • •

18. *Describe a leader you admire.*

Sample Answer: I've always admired the president of my company. He's visible, he doesn't want a special parking place or table in the cafeteria, and he gives you the feeling that he's just another member of the team.

Advice: The candidate should describe a former manager or supervisor he or she respected and would most likely emulate. Ask the candidate to describe qualities and characteristics of people that he or she considers impressive in terms of leading, motivating, or strategizing.

Passion for the Business

A skilled professional who brings a lot of passion to his or her work is quite likely to be a superlative performer who can drive your business forward. People who are highly passionate about their work often perform way over the levels their skills and experience would have led one to expect. There are three different types of passion you should look for: passion for the industry/career path, passion for working at a particular company, and passion for a particular position. However, all too often a candidate who has lots of passion in one of these areas may have little passion in the others. And, of course, if the candidate is highly passionate about the industry and the job but not the potential employer, he or she is are more likely to stay with the new employer for only a short period of time.

1. Why do you want this job?

Sample Answer: I've always wanted to work in an industry that makes tools. One of my hobbies is home improvement projects, so I've collected a number of saws manufactured by your company.

Advice: Be wary of the candidate who simply lists job functions and responsibilities as opposed to demonstrating in-depth knowledge about the position, your company, and the industry. The candidate should go beyond mere job description and tell you why he or she is truly excited about the job and ready to make an impact from the start. What is it about the position that the candidate finds so appealing or unique as compared to other positions for which he or she is interviewing?

2. *Why do you want to work for this company?*

Sample Answer: I lost a bid several years ago to your company. I realized then that, with similar products, the company with the best service record will survive in the long run.

Advice: What does the candidate like about your company other than its products and services? For example, if your company is an entrepreneurial start-up, does the candidate think he or she has the temperament and personality to fit in with the other members of your company? If your company is more structured and bureaucratic, has the candidate demonstrated that he or she has the qualities to succeed in such an environment? What type of environment does the candidate feel most comfortable and effective in, and does it match the type of environment at your company?

• • •

3. *What excites you about this industry?*

Sample Answer: I've always wanted to be an architect; growing up, I used to enjoy sketching houses and drawing room arrangements. As a teen, I did the rough sketches for the design of a house my parents eventually built.

Advice: Ask the candidate to give specific reasons why he or she believes your industry is *the* place to work. The response should include reasons from both work experience and personal values. Do not accept the standard rhetoric of "I see plastics as being the industry of the future." You want to make sure the candidate has taken the time to get to know companies, people, products, and services within the industry and can, in all confidence, articulate why the industry holds such promise.

Passion for the Business

4. Describe our competition as you see it.

Sample Answer: Most of your competitors try to do too many different things. As a result, they have difficulty expanding and maintaining consistent quality.

Advice: Has the candidate done his or her homework and thoroughly researched your industry? Does the candidate have a clear sense of how the competition is attacking the marketplace? Can the candidate articulate your competitor's strategic direction and predict what it will be doing in the next year to eighteen months? You need to make sure the candidate has a strong grasp of what the players in your industry are doing to differentiate their products or services from others', and how they are doing it. Does the candidate see the "big picture" and understand the different market strengths of your company's competitors?

• • •

5. Tell me what you know about our company.

Sample Answer: I served as an intern to a restaurant analyst last summer, so I followed all the steak house chains closely. I've noticed that you focus on a limited but consistent menu with great results.

Advice: Look for the candidate to go beyond traditional sources of information, such as the *Wall Street Journal* or annual reports, and give you in-depth information about your company and its position in the industry. Can the candidate tell you what threats to your market position might exist in the near future? Does the candidate have a good feel for your products or services, and can he or she tell you what legitimate opportunities exist in the marketplace for your company?

Passion for the Business

6. *Tell me what you think are our distinctive advantages within this industry.*

Sample Answer: With your low-cost production methods, you seem to be in a better position than your closest rival to spend aggressively on R and D—even in a down year.

Advice: Get the candidate to give you concrete examples of what he or she thinks are your competitive advantages. If your industry is in a state of transition, is the candidate aware of the transition and the ways in which your company can take advantage of it? Are you convinced that the advantages cited by the candidate are realistic, given your competitive position in your industry? Can the candidate differentiate the market strengths and weaknesses of the major players in your industry?

• • •

7. *What are your major interests in our company?*

Sample Answer: I'm most interested in your Latin American developments. My father was an army officer, and we lived in Latin America for three years. I know that you have just entered joint ventures with two processing companies in Chile.

Advice: Test the candidate's knowledge of your products or services beyond what he or she might find in marketing literature or advertising pieces. Does the candidate have some intimate knowledge of your field operations or of a division that he or she finds particularly appealing as a place to grow and contribute? Why is the candidate's interest in a particular area of the company so strong? Will the candidate be able to sustain this interest in your company for several years, and if so, how?

Passion for the Business

8. ## Why would you be especially good working in this business?

Sample Answer: I was a pastry chef, so I understand dessert products and can help you in new product development, especially in the areas of preservatives and flavoring.

Advice: The candidate must show not only enthusiasm for the product or service but some reasonable knowledge of successful product or service strategies. Look for personal qualities, and ask for examples that demonstrate business acumen and indicate that the candidate will be successful in your industry and, more specifically, at your company.

• • •

9. ## What would you do differently if you ran this company?

Sample Answer: I might investigate whether to sell off the light-manufacturing business and start an aggressive supplier-relations campaign.

Advice: This is a classic question that tests the candidate's knowledge of your business as well as his or her perception of where your company is headed in the next year to eighteen months. What areas of the company does the candidate believe need improvement or possibly an overhaul? You should also measure the candidate's willingness to take risks. How frank would he or she be in taking immediate steps to move into new markets or to develop new products or services?

10. *Why do you think this company or industry can hold your interest over the long haul?*

Sample Answer: The technology in this industry is changing so rapidly that I see plenty of room for job fulfillment, regardless of promotions. I'm especially interested in multimedia training applications.

Advice: Here the candidate must demonstrate a significant commitment to the industry and your company. You want to make sure that this candidate isn't merely job hopping or testing the waters. The candidate must demonstrate enthusiasm and excitement for the industry and give solid reasons why he or she will stick around and not jump ship at a moment's notice.

• • •

11. *Tell me where you think you'd like to be in five years.*

Sample Answer: I'd really like to have the opportunity to work in operations management. I'd also like the chance to develop my communication skills, perhaps by managing a small staff.

Advice: You should not be looking for job titles here, but rather for some logical progression of duties and responsibilities that indicates whether the candidate really wants to be in your industry. You need to find out during the interview, rather than three months into the job, if the candidate is looking to start a business or has some other long-term agenda. Dig into the candidate's thoughts on what he or she is looking for in terms of level of responsibility and professional growth.

Passion for the Business

12. *What would you do if one of our competitors offered you a position?*

Sample Answer: I'd say no. I'm not interested in other players in this industry. I want to work for your company because I won a number of races wearing 100

your brand. I know I'd be convincing selling to retailers.

Advice: You want to find out if the candidate is serious about working in your industry or is just shopping around. Has the candidate done his or her homework and thoroughly researched your industry? Does he or she know what your competitors are up to and what types of opportunities exist at those companies? A candidate who displays strong industry knowledge and is intimately aware of your competitors' agendas will be a more valuable hire.

• • •

13. *Tell me what you know about the industry.*

Sample Answer: None of the players in the industry have franchised. I believe that you could now franchise without losing your consistency. You have good management in place with good rules and training procedures. Your competitors either lack the skilled trainers or don't have the quality reputation to attract good franchisees. By franchising you could capture a large portion of the expected 14 percent increase in the total market over the next two years.

Advice: If you press candidates on their current knowledge of the industry, you will quickly separate the tire kickers from those who truly want to be in your industry. Look for more than what someone might find in a local library or an annual report. Candidates should be able to give you substantive evidence of industry trends extending at least over a year to eighteen months and tell you who the players will be during this time period.

14. What is your favorite product made by our company?

Sample Answer: I've used Softer Than Ever shampoo for years. In fact, my initial contact with the company was with the brand manager for Softer Than Ever. She encouraged me to apply for an HR position here.

Advice: Why does the candidate find your product more appealing or interesting than a competitor's product? What features does the candidate admire most about your product, and how would he or she sell the product to a prospective customer? You want to measure the candidate's knowledge of your company and the positioning of your products against the competition.

• • •

15. Where do you think we are the most vulnerable as a business?

Sample Answer: Your cash position and strong product presence make you an attractive target for a takeover. That's my only major concern. I've already worked for one organization that was merged. However, I also know I can weather the storm.

Advice: The candidate should be able to pinpoint areas where your company could be doing better than the competition or is getting beaten out by competitors. Does the candidate have ideas about how your company can outmaneuver the competition and gain market share? This question will quickly help you determine if the candidate is up to speed on your competitive situation and if he or she can think strategically.

16. What do you think of our newest product and ads?

Sample Answer: It seems that your new ads are trying to show that breakfast time is family time, with a certain wholesomeness. Are you doing this to balance against the recent bad press about high-fat foods without attacking the issue directly?

Advice: What is the candidate's depth of knowledge about your product line, your product planning, and your strategy in positioning the company within the industry? Does the candidate have the skill and ability to analyze your advertising strategy and offer comments that would suggest he or she could step in and add value to your department tomorrow?

• • •

17. Describe your ideal career.

Sample Answer: I'd like to stay in a field related to training no matter what happens. I was too interested in business to work at a university, but I believe teaching is somehow in my blood. I've been good at sales because I took the time to educate my clients. Now I look forward to training the new hires.

Advice: Rather than looking for specific job titles here, you want to see some progression in career development that follows naturally from prior positions. The candidate should be prepared to discuss what is motivating him or her to seek your position, and what he or she expects from your company in the next several years. You want the candidate to give you an answer that indicates a career track that your company can reasonably offer over the next several years.

Passion for the Business

18. *How do you stay current?*

Sample Answer: I pore over the *Wall Street Journal*, *New York Times*, *Institutional Investor*, and several mutual fund newsletters. And I have a number of friends who are analysts.

Advice: The candidate should list journals, books, periodicals, and any other material relevant to your industry, as well as any general business publications. Find out what particular types of articles and/or issues attract the candidate and how he or she uses this information at work. Does the candidate belong to any special trade associations or groups that enhance his or her professional development?

• • •

19. *If you had unlimited time and financial resources, how would you spend them?*

Sample Answer: I'd love to be able to take several executive seminars on financial management that aren't geared toward financial experts. I'd also love to be able to shut down my department long enough to send everyone through an Outward Bound program. Then I'd probably travel, look at foreign competitors, and enjoy the food along the way.

Advice: This question asks the candidate to pick those activities he or she truly enjoys and would commit to for extended periods. The activities the candidate chooses should reveal personal values and character traits. (For instance, does the candidate enjoy participating in outdoor activities? Traveling? Writing plays or short stories? Building models or remodeling houses?) You might also gain some insight into what kind of work environment the candidate may be the most comfortable in.

Personal Interests

Strong personal interests can indicate a more balanced lifestyle and can help professionals to recharge their batteries and avoid getting burned out. The types of activities individuals enjoy in their spare time may give you further insight into how they might approach work issues. Do they stick with one or two activities and really excel at them, or do they experiment with a broad variety of pursuits? Of course, as in many other areas of interviewing, you need to be cautious when asking seemingly innocent personal questions—they may be interpreted as being discriminatory.

1. Tell me about an activity you've remained interested in outside of work over the last several years.

Sample Answer: I've been involved in fund-raising for the Cancer Society ever since my grandmother died from the disease. I hope they continue to be successful in saving people's lives.

Advice: Look for an ongoing commitment to some interest or hobby. The candidate must have interests outside the workplace to avoid burning out too quickly. These interests can range from civic and political activities, to sports or hobbies such as coin collecting, model railroading, and painting. How did the candidate first become interested in the activity, and why has it held his or her interest for so long? Does the candidate demonstrate some depth or expertise in this particular hobby or interest? What level of enthusiasm does he or she exhibit when talking about this outside interest? Make sure not to discriminate against a candidate whose membership or participation in an organization indicates a particular race, color, national origin, religion, sex, physical handicap, age, or other characteristic protected by federal or local employment laws.

2. What outside activities complement your work interests?

Sample Answer: I really enjoy chess. It is a game that demands strategy, a lot of thought, and a competitive attitude, and that's how I approach my work.

Advice: Look for specific examples of what the candidate does during his or her spare time. What would the candidate do if your company were to offer a week away from work at the company's expense? Where would the candidate go? You want this person to demonstrate a well-rounded lifestyle that will enhance his or her professional development. Make sure not to discriminate against a candidate whose membership or participation in an organization indicates a particular race, color, national origin, religion, sex, physical handicap, age, or other characteristic protected by federal or local employment laws.

• • •

3. What do you do in your spare time?

Sample Answer: I really enjoy outside activities, especially camping. I've learned a lot about different fabrics that are good for various weather conditions. That's why I'm so interested in your textile operations.

Advice: What does the candidate like to do on a typical weekend or a free day? You want evidence here that the candidate can keep fresh and invigorated by participating in outside activities, so he or she will remain a strong contributor to your organization. The candidate should show a healthy balance in his or her life. In the case of a candidate who must relocate, you should be concerned that the activities offered in your area will be of ongoing interest. For instance, if the candidate likes to surf on a regular basis, a position on Wall Street may not be particularly desirable. Make sure not to discriminate against a candidate whose membership or participation in an organization indicates a particular race, color, national origin, religion, sex, physical handicap, age, or other characteristic protected by federal or local employment laws.

• • •

4. If you had unlimited leisure time, how would you spend it?

Sample Answer: I don't think I could ever be happy with a lot of spare time. I'd probably travel, learn another language, and spend more time doing charity work.

Advice: This is another question that basically asks the candidate to describe those activities he or she truly enjoys and would commit to for extended periods. The activities should give you some indication of the candidate's values and personality. You won't learn much here about work-related skills or ability to the job, but you should be able to form an opinion about the candidate's balance between work, family, and leisure.

• • •

5. If you found yourself getting burned out, what might you do to revitalize your energy?

Sample Answer: I don't allow myself to get involved in a routine to the point that I get burned out. I'm the type of person who always asks for new assignments to stay motivated.

Advice: Burnout is always a threat in corporate America, even for the best and most disciplined employees. Here again it is important to discover if the candidate has a wide range of interests outside of work and can effectively balance job responsibilities with an active lifestyle. Working hard becomes less of a sin if the candidate plays hard as well.

Personal Interests

6. Do you have a balanced lifestyle?

Sample Answer: I make an effort to get out of the office at a reasonable hour twice a week. I go home and walk three miles with my dog. That's one of the most relaxing things I do, but it also often helps me think of solutions for problems at work, even though I'm not consciously trying to solve those problems.

Advice: With this question you are looking for examples of how the candidate can juggle work and outside activities without overextending him- or herself. Candidates who have a well-rounded background often are less likely to suffer burnout from a demanding workplace. Can the candidate give sufficient attention to both work and outside activities without upsetting the balance, and respond to quickly changing circumstances that may demand disproportionate time at work at the expense of the outside activities?

• • •

7. Tell me about a time you were in a relaxed setting away from work and got an idea that helped in your work.

Sample Answer: I was on vacation in Mexico and saw a woman hanging her laundry and using a homemade seesaw to lift her laundry basket when she needed something out of it. It gave me an idea for a new type of scaffolding, which I designed when I got back to work. Now our brick masons have a rotating bench that keeps their materials at waist level, which reduces back fatigue.

Advice: You are looking for the candidate's awareness of opportunities outside the workplace to seize ideas or concepts that might benefit his or her company. Be prepared to listen to a story, and don't be surprised if some off-the-wall quirkiness led the candidate to an idea that improved his or her last job. Often individuals who are far removed from a stressful workplace environment come up with unusual and creative ideas to help their company improve its bottom line.

Personal Interests

8. *How is your personality reflected in the kinds of activities you enjoy?*

Sample Answer: I love to cook and entertain. That's the salesman coming out in me. I love sharing experiences with people, and I'm very outgoing. I don't enjoy being alone. I always feel as if I should be doing "something."

Advice: Individuals who enjoy high-risk activities outside the workplace may exhibit that type of behavior on the job. This question is used to determine how outside activities relate to the skills and talents the candidate uses on a daily basis to perform his or her job.

• • •

9. *What kinds of leisure activities help you perform your work better?*

Sample Answer: I enjoy sitting outside during lunch and talking with students. It gives me a chance to get fresh air, but it also helps the students get comfortable with me, so they are more likely to seek my help when they need it.

Advice: What does the candidate like to do on a typical weekend or free day? You want evidence that the candidate can keep fresh and invigorated by participating in outside activities so that he or she will continue to be a strong asset to your organization's work force. The candidate should show a balance in his or her life choices. In the case of a candidate who has to move, you may want to ensure that the activities offered in your area will be of particular interest. For instance, if the candidate likes to snow ski on a regular basis, a position in Florida may not be what he or she wants. Look for a more than passing interest in outside activities that can help with the development of a well-rounded employee.

10. *Our company believes that employees should give something back to the community. How do you feel about that?*

Sample Answer: I believe that, too. In my last job as manager, I told each of my employees they could spend one Friday afternoon a month at a charity of their choice on company time as long as they weren't all gone on the same Fridays. Ironically, productivity didn't decrease at all; they got more done in the morning, and apparently Friday afternoons were never that productive anyway. I spend my afternoons with an adult reading program.

Advice: This question tests the candidate's willingness to give as well as to receive, including any volunteer or charity work outside the normal business day. Ask the candidate for one or two examples of how he or she gives back to the community, apart from making donations of money. What does the candidate do specifically to help others outside of work be more productive and have a more fulfilling life? Make sure not to discriminate against a candidate whose membership or participation in an organization indicates a particular race, color, national origin, religion, sex, physical handicap, age, or other characteristic protected by federal or local employment laws.

• • •

11. *What community projects that can use your professional skills are particularly interesting to you?*

Sample Answer: As a marketing person, I've offered free advice to our local high school for its fund-raisers and also to a local real estate office whose success could help my rural community's real estate values.

Advice: Here you want the candidate to describe projects that make use of the skills routinely required in the open position. Why was the candidate attracted to a community project in the first place? What skills or new experience did he or she gain by working on this project? Is it readily apparent that these projects hold some value with respect to the duties of the job you're seeking to fill?

• • •

12. *Describe how a sport or hobby has taught you a lesson in teamwork or discipline.*

Sample Answer: My debate-team coach in high school taught me to help out team members when they needed it. I found that if I did, someone was always willing to help me in return when I needed it. I've applied that principal in all of my work groups, especially on the trading floor.

Advice: Here you are looking not so much at the nature of the sport or hobby as at the value of it, and the experience gained by the candidate while interacting in a

competitive environment. How did the candidate handle the pressure of winning? What lessons did he or she take away from the experience? You want to know, basically, if the candidate is able to put ego on the shelf for the benefit of his or her teammates.

Personal Interests

13. Tell me about an interest that you outgrew.

Sample Answer: Early on, I wanted to be a research physician. Then I spent time in a chemistry lab and realized I didn't like the next twelve years of lab work that I saw before me. That's why I chose medical equipment marketing instead. It brings together my respect for the medical profession with a job activity that's more suited to my personality.

Advice: Ideally, you want the candidate to talk about an early career aspiration, project, or hobby that did not sustain his or her interest over the long haul. What factors led the candidate to move on to other projects, or to develop new career goals? You also want to find out if this move is symptomatic of the candidate; in other words, does he or she quickly lose interest or become easily distracted and less likely to commit to following through on a goal?

• • •

14. What do you do to relax?

Sample Answer: I have a great family. Weekends are like a vacation for me. When I'm at work, I focus on work, but when I'm home on weekends, my family gets my full attention.

Advice: Burnout and stress are common enemies of corporate professionals, especially in this age of downsizing and reorganization. You want a clear demonstration from the candidate that he or she can leave work at the office and engage in stimulating, rejuvenating activities. What types of activities does the candidate enjoy outside of work? Does he or she believe in a good balance between work and play? You want the candidate to demonstrate a well-rounded lifestyle that will enhance his or her professional development.

15. *When you aren't at work, do you prefer an agenda, or are you spontaneous?*

Sample Answer: My workday is very structured because I'm in four or five meetings daily. On weekends I like to have a plan but be flexible enough to try something new at the last minute.

Advice: Does the candidate prefer rigidity in his or her schedule outside the office? If the candidate can leave the office behind and is able to relax in an unstructured, unplanned environment, the chances are good that he or she will return to work renewed and invigorated.

• • •

16. *Tell me about a character in a book or movie that you identified with.*

Sample Answer: No one particular book or movie stands out in my mind. However, I am often inspired by stories of people who have succeeded despite adversity.

Advice: Look for the candidate to draw parallels between literature and his or her professional life. What is it about a book that attracted the candidate in the first place? Did he or she find lessons to apply to work? Would the candidate recommend the book to a colleague or supervisor, and why?

Management Style, Creativity, Leadership

4 s you evaluate candidates for more senior, decision-making positions, the factors that are often difficult to weigh, such as creativity and leadership skills, take on increased importance. In a fairly structured environment, many people can perform well without a lot of creativity, leadership skills, or a well-balanced management style. But in more loosely structured organizations and in more senior positions, these factors are crucial for achieving high levels of performance.

1. What is the most creative or innovative idea you have ever had?

Sample Answer: During a summer job at a cellular phone company I noticed that all the sales inquiries were distributed haphazardly to the sales assistants. I developed a system of grouping sales inquiries according to category, region, and size of company.

Advice: Does the candidate have a creative style that will work well in your organization? You will want to determine how the candidate's creative thinking is similar to or different from the way your company approaches the creative process, and eliciting several examples of creativity from the candidate will be helpful here.

2. Give me an example of how you have overcome an obstacle in a creative way.

Sample Answer: Our company could never get an appointment with a major Fortune 500 company. I contacted a VP's assistant and set up a presentation. It went so well that she scheduled us on the spot.

Advice: Have the candidate describe how he or she tackled a tough assignment and developed a creative solution. If your work environment demands a flexible, adaptive individual with a creative bent, ask for examples of how the candidate has been able to eliminate an obstacle that hindered progress on a project or task. You want a specific example here that will apply to the position for which you are hiring.

• • •

3. Why do you think that some companies with good products fail?

Sample Answer: Any product must continually adapt to meet the changing needs and demands of the consumer. In order to succeed, companies must get employees to "buy in" to the product.

Advice: This question tests the candidate's ability to analyze a company's strategic positioning, strengths, and weaknesses relative to the marketplace. Does the candidate have a strong grasp of your company's marketing and sales strategies, resources devoted to product planning and marketing, talent and skill level, and overall mission and direction? You want to determine if the candidate has the ability to think critically and give an objective evaluation of what a company needs to do to market its products successfully.

4. Describe a time when an existing process just didn't work.

Sample Answer: The order entry system at the telecommunications company where I worked was a mess. Orders weren't being processed correctly or in a timely manner. I did a work flow analysis to determine the bottlenecks, then convinced my boss that we needed to spend $150,000 to $200,000 on a new computer system.

Advice: Encourage the candidate to describe an internal situation in which there was an information bottleneck or a flawed methodology. How did the candidate resolve the situation? Did he or she inherit the problem, or was it a result of the candidate's failing to anticipate possible roadblocks when working on a project or system? What steps did the candidate take to rectify the situation and prevent the problem from reoccurring?

• • •

5. How would a former subordinate or associate describe your leadership style?

Sample Answer: My colleagues would probably say that I'm the strong, silent type when it comes to leadership. I don't make a big deal about being in charge or giving orders.

Advice: If the candidate's former colleagues were sitting in the interview, what would they say about the candidate's ability to manage others? Do you accept the response to this question, given the managerial background and accomplishments outlined on the candidate's resume? Based on the response you receive, do you think the candidate could lead members of your department? Look for some indication of his or her ability to grow and influence others in your department for the short and long term.

6. Describe an improvement you personally initiated.

Sample Answer: I improved an outdated inventory management system for all laboratory supplies and equipment at Memorial Hospital. I decreased inventory costs while raising quality.

Advice: You want a specific example here of how the candidate took the bull by the horns and came up with a creative solution. How did the candidate analyze the problem? What steps did he or she take to determine the improvements necessary to enhance a project or task? Is the improvement significant in your eyes?

• • •

7. Tell me about a time you had to persuade others to adopt your idea.

Sample Answer: Our customer retention at the biotech company where I worked was poor. I thought we could take the first step in alleviating this problem by doing a thorough customer attitude survey, which my boss thought would be a waste of time. I finally persuaded him that we could uncover some of the core reasons why retention had been getting progressively worse.

Advice: Probe the candidate's background and ask for examples of times when he or she was successful in convincing others to accept an idea or concept. What did the candidate do or say to sell others on the idea? Did the candidate use visual aids or physical samples of products or items to get others to see the value in the idea? You are testing here not only the communicative powers of the candidate but also his or her creativity when persuading others to buy in to an idea. Why was there resistance to the idea in the first place, and how did the candidate overcome this resistance?

Management Style, Creativity, Leadership

8. *What would your last supervisor say about your initiative?*

Sample Answer: She would probably say that I am a real go-getter with plenty of ideas. She would also say, most likely, that I am not bashful when it comes to recommending process or procedural improvements.

Advice: You want the candidate to describe situations in which he or she eagerly dived into a project or other assignment, more than willing to be first in line to make a good situation even better. Did the candidate have to be prodded into taking the lead on projects or tasks? Or can he or she give examples of times when a supervisor recommended the candidate for challenging assignments above and beyond the normal daily routine?

• • •

9. *Have your past job appraisals adequately portrayed your leadership abilities?*

Sample Answer: Although I've had limited opportunity to demonstrate my leadership abilities in my previous job, I'm certain my references would mention that I am extremely thorough and dependable.

Advice: How has the candidate fared in job appraisals with respect to leadership qualities, if leadership was a factor in the candidate's appraisal? You should try to determine what approach the candidate takes in providing leadership either on a team or in a supervisory role. Leadership means different things to different people, and it will be helpful to find out how the candidate, and others, perceive his or her leadership style.

10. Tell me about one of your projects that failed.

Sample Answer: During the last hurricane in 1992 my insurance company was inundated with claims. I thought I could single-handedly take care of all the claims in my area, but when reality set in, I discovered otherwise. I had to get help from the investigators to get all the work done.

Advice: How does the candidate deal with failure? How resourceful is he or she in sticking to the task at hand until a solution is found? What did the candidate learn from this failure? Projects can fail because of external as much as internal factors, so get the candidate to give an honest appraisal of what happened, why it happened, and what he or she would do differently, given the chance.

• • •

11. How resourceful are you?

Sample Answer: For my first product launch I decided to get three of our largest customers to videotape an endorsement for use in our marketing campaign. The endorsements helped us exceed our sales goals.

Advice: The candidate should have plenty of examples of times when he or she used creative or technical skills to solve a problem. You want evidence that the candidate can respond to a problem situation by using his or her ingenuity to see the matter through to a successful resolution.

12. Give me proof of your persuasiveness.

Sample Answer: On my last job I analyzed communication expenditures for a major utility. I had to get the consensus of employees in several different areas. After a frustrating month I finally got their cooperation, the project went flawlessly, and I received a bonus for my efforts.

Advice: How has the candidate convinced either coworkers or supervisors that ideas or plans should be implemented? Not everyone has the ability to argue persuasively for a cause or idea, so in this case you should assess the candidate's willingness to recognize a problem and ability to convince others to adopt his or her solution.

• • •

13. How have you demonstrated leadership by example?

Sample Answer: On a recent hiking trip in the Canadian Rockies, I volunteered to lead novice hikers through some rough terrain. I made sure they understood and appreciated their surroundings.

Advice: Obviously, you want the candidate to describe a time when he or she effectively showed others what needed to be done in a situation that called for leadership. What steps did the candidate take to get others to follow? Do you feel comfortable with the candidate's leadership qualities based on the answer to this question? Would you feel confident placing the candidate in a leadership position within your department or organization?

14. Describe situations in which you are most comfortable as the leader.

Sample Answer: One of my talents is to take complex issues or problems and break them down into their simplest parts. As a result, people tend to seek out my advice when a major project is running into difficulty.

Advice: Encourage the candidate to describe particular instances when he or she immediately assumed a leadership role. What is it about a situation that brought out the candidate's leadership qualities? How did others respond to the candidate? Did the candidate's boss recognize that he or she would be a natural leader given the set of circumstances? You should also consider if the types of situations the candidate describes would occur in your department. Are you confident the candidate can lead your employees in those situations?

• • •

15. In what situations are you an effective contributor if you are not the leader?

Sample Answer: I am always willing to lend support to projects that are not under my direct supervision. Very often other project teams will seek me out for solutions to problems.

Advice: Some candidates may feel they are better suited to contribute to a team effort when they are not leading the team. You should press the candidate to describe how he or she can best contribute to your department and why he or she does not feel comfortable in the role of leader. Are there situations in which the candidate might envision him- or herself leading members of your department?

Management Style, Creativity, Leadership

 16. *Describe your comfort level working with people of higher rank and people of lower rank.*

Sample Answer: The person who delivers our mail twice a day has become a good friend. I have invited him to my house to meet my family, and we often go to baseball games together on the weekends. I also get together with my supervisor and his wife for occasional dinners.

Advice: Expect the candidate to provide examples of how he or she interacts with senior management as well as with junior staff members, and communicates effectively with members of both ranks. Try to determine what skills or language the candidate uses to relate to both junior- and senior-level personnel on a daily basis. Is there one particular group of individuals that the candidate generally prefers dealing with, and if so, why?

• • •

17. *Tell me about a time you had to alter your leadership style.*

Sample Answer: I see myself as a strong leader who can delegate. When I took on a project to increase our overseas sales, I quickly developed a strategy and assigned tasks. Later I discovered that several employees with international backgrounds were not responding well to this management style. I decided to work with them as a team to ensure a smooth operation.

Advice: What events or individuals caused the candidate to rethink or re-evaluate how to lead and manage employees? Did the candidate change his or her style permanently or make a one-time-only exception? Carefully weigh the situation against the candidate's actions and ask yourself if you would have acted in the same manner.

18. Tell me about a good process that you made even better.

Sample Answer: Even though our account team had an effective method for media placements, we improved the process of media buying by targeting regions, product categories, and customer profiles.

Advice: Here the candidate should describe a time in which he or she stepped in to improve an internal methodology or policy that helped his or her company financially or otherwise. What, specifically, did the candidate do to effect changes, and how and when did the company feel the effect of those changes? What was lacking prior to the candidate's improvements? Ask for a concrete example, complete with a brief history of the situation and the steps the candidate took to make the department or company more effective. When a system is working, it is often hard to pinpoint what can be done to make it work more efficiently, yet you want the candidate to explain how he or she was able to zero in on exactly what needed to be done.

Skills and Ability to Do the Job

You will almost always determine if the candidate has the basic skills to do the job early on in the hiring process, such as during the first resume sort or during an initial telephone interview. But even if only a fairly routine skill set is necessary to perform a job satisfactorily, there may be sizable differences between one candidate and another in their abilities to perform particular aspects of the job. Probe a candidate to assess his or her job skills with questions like "What skills do you think are most critical for this job?" in order to gain insight into how the candidate will approach his or her work.

1. What sets you apart from the crowd?

Sample Answer: Once I'm committed to a job or a project, I like to tackle it with tremendous intensity. I like to find out everything I can about a task and exceed the expectations of my boss.

Advice: Ask the candidate to enumerate skills that make him or her unique and attractive to companies that have large talent pools to choose from. The candidate may also bring up intangible abilities that do not relate directly to the job but that could be attractive down the line. If the candidate can cite only the standard skills that the job calls for, he or she may not be a value-added hire for the future.

2. ## What are the weaknesses in your skills relative to these job requirements?

Sample Answer: Well, one of my weaknesses is that I tend to take on a little too much responsibility. I need to recognize when I do this and learn to ask my supervisors and coworkers for help from time to time.

Advice: Here you want the candidate to assess honestly the requisite skills he or she may lack. The response "I have no weaknesses" indicates a naïve or immature approach to self-improvement and self-development. Encourage the candidate to focus on his or her skill set and possible areas of improvement.

• • •

3. ## Tell me about your strengths.

Sample Answer: My strengths include interpersonal skills, analytical ability, and a keen ability to spot trends and opportunities that can help position my company and capitalize its strengths.

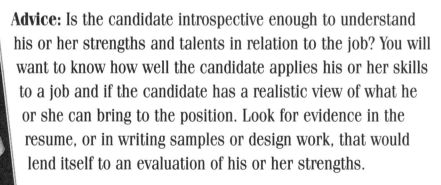

Advice: Is the candidate introspective enough to understand his or her strengths and talents in relation to the job? You will want to know how well the candidate applies his or her skills to a job and if the candidate has a realistic view of what he or she can bring to the position. Look for evidence in the resume, or in writing samples or design work, that would lend itself to an evaluation of his or her strengths.

4. *What are your weaknesses?*

Sample Answer: When I take on a major project or problem, I like to get totally engrossed in it. The last environment I worked in was very social, and I ruffled a lot of coworkers when I worked through lunches on several occasions.

Advice: You want the candidate to assess honestly what he or she can improve upon for future success. A response of "I have no weaknesses" indicates a naïve or immature approach to self-improvement and self-development. In addition, beware of a candidate who responds with an answer such as "I work too hard" or "I am too much of a perfectionist." Many candidates try to turn a negative into a positive with such answers, and it is your responsibility to dig deeper by asking for specific examples.

• • •

5. *How is your experience relevant to this job?*

Sample Answer: The job description, as I understand it, calls for strong written and verbal communication skills. My experience as a writer and amateur actor incorporates both those skills.

Advice: Does the candidate have the maturity to know which skills fit a project? The hiring manager must make sure the candidate understands and can clearly articulate the skills needed for the job. You do not need to probe too deeply to reveal these skills. The applicant should be prepared to talk about them, as well as ways in which his or her experience can contribute to your opening.

Skills and Ability to Do the Job

6. ### What is your dream job?

Sample Answer: My dream job would include all of the responsibilities and duties in this position you are trying to fill. In addition, I thrive in a fast-moving environment with constant change.

Advice: You are not looking for a job title here; rather, you want the candidate to give you a snapshot of the direction in which he or she is headed on a particular career path. If the candidate had a choice of any position, company, and industry, what would that choice be? Make sure the candidate's response is based on reality insofar as his or her background and experience are concerned, and not some pie-in-the-sky fantasy job that would be difficult, if not impossible, to achieve.

• • •

7. ### What skills do you think are most critical to this job?

Sample Answer: The ability to evaluate all of the regulatory and competitive requirements for your new product is critical. I've had considerable experience in the area of strategic marketing and regulatory policy analysis in my most recent job.

Advice: As a hiring manager, you are looking to discover how the candidate applies his or her unique skills to a job. Ideally, the candidate should also demonstrate an understanding of how to transfer long-used skills to a new environment. The differences between one job and the next may be dramatic or subtle, but the candidate should at least show an awareness that some adjustment will be necessary.

Skills and Ability to Do the Job

8. **Compared to others with a similar background in this field, how would you evaluate yourself?**

Sample Answer: I'm an excellent problem solver. I can readily shift my focus from the big strategic picture to small details and quickly get to the heart of the major issues.

Advice: Look for the candidate to discuss one or two strengths that set him or her apart from the typical candidate for this position. Any skill or talent the candidate offers should have a direct bearing on the types of tasks and responsibilities required in the job. Also try to gauge how confident the candidate is in assessing the added value he or she will bring to your company. Ask yourself if this candidate will add value not only in the short term but also down the road as your company or department expands.

• • •

9. **Have you ever been fired or asked to resign?**

Sample Answer: One summer, while employed as an intern at a software company, the president decided to outsource all the work done by our department. This made my position obsolete, and only permanent employees were transferred to other departments.

Advice: You want to see here if the candidate is willing to confront this issue directly and deal with it head on. What has the candidate learned from the experience of being fired or laid off? Does he or she still harbor resentment for past supervisors or coworkers? You don't want to hire someone who is still dealing with the emotional aspects of being fired or asked to resign. Try to relate this question to the job history on the candidate's resume. If the answer to this question is no, a good follow-up question might be "What job were you most anxious to leave, and why?"

10. What are your key skills?

Sample Answer: After working six years as a senior systems analyst, I have developed a number of key skills, including business modeling, process re-engineering, software package evaluation, and excellent programming skills in UNIX and C environments.

Advice: Get the candidate to go beyond skills and tell you what he or she can contribute to your department or organization that will make a difference right away. What does the candidate have to offer your company that other applicants do not possess? What skills does he or she expect to acquire in your opening in the short term and over the next few years? Ideally, the candidate will cite more than the usual verbal and written skills that you are likely to hear in many interviews, and touch upon attributes that truly set him or her apart from other candidates.

• • •

11. What one weakness or bad habit would you like to work on first?

Sample Answer: I need to be more thorough in presenting suppliers' bids to top management. Previously, I merely presented the bottom-line price of the product, but other costs, such as freight setup costs and variable unit prices, have been significant factors in choosing vendors.

Advice: Candidates may be reluctant to dwell on a weakness because, understandably, they are hesitant to showcase the negative in an interview. Expect an answer that cites a skill or ability the candidate would like to improve but that would not significantly impact the job in question. What steps will the candidates take to eliminate this weakness and turn it into a positive?

Skills and Ability to Do the Job

12. **What skills would you like to develop in this job?**

Sample Answer: I would like to develop my negotiating skills. I have had considerable experience interpreting and implementing large contracts, but my experience in negotiating has been limited to minor contracts.

Advice: This question obviously looks forward to the candidate's career development in your company and the types of activities and challenges he or she is looking forward to as part of the job. The candidate should be thinking about what he or she would like to learn in a new environment. Get the candidate to pinpoint specific aspects of your opening that he or she believes will enhance or improve current skills.

• • •

13. **If you had to stay in your current job, what would you spend more time doing?**

Sample Answer: If I had to stay in my current job, I would like to gain more experience in labor negotiating. In particular, I'd like to help negotiate labor contracts, resolve grievances at the step-4 level, and prepare grievances for arbitration.

Advice: This question goes to the heart of not only what the candidate enjoys doing on a daily basis but what he or she looks forward to doing in a new job. Are these expectations consistent with the duties and responsibilities your opening offers? Does the candidate enjoy daily tasks that are somewhat repetitive and boring? If so, this may be an indication that the candidate is not really looking forward to new challenges.

Skills and Ability to Do the Job

14. *How did you enrich your current or past job?*

Sample Answer: By taking night courses in marketing and graphic design, I have been able to handle tasks outside the scope of my original job description.

Advice: You are more interested here in the candidate's career aspirations and development than in specific day-to-day tasks and responsibilities. If your position or company does not offer much more than what the candidate already has, the candidate may leave after a relatively short period of time, making the hiring decision a costly one.

• • •

15. *To what do you attribute your job successes?*

Sample Answer: I never assume our customers are satisfied with our product. I do my best to follow up with every customer to get feedback. The customer always appreciates this follow-up, especially when something has not gone right and I have the opportunity to correct the problem on a timely basis.

Advice: Don't look for skill sets but, rather, for qualities or personal characteristics that separate this candidate from others who are applying for the position. Has the candidate displayed one particular quality or characteristic that has consistently led to professional success over the years? Was there a common thread running through the candidate's past positions, such as the ability to persuade or some analytical skill that has served the candidate well, even in different companies or industries?

Skills and Ability to Do the Job

16. *Tell me about a project in which you were disappointed with your personal performance.*

Sample Answer: In my first job out of college, as a marketing assistant, I developed a market analysis of a competitor's product. Unfortunately, top management rejected my conclusions because I presented a weak slide show that failed to demonstrate our product's superiority.

Advice: If the candidate had to do it all over again, what would he or she do differently to effect a positive outcome? How a candidate deals with failure on a daily basis is almost as important as how he or she handles success. Look for signs that the candidate was able to overcome the disappointment and learn from the experience. How did the candidate confront his or her shortcomings, and what steps were taken to improve work performance?

• • •

17. *What aspects of your work earn the most respect?*

Sample Answer: As a sales representative, I have been consistently praised for my ability to deliver the right solution at the right price for my customers. I attribute this to my ability to listen to and analyze my clients' needs.

Advice: What aspects of the candidate's performance earn consistent praise from supervisors and coworkers? Ask the candidate for examples of the type of successes that have drawn the attention of internal personnel, as well as external people who have a direct relationship with the company. Would this type of output normally command your attention, or the attention of other people in your department or company? What would the candidate like to improve upon in his or her next position to gain even further recognition?

Skills and Ability to Do the Job

18. What aspects of your work are most often criticized?

Sample Answer: I don't know if you would characterize this as a criticism, but I need to show a little more patience and not get down on myself if my projects do not flow smoothly from start to finish.

Advice: Candidates may hesitate in answering this question because criticism of one's work is a very personal issue and not easily dealt with in an interview. In all likelihood the candidate will try to minimize these aspects by showing how the criticism was minor and had little to do with the overall results of the work produced. Ideally, the candidate should talk about criticism that occurred early in his or her career and demonstrate the steps that were taken to improve the quality of output.

• • •

19. Does the frequent travel required for this work fit into your lifestyle?

Sample Answer: The frequent travel in this consulting position is no problem for me or my family. I expect to be traveling to client sites on a regular basis.

Advice: This question can bring about a response that may or may not be close to the truth. Some candidates may indicate that travel is never a problem while knowing the statement is perhaps only 75 percent accurate and may ultimately be a deciding factor if an offer is made. Try to gauge the candidate's body language and tone of voice here. Does he or she respond immediately and unequivocally that there will be no problem with travel, or hesitate slightly and seem uneasy even while claiming that travel is okay?

Skills and Ability to Do the Job

20. *Why have you changed jobs so frequently?*

Sample Answer: My frequent job changes over the last five years have resulted primarily from the rapid changes in the field. My career to date has been based on government contracts that have fluctuated for several years.

Advice: Know the reason for each job change. Was it due to external economic or market forces, or was the problem internal? Were there personality clashes? Make sure you are convinced that the candidate's answer is honest and believable. Encourage the candidate to be succinct and honest in the appraisal of each job change.

Career Aspirations

Generally your biggest concern is how long the candidate is going to stay with your firm. You may also be concerned with how long he or she is going to feel challenged in the position. The worst thing is to have an employee who stays in a position but doesn't like it and complains all the time. However, at the same time, a candidate for a professional position who has no aspiration for growth in his or her career should cause you to wonder if you are interviewing someone who really wants to work, or just show up and collect a paycheck. While you need to seek balance in career aspirations, the candidate's previous track record and length of job tenures should give you a strong indication of what you should be more concerned about. Should you be more concerned about the candidate's likelihood of jumping ship within a few months, or should you be more concerned that the candidate will not bring any career development aspirations and energy to the firm?

1. Where do you want to be in five years?

Sample Answer: In five years I'd like to have progressed to the point where I have bottom-line responsibility and the chance to lead a manufacturing operations unit.

Advice: The candidate's answer should include a well-thought-out plan that demonstrates increasing responsibility without emphasizing job titles or pay structures. You want to make sure the candidate has done some homework on your company or industry and has a strong feel for where he or she could eventually move from the position you're trying to fill. The candidate's plan should indicate a logical path of upward mobility that makes sense to you, given what your company can offer.

Career Aspirations

2. Tell me about your long-term career goals.

Sample Answer: My career goals beyond five years are to become an industry expert and to reach middle management within an organization.

Advice: What lies beyond the immediate job? The hiring manager should discover the candidate's goals, aspirations, dreams, hopes, and objectives. The answer here should reflect both short-term and long-term goals and should not focus on job titles. Rather, you need the candidate to give you a series of job responsibilities and duties that reflect upward mobility and positive career development.

• • •

3. Why is this job the right one for you at this time in your career?

Sample Answer: This job would build on my extensive technical background both in the navy as a communications officer and in the two software companies where I have worked. I think I'm now ready to assume a broader responsibility as a project manager.

Advice: You are interested here in the candidate's short-term aspirations, such as a desire to learn more about industry products, services, and trends; to take on more responsibility; to increase education; to break into leading-edge technology. The candidate's answer should focus on what he or she can offer to the company in the next six to twelve months rather than on any long-term strategic goals.

Career Aspirations

4. *If you could start your professional life all over again, what career direction would you take?*

Sample Answer: I have always enjoyed consumer sales. Looking back, I wish I had gotten more experience in market research to understand both quantitative and qualitative models.

Advice: The candidate's answer must have a logical and rational basis that reflects a desire for industry and product knowledge. Is there a realistic plan for a new career based on the skills and abilities described in the candidate's resume? Why is he or she interested in this new career? Look for concrete examples of accomplishments that point toward such a career.

• • •

5. *What achievements have eluded you?*

Sample Answer: Although I have enjoyed success as a controller, I've never had the opportunity to work in a treasury department. Based on my finance degree and other extensive experience, I'm now convinced that I am ready to handle that responsibility.

Advice: The candidate should be prepared to discuss any and all professional goals that have thus far escaped him or her. Why haven't these goals been accomplished? You want to make sure that the candidate has left behind any excess emotional baggage, such as negative feelings and resentment for a prior supervisor or colleague, and is ready for a new start with your company.

6. *How would you compare this job to others you are pursuing?*

Sample Answer: I've focused my job search primarily on financial consulting positions with major accounting firms. All of these positions require strong quantitative ability, quick decision making, and good interpersonal skills.

Advice: Have the candidate discuss other positions that he or she is considering, and find out what attracts him or her to those positions. If the candidate is looking at a variety of job titles, or at companies in different industries, he or she may just be looking for a job and lack a clear career direction. This job seeker, then, might be less inclined to stick around should the pressure mount or should greener pastures appear elsewhere. If the candidate is not offered this job, what other options are available, and where will he or she most likely end up?

• • •

7. *Have you progressed in your career as you expected?*

Sample Answer: My position with a major gas company has included six years of progressive experience in pricing analysis, capital budget planning, and financial modeling. I believe I'm ready to take on departmental responsibility for your corporate finance department.

Advice: You are not looking for specific job titles here; rather, you want to know that the candidate is interested in working with, or developing, products in your industry. Is the candidate realistic about goals and aspirations? Does he or she have the background, skills, and experience necessary to get there?

Career Aspirations

8. Tell me about your salary expectations.

Sample Answer: Current salary information published by our national association indicates a range of thirty to forty thousand dollars a year. Although I'm not certain how your salaries compare to the national norm, I have a feeling that my salary would be in the upper end of this range. What is the range for this position?

Advice: You are looking for a salary range not only for this position but for what the candidate hopes to be earning in the near future. The candidate's salary goals should be realistic for the industry and the position, as well as for future positions. Obviously, if the candidate is looking for a salary level well above what is normal, the likelihood of reaching an eventual agreement on wages is slim.

• • •

9. Why did you stay in your last position so long?

Sample Answer: I wanted to complete an advanced technical degree at an evening university; I also had two long-term assignments during which I was loaned out to different departments.

Advice: Beware of a lack of motivation to move up the ladder. Was the candidate stunted in his or her attempts to progress? Was there a general lack of upward mobility in the organization, or in the candidate's specific department? Is the candidate simply complacent and perhaps now worried about losing his or her job?

10. *Have you ever been passed up for a promotion that you believe you were qualified for?*

Sample Answer: After six months as a financial analyst, I was the most talented candidate for a senior position that became available in the department. My boss decided to give the position to another candidate who had more seniority. At the time I was disappointed and surprised, but in retrospect I agree with his decision and would make the same decision myself now.

Advice: Find out if the candidate has a realistic view of his or her achievements and skills. If the candidate dwells on emotional issues caused by being bypassed for a job, this should be a warning that the candidate may not be able to assess reasonably what he or she can offer your company.

• • •

 11. *Because this will be your first job, how do you know you will like the career path you have chosen?*

Sample Answer: Although it's true that I have never had a job in your industry, I have talked to many friends and alumni at my school who have been successful in your company. I always ask them the questions, What is the most frustrating thing about your job, and, What is the most rewarding thing about your job? With this information, I'm confident that I will be able to adapt quickly to your culture and find the next few years rewarding based on my goals and values.

Advice: Ideally, the candidate will provide ample evidence, from part-time jobs during the academic year to summer internships, that highlight those strengths and abilities that would be an asset to your department. Why is this career direction so appealing to the candidate, and why will he or she excel in this industry as opposed to another? Will this career path continue to hold the candidate's interest for the next several years, and if so, why?

Career Aspirations

12. What are your aspirations beyond this job?

Sample Answer: I see myself developing my marketing skills as a marketing analyst, then as a brand manager, and finally as a category manager.

Advice: Watch for candidates who discuss at length long-range plans that include positions significantly higher on the organizational chart than your current opening. This is an indication that the candidate wants to move up quickly and is not really interested in working this particular job for any length of time. It is perfectly natural to expect that a candidate has some long-term plan, but you should be concerned if his or her answer focuses too heavily on senior management job titles.

• • •

13. What new challenges would you enjoy?

Sample Answer: My extensive experience in the hospitality industry includes food and beverage management. I believe this experience, combined with hotel management experience, will serve me very well as a conference sales manager.

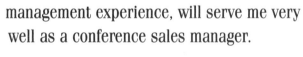

Advice: The candidate should be prepared to discuss any and all professional goals that have eluded him or her so far. Find out what he or she would find challenging in your current opening. Ask for specific examples of tasks or responsibilities that the candidate believes are missing in his or her current job, and that would represent something of a professional milestone to achieve at your company.

14. *How long do you think you would continue to grow in this job?*

Sample Answer: My own personal measure of growth in a job is the acquiring of new skills, new knowledge, and new insights into the industry. As long as I can measure this type of growth, I consider myself successful.

Advice: You are testing here to see how interested the candidate really is in your position and whether he or she anticipates sufficient growth possibilities in the job over the next few years. You also want to know if the candidate is motivated to reshape the position over a period of time to encompass new responsibilities. How eager is this job seeker to expand his or her knowledge base and contribute to the growth of your company while remaining in the position for which he or she is interviewing?

• • •

15. *What career path interests you within the company?*

Sample Answer: I would like to work toward the job of a senior project manager within your commercial real estate firm. My background includes working in several areas within commercial real estate, including sales and finance.

Advice: The candidate should offer convincing proof that he or she has a well-defined career plan that makes sense within your company. Has the candidate carefully thought through a logical career progression based on past experience and future expectations? What does the candidate's answer reveal about his or her ability to assess one's own strengths and capabilities realistically and match them to an appropriate career direction?

16. *I see you've been out of work for a while. What difficulties have you had in finding a job suited to your interests?*

Sample Answer: It's true I've been out of my field for the last four years, but I've had a number of tempting offers to jump back in. However, I thought it was important to stay at home with my new baby and also continue a part-time family business.

Advice: You want to test the candidate's ability to assess realistically his or her skills in relation to jobs for which he or she is applying. Does the candidate have reasonable expectations, or a pie-in-the-sky approach that, so far, has yielded nothing in the way of a substantial offer?

• • •

17. *What do you reasonably expect to earn within five years?*

Sample Answer: My expectation for the next five years is that my contributions will be recognized and appropriately rewarded.

Advice: The candidate should have some realistic expectation of salary goals that are in line with your industry pay scale. Don't be surprised if the candidate turns this question around to ask you what he or she could reasonably expect to earn if they remain with your company for the next few years. The figure quoted by the candidate should be in a range that is neither too low nor too high for the candidate's background and experience, and for the position he or she expects to occupy in five years.

Career Aspirations

18. *Have you ever taken a job that didn't fit into your long-term plan?*

Sample Answer: Back in the late eighties, when Wall Street was booming, I was lured away with a high-paying offer to go with a firm that was trading commodities on the Asian market. Even though I had success in the job, I quickly realized that it was not fulfilling.

Advice: If the candidate frankly admits to having taken one or two positions that did not fit with his or her career aspirations, you should not be overly concerned. However, a candidate who cites several jobs, clearly disparate in terms of responsibilities and upward mobility, may be fishing around, with little or no idea of what he or she really wants in the way of a long-term career.

Problem-Solving Ability

ifferent people solve problems differently—and all too many people try to skirt problem issues altogether or try to downplay their significance. These questions give you insight into a candidate's mindset in approaching problems, making decisions, and dealing with frustrating situations. Do candidates talk freely and easily about problem situations? Do they talk defensively about their actions in dealing with specific problems? Do you see a balance between how they acted as individuals and how they acted in concert with others? How would their problem-solving style fit in at your firm?

1. How do you value or measure the success of your work?

Sample Answer: I measure the reactions of customers. When my customers call me with a referral, I know they are happy.

Advice: Does the candidate consider him- or herself successful upon the completion of a certain number of tasks in a given day? Or do those tasks have to be accomplished in the most efficient manner possible to be considered a success? Is the candidate's measure of success consistent with your own ideas about what constitutes success in your company? Has the candidate successfully achieved all of his or her goals to date?

Problem-Solving Ability

2. ## How pragmatic or practical are you?

Sample Answer: Here's an example. Before looking for a house, I made a list of my needs, including what I could afford and the house's proximity to work and shopping areas, and I found that that list saved me a lot of unnecessary trips. As a result, I was able to locate what I was looking for within three months.

Advice: Have the candidate give examples of his or her approach to handling day-to-day assignments, as well as long-term planning. Does the candidate tend to think abstractly, or does he or she have a commonsense, nuts-and-bolts approach? Can the candidate develop practical solutions to complex problems? What drives his or her thought process? Is it realistic?

• • •

3. ## How do you balance your reliance on facts with intuition?

Sample Answer: In my last position as a market analyst our research indicated that we should launch our new sportswear line in May. My instincts told me that I should move up the launch date by sixty days. We did that, and as a result our sales tripled.

Advice: Does the candidate rely on gut instinct or a programmed approach to solving problems? Do you feel comfortable with the approach laid out by the candidate? What does the job require as far as problem-solving ability is concerned? Are there other managers who will expect a particular methodology different from that which the candidate offers? Can the candidate be flexible in his or her approach to solving a problem?

4. What was your greatest problem in your last job?

Sample Answer: I had to implement a new e-mail system but had a lot of difficulty getting some of our older employees to use it. So I came up with a witty saying or a joke for each day's first e-mail to help ease the transition.

Advice: Make sure you get the candidate to discuss the core of the problem and the reasons why he or she considered the problem a formidable challenge. Be sure the candidate provides details about how he or she approached and resolved the issue. Could you see this problem occurring within your department or organization? Are you comfortable with how the candidate tackled the issue, and with his or her final solution?

• • •

5. Tell me about a problem that you were unable to anticipate.

Sample Answer: My boss asked me to solve an ongoing scheduling problem. I failed to realize that the person who lived with the problem would see me as the antagonist. If I had included him in the process of solving the problem, the antagonism would have been avoided.

Advice: Ask the candidate to describe a problem that came "out of left field." What did he or she do to solve this unanticipated problem? Why did he or she fail to anticipate it? Make sure you get details about how the candidate broke down the problem and came to a resolution. Was the situation a one-time issue, or something the candidate confronted on a regular basis? You need to feel confident that the candidate has the emotional makeup and the ability to deal with the unexpected—no matter how severe the problem.

Problem-Solving Ability

 6. *Tell me about a time you believed it necessary to act on an unpopular decision.*

Sample Answer: I had to start a policy of no food in the work areas, including private office suites, in order to protect computer equipment. This was done to ensure fairness for everyone, from clerical workers to executives.

Advice: Here you want to find out how the candidate reacted to an unpopular decision. Did he or she try to influence the decision? What could the candidate have done to influence the unpopular decision before it was implemented or before he or she was required to take action? Did he or she ultimately accept the decision, make an effort to fully understand the rationale behind the decision, and go forward and implement the decision? How would the candidate handle the same situation again, based on the outcome of this decision?

• • •

 7. *Describe a time when a problem was not resolved to your satisfaction.*

Sample Answer: I once thought that we had let our customer down and didn't respond quickly enough to resolve the problem. The customer wanted a discount, which we should have offered in the first place. We could have created some goodwill.

Advice: The candidate should provide a detailed description of a problem that he or she could not resolve or that was not resolved to the candidate's satisfaction. You are looking here for evidence that the candidate recognized the scope of the problem but failed either to take the necessary steps to solve it or to seek advice from others. Did external forces hamper the candidate's efforts to resolve the problem? Were there any internal issues? Did he or she learn as a result of this experience?

8. In what situations do you have difficulty making choices?

Sample Answer: I'm not altogether comfortable with market surveys, so I rely on our staff librarians and researchers to help me analyze data.

Advice: Look for examples of times when the candidate had to deal with several options and could not decide on the best. What bogged the candidate down and prevented action? Did the candidate have a clear understanding of what was called for? If your department or company relies heavily on proactive individuals who are quick thinkers, you must be sure the candidate will respond accordingly and be productive.

• • •

9. Describe a situation in which you concluded the risks far outweighed the rewards.

Sample Answer: Five years before our distribution facility was scheduled for an overhaul, I had the opportunity to buy the shipping equipment we would need for only thirty cents on the dollar. But I decided the market was too uncertain to make the investment at that time.

Advice: You are looking here for the candidate's willingness to take risks at any cost and his or her ability to evaluate when taking a risk is appropriate—even in lieu of short-term benefits. How did the candidate arrive at the decision to take a chance over going a safer route? What factors went into his or her decision-making process? Try to determine whether the action was out of character for the candidate or if he or she would do the same again.

Problem-Solving Ability

10. How have your technical skills been an asset?

Sample Answer: My part-time college job with the student newspaper taught me a great deal about desktop publishing and page layout. As my marketing career progressed, I found myself using these skills to communicate my needs to graphic designers, thus avoiding costly revisions.

Advice: Encourage the candidate to describe skills that played a key role in his or her last position and what skills he or she believes will prove valuable in your position. How do you measure the value of the candidate's skills as they relate to the requirements of your position? What skills could he or she be using to even greater effect?

• • •

11. Describe a situation in which you applied technical skills to solve a problem.

Sample Answer: One of our components kept arriving at distribution points with stress cracks. I discovered that the storage area at one of the shipping companies lacked proper ventilation. We are now using a different labeling system to warn our shipping companies to avoid temperature extremes.

Advice: The candidate should describe a problem he or she resolved using technical capabilities. Is the candidate able to produce a substantive example? Might the same capabilities or approach be a benefit to your company?

12. *How do your technical skills, combined with other skills, add to your effectiveness on the job?*

Sample Answer: My strong economics background combined with my professional experience with computers provides a balanced skill set that allows me to perform top-notch financial research on the computer industry.

Advice: With this question look for the candidate to provide you with the complete package of his or her skills and capabilities. In other words, if you hire this person tomorrow, what can he or she bring to the table, in addition to technical prowess, that will prove the candidate a versatile contributor right from the start? Do you find this particular combination of skills impressive and believable, given the candidate's background and experience?

• • •

13. *Describe how you've used a problem-solving process.*

Sample Answer: We had many customers who arranged multiple free hotel stays around the country using our 100 percent satisfaction guarantee. I led a PC task force that set up a warning system flagging any guest name that corresponded to a previous reported complaint or "free" service. Our satisfaction rate improved and fraudulent cases decreased.

Advice: Look for the candidate to give you a thorough step-by-step analysis of how he or she tackled a problem and why he or she chose a certain methodology to arrive at a solution. Would you have repeated the process given the same set of circumstances? Would the candidate have the same success using this methodology in your department and applying it to problems your department encounters on a regular basis?

Problem-Solving Ability

14. What is your logic or framework for solving a problem?

Sample Answer: When I tackle a problem, I start by writing down all the possible causes I can think of. I look for relationships among causes, grouping together symptoms of bigger problems. This method has often proved very successful in identifying the root of a problem.

Advice: You want to test the candidate's ability to break down a problem into its basic parts and develop a blueprint for arriving at a solution. How does the candidate think through a problem, including its setup? Does he or she use a flowchart or a diagram, or does the candidate lean more toward abstract problem-solving techniques? Does the candidate's thought process seem to be feasible for what you need in your department?

• • •

15. Have you ever resolved a long-standing problem?

Sample Answer: We used to batch our hotel guests' faxes to save administrative time and money. Our guests were not happy, so I arranged for a leased "guest only" fax machine.

Advice: Ask the candidate to describe a situation in which he or she was able to identify the core of a problem and resolve it to his or her satisfaction. What led the candidate to the resolution? Were there specific steps that he or she used to break the problem down? Did this process help the candidate see the problem in a new light and perhaps make a difference in the final outcome? Be prepared for a story with plenty of detail, and pay attention to the candidate's thought process to see if he or she can revisit a problem with a fresh perspective.

Problem-Solving Ability

16. *Tell me about the most difficult problem you've dealt with.*

Sample Answer: I was once promoted over a colleague who had more seniority and with whom I had worked for five years. He resented the promotion tremendously, so I talked with him about it to make sure he knew the situation was not personal.

Advice: The candidate should offer an example of how he or she tackled a difficult situation and managed to resolve the situation to the satisfaction of the boss. Did the candidate see the problem coming, or was it "out of left field"? What skills were employed to successfully overcome any obstacles in solving the problem? How difficult was the problem in your own estimation?

• • •

17. *Tell me about a time when there was no set procedure or precedent to help you attack a problem.*

Sample Answer: That would be the time I was the first employee in a newly created position. I spent the first week developing an understanding of the history that had led to the creation of the position. Then I found that setting priorities for the job became clear and obvious.

Advice: What is the candidate's comfort level in tackling problems without a blueprint? Here you are testing the candidate's ability to think and to act quickly and decisively, using whatever tools or resources at his or her disposal, to come up with a plan that identifies and overcomes a problem. Can the candidate react and follow through with a workable plan without any guidance, or with no organizational structure in place, to assist in solving the problem?

18. *Tell me about a time when you failed to resolve a conflict.*

Sample Answer: I was not able to keep a good employee who had been in our manufacturing facility for ten years. His position was rewritten to require computer skills. He refused to take additional training, so I had to replace him.

Advice: Have the candidate to describe a situation in which he or she could not effect a positive outcome. The candidate should openly and honestly discuss the failure and the steps or measures taken to try to prevent the conflict. In hindsight, what would the candidate do differently if he or she faced a similar conflict in your department?

Recruiter's Wrap-up Questions

n wrapping up an interview, you always want to end on a positive note. You also want to give the candidate the courtesy of answering any questions that he or she might have. Remember that for many candidates, job interviewing is a tense and frustrating experience. Keep your cool and act professional and warm regardless of how you feel about the candidate's performance during the interview.

1. That's all I have. Do you have any questions for me?

Sample Answer: I'm really interested in your expansion plans for the Pacific Rim. What can you tell me about the role the global-product managers will play in supporting that effort?

Advice: This should be a final test to discover if the candidate has any concerns about performing the job, as well as the candidate's depth of interest in the job. The candidate should have several questions for you, and you should be able to determine from those questions whether he or she is serious about the job or is merely shopping around.

• • •

2. Finally, is there anything else about your background that would be helpful for me to know?

Sample Answer: In addition to having all the basic qualifications, my proved ability to work with a diverse group of people would be a tremendous asset in this position.

Recruiter's Wrap-up Questions

Advice: You want to see here if the candidate has the maturity and the confidence to discuss any areas of his or her background not covered in the interview. Is he or she serious about discussing suitability for the job or just shopping around?

• • •

3. Those are all the questions I have. Is there anything else you want to tell me?

Sample Answer: I just want to remind you that I'm available on a project basis until I finish school in June. In any event, I would jump at the chance to be an assistant brand manager.

Advice: Listen carefully to determine the candidate's motives. Is he or she self-centered, thinking only about him- or herself, or really interested in your company and the job? The candidate should ask about specific responsibilities and duties rather than vacation time, bonus structures, and other company benefits. Any questions the candidate asks should be job or company related and express a sincere interest in working for your company.

• • •

4. As we wrap up this interview, tell me—do you really want this job?

Sample Answer: I believe I have all of the qualifications, and I'm ready to start tomorrow.

Advice: You are essentially asking the applicant to make one final sales pitch for the job. He or she should demonstrate a sincere desire to start working for you as soon as possible. Any last-minute concerns may come up at this time, but you want to hear that he or she wants the job and is eminently qualified to handle the position.

ACCOUNTING MANAGER

Growing auto repair shop seeking top-flight Accountant with aggressive, hands-on accounting management skills including AP/AR. Knowledge of auto repair industry and Quick-books a +. Fax resume and salary requirements to 508

Accountant: Accounts Receivable

National automobile rental agency seeks organized, detail-oriented entry level individual to coordinate accounting for credit card transactions and associated receivables related to business in its busy Hartford aeroplex office. Motivated individual with demonstrated ability to juggle multi-tasks must have BA in accounting. Interested applicants are invited to submit resumes to Car-4-A-Day, 120 Airport Way, West Hartford, CT 06107.

BANK TELLERS

IMMEDIATE OPENINGS!

Immediate openings in all branches of AtlantaBank for experienced Bank Tellers. Growth potential. for the motivated. Fax resume to Business Resources at 404-555-6778.

BOOKKEEPING/ ACCOUNTING

Small medical office requires the services of savvy bookkeeping/accounting professional to oversee financial responsibilities for two busy family practice physicians. Experienced required in receivables, payables, and aggressive, but gracious, bill collections. 5+ years experience necessary with medical office background a definite +. Qualified applicants should fax resume and salary requirements to 514-555-3467.

Computer Technician

Chicago's largest electronic imaging service bureau is expanding rapidly with new branches opening in seven metro locations. Full-time experienced graphics output wiz with hands-on laser printer, digital printer, Iris Imaging, flatbed and drum scanning, Linotronic, Macintosh, and PC troubleshooting capabilities sought immediately to travel locations as required to keep us up and running and number one. Fax resume to 312-555-9999.

CUSTOMER SERVICE REPRESENTATIVE

Residential Interior Decorator pursuing creative individual with an avid interest in home decor to assist interior designers in servicing clientele. A background in design or demonstrated applied arts skills required. If you are also energetic, intuitive, wild about color and texture, eager to learn the trade, and flow with the trends, send us your resume today. TrendSetter Interiors, P.O. Box 950, Miami, FL 03111.

Electrical Engineer

Westerlund Ambitronics is searching for an electrical engineer with ten+ years in the home lighting system design and installation field. Excellent communication skills required to work closely with owners, architects and building contractors. management and marketing skills a definite plus. Excellent salary, company car and great benefits package. Please forward resume and salary expectations to N.K. Westerlund, Westerlund Ambitronics, 151 Razor Back Road, Rutland, Vermont 05701.

EVENT DIRECTOR

Centre Dome North desperately seeking a energetic, organized, multi-talented events coordinator to oversee planning and execution of sports, convention, trade show, fund-raising, and other events held at the dome. Must be able to prepare and target budgets, source and contract vendors, and manage time schedules. Outgoing, diplomatic personality required for close work with clients. Ten years experience corporate or facility events planning experience a must. Business background or education a +. Fax or send resume and salary requirements to Human Resources, Dept. C, Centre Dome North, 1045 Highland Street, Redlands, CA 00000, Fax: 804-555-5566. Equal Opportunity Employer

Field Recruiter

Fast paced personnel placement agency seeks well organized, charismatic communicator with strong networking skills to recruit and place professionals in high level positions at prestigious firms. Travel required. Fax resume to 617-555-8989.

Graphic Designer

Highly creative graphic designer sought to develop business communication, presentation, internet presence, and direct mail pieces for American Crafter's Catalogue Company..We represent internationally recognized artisans and require collateral and multimedia materials that reflect elegance and quality. The ideal candidate will be skilled in QuarkXpress, Director, Photoshop and Illustrator. He or she will have a minimum of five years retail/direct marketing design experience; will be capable of producing CD-ROM and Web Site graphics. If your portfolio is exceptional, your attitude dedicated, your imagination beyond limits—send three non-returnable samples, your resume and salary requirements to ACCC, P.O. Box 45, Charlotte, NC 28201. All submittals will be acknowledged. ACCC is an equal opportunity employer.

IMPORT CLERK

International freight forwarder has immediate opening for Ocean Import Clerk. One year experience required. Full time position with excellent benefits. EOE. Please call 212-555-5656 for appointment.

Legal Secretary

Part time legal secretary sought for busy law firm. Flexible hours—mother's, evenings, weekends OK with potential for full time in the future. Excellent Word Perfect 5.2 skills and experience required. Fax resume to 617-555-8900. EOE. .

LEGAL SECRETARY

Experienced legal secretary sought by Waltham firm. Top pay for top skills and credentials. Mr. Walters 617-555-9350..

Marketing Coordinator

Leading construction management company seeking organized, motivated individual with excellent administrative, interpersonal and communication skills to support marketing management team. Work includes PR implementation, media contact, event and presentation coordination and database management. WP and ACT! required. Writing and design skills a definite plus. Excellent entry position with advancement potential. Degree preferred. Fax resume 518-555-9900.

MARKETING DIRECTOR

West Coast Gourmet Coffee purveyor with chain of trendy coffee bars and catalog mail order service conducting a search for a savvy, proven marketing director to position our company for success along the Northeast Corridor—Maine to Florida. This is a start-up opportunity integrating West Coast marketing resources with your own team development. Your resume must demonstrate extensive knowledge of the gourmet food industry, proven market development and penetration skills and fast track results. If you think you can place our name on the public's palette in six months—you're the key player we're looking for. Forward resume in confidence to Dept. G, The Daily Hemisphere, P.O. Box 780, 99 Planet Drive, Portland, OR 97201

Medical Receptionist/Secretary

Full time medical receptionist/secretary sought for busy four physician office in Troy. Knowledge of managed care procedures, familiarity with national and local medical plans, computer billing using Medi-Bill 3.1, appointment scheduling, and diplomatic, caring attitude all necessary. References required. Salary negotiable dependent upon experience. Benefits. Equal Opportunity Employer. Send resume to 45 East Main Street, Troy, NY 12180.

NURSING SUPERVISOR Psychiatric Home Care

Home care organization seeks Master's prepared psychiatric nurse with seven years acute experience and a minimum of two years home care experience. Demonstrated management skills required to schedule and oversee activities of ten visiting nurses and associated staff. Must have excellent communication and organizational abilities. Full benefits package. Send resume in confidence to HCS, Department PY, Code 3456, P.O. Box 78, Omaha, NB 68112.

SUNDAY CLASSIFIEDS GET RESULTS!

More regional companies, large and small rely on the Sunday Sphere Classifieds to attract the top candidates for their job openings than any other search vehicle. Searching for the right applicant? Have your query in by Wednesday.

BUILDING AN INTERVIEW

SPECIAL SITUATION QUESTIONS

In this section we give you the opportunity to pick questions that address a particular aspect of a candidate's employment history. These questions are divided into categories that assess matters like how the candidate handles stress on the job, what the candidate has been doing since being terminated from a previous job, and why a candidate is returning to the work force or making a career change. Each of these situations reflects a mixture of personal and professional experiences that the questions will shed light on in helping you to determine what the candidate gained from the experience and how that experience will help him or her succeed in your position. For candidates who have changed jobs frequently, been fired or laid off, or are changing careers, these questions can alert you to any "red flags" you need to be aware of in terms of hiring somone else's problem employee.

Frequent Job Changes

hen interviewing a frequent job changer, a fair degree of skepticism is called for. This candidate probably performed pretty well at interviews at companies and then quit a short while later. Why? Was the candidate candid during interviews with previous employers? Does he have an unrealistic view of his potential career path? Does he simply find it difficult or boring to do the same work at the same place for more than a brief period of time? Use these questions to probe as carefully as possible, but don't discount a candidate's prior track record either.

1. Why are you ready to leave your current job after a relatively short period of time?

Sample Answer: I've gone as far as I can go unless someone vacates a position. I've learned the job and no longer feel I am growing professionally.

Advice: Know the reason for each job change. How does the candidate perceive the reason? Was the problem external economic or market forces, or was it an internal issue? Were there personality clashes? The candidate's answer should be honest and believable. Encourage the candidate to be succinct and frank in the appraisal of each job change.

Frequent Job Changes

2. What do you want out of your next job that you haven't found yet?

Sample Answer: I haven't had the opportunity to oversee a budget. This is important to me because I want to begin developing skills that will help me move into general management.

Advice: Past job changes should have taught the candidate what he or she wants and doesn't want in the next job. Therefore, the candidate should have a list of responsibilities, challenges, and opportunities he or she has yet to encounter. Inquire about the specifics of what he or she wants to do for the next six to twelve months.

• • •

3. How have your motivations changed over the last few years?

Sample Answer: Recently I have found myself spending more time with customers. I would like to strike a balance between systems design and troubleshooting at the client site.

Advice: What did the candidate learn from each job change? What does it mean to him or her to have made these changes? Try to determine what the candidate has gained from each transition to a new job opportunity, and how each change has altered the candidate's career goals. What motivates the candidate to seek your particular opening?

4. ## Why is this job especially suited to you?

Sample Answer: In my past jobs I have used a variety of management styles and worked in a variety of cultures. Therefore, I have the flexibility to adapt quickly to ongoing changes in a rapidly growing company such as yours.

Advice: Again, the candidate should have a good idea of what he or she wants to do and, therefore, should be able to name specific areas of responsibility in your position that are attractive. Both the personality and the skills of the candidate should be clearly compatible with the position. Is the candidate emotionally mature enough to handle the demands of the job? What will keep the candidate from leaving if the going gets tough?

• • •

5. ## Tell me about your goals and objectives over the next five years.

Sample Answer: I have now acquired a high level of technical skills and a knowledge of at least three different industries. I'm ready to put this experience to work for you.

Advice: You don't want to hear about grandiose titles or plush corner-office space. Rather, the candidate should have a well-thought-out plan that includes a logical career progression and builds upon the experience acquired from past positions. No one really knows what will happen over the next five years, but the candidate should demonstrate a consistent focus and a purpose for career development.

6. *How can I be assured that you'll stay with us for more than a year or two if we hire you?*

Sample Answer: I've carefully considered the day-to-day duties of this position and know that this is exactly the kind of work that I would find stimulating over a long period of time. I also know that to build my career I will need a longer tenure in my next position.

Advice: How has the candidate grown and developed as a person? What conclusions can you draw about his or her maturity and outlook? What skills and experiences has the candidate accumulated through previous positions? You are looking for evidence that he or she has learned from the past and will be able to settle down in one position long enough to establish him- or herself.

• • •

 7. *If we were to hire you and you ended up resigning, what would be the most likely reason?*

Sample Answer: I am sure that I will be satisfied with this position for a long time. Also, I am determined to stay with my next position. I could not imagine leaving unless the situation dramatically changed, such as a significant reduction of my responsibilities.

Advice: No one can prevent someone from changing his or her mind and leaving, but because the hiring process is expensive and time-consuming, you must be reasonably sure that if the candidate does decide to leave, it will be for something that has nothing to do with his or her career plans at the time of the interview. The candidate must convince you that the only reason he or she would leave would be something unforeseen and unrelated to your company or the industry.

Frequent Job Changes

8. *What is the single most important lesson you have learned over your last three jobs?*

Sample Answer: I have learned to appreciate and accept the fact that every executive has his or her own management style and that I must learn to adapt my style to perform at the highest level possible.

Advice: One common thread should bind each of the candidate's last three positions, and it should not be an error in judgment or weak decision making that the candidate may be prone to repeat at your company. Look for the candidate to describe an ongoing experience or acquired knowledge that was strengthened through each new position and would add value to your opening.

Re-entering the Work Force

Is the candidate truly committed to re-entering the workforce—or is she just "testing the waters"? Is she confident about having the ability to perform the work? Does she have a realistic view of how her skills and background will fit into today's workplace? How have any unpaid or volunteer activities, including childrearing, added to her abilities to perform in the workplace?

1. *Because you have not worked in the private sector for a number of years, give me an example of how your professional skills have been challenged during that period.*

Sample Answer: Several years ago I joined an advisory board to aid a senior citizens' home. By working closely with and soliciting the active participation of the home's management, I was able to implement several projects.

Advice: You must try to discover whether the candidate is ready to come back to a high-pressure, demanding environment. Is the candidate in touch with what is happening in today's working world, and can he or she adjust and adapt? If the candidate offers examples of volunteer work, how does that work relate to the job at hand? What skills or experience can the candidate offer that are unique and valuable to your company?

2. Why do you want to work in this industry?

Sample Answer: I have been very active in an environmental group that has been successful in placing referendums on ballots for clean water acts. This experience was very stimulating and has led me here today.

Advice: What kind of experience is the candidate looking for with your company? What is the candidate's overall goal, and how does working in this industry help to achieve that goal? The candidate should give concrete and compelling reasons for specifically choosing your industry. You want to dig into the candidate's knowledge of key industry players, trends and forecasts, to ensure that the candidate's motivation is high.

• • •

3. How do you define success when it comes to balancing your lifestyle needs with your professional job?

Sample Answer: I expect to work an average of fifty to fifty-five hours per week. I'd like to devote the rest of my time to pursuing my master's degree, getting to the gym two to three times per week, and spending some quality time every weekend with my new husband.

Advice: Find out what the candidate values in his or her work as well as outside the workplace. Can he or she effectively devote the time needed to excel in the position and remain attentive to outside interests? How is this balance achieved? Is it a struggle? You want to make sure that his or her attention is not skewed in favor of either work or play and that he or she is aware of the demands of re-entering the work force and the need to play professional catch-up.

4. **What do you expect will be your biggest challenge returning to the professional world after a long absence?**

Sample Answer: The biggest problem I'll face will be working with a diverse group of employees in an environment that requires a high level of teamwork. In anticipation of this adjustment, I recently joined a "good government task force" to work with a group of over fifty professional and business leaders to develop a blueprint for a better form of city government.

Advice: The candidate should be realistic in an evaluation of what lies ahead in this new job. What will it take to succeed in the job? How will he or she approach and meet the challenge? You are looking for commitment here, as well as for the candidate's own intelligent assessment of how to become productive for your company.

• • •

5. **What aspects of your past jobs have given you the most confidence?**

Sample Answer: I've always had success working with a diverse group of people—in my previous career in educational sales and in my volunteer work when my children were younger.

Advice: You are looking for experiences, tasks, or accomplishments that relate to the current opening. The candidate should be upbeat when describing past jobs and the responsibilities within those positions. You do not want to hear a regurgitation of the job description in question. Have the candidate focus on those aspects of previous positions that he or she performed the best.

6. What do you want to achieve or develop in this job?

Sample Answer: I seek the challenge of a market-driven company where I can grow and advance based upon my contributions. Volunteer work, though satisfying, just doesn't offer this growth and reward potential.

Advice: What kind of experience is the candidate looking for in this new position? What is the candidate's overall goal, and how does he or she think this position will help achieve that goal? You want to find out what the candidate can do to contribute to your department and what he or she can accomplish in this position. Does the candidate have a clear picture of what he or she can bring to your department in terms of specific accomplishments?

Career Changers

s the candidate familiar and comfortable with the day-to-day tasks of this new line of work? Is he or she realistic about starting at a lower level than he or she may be accustomed to in order to change careers? Is he or she comfortable with any financial sacrifice that the move may involve? Is this candidate really committed to the new career path—or still toying with several possible alternatives?

1. Tell me about your people skills and how they relate to this job.

Sample Answer: I always share credit with my entire office. We laugh and enjoy each other as we carry out our responsibilities. I'm convinced that my old career enabled me to develop interpersonal skills that can be applied to a diverse work force like the one in this job.

Advice: The candidate should provide several examples of how he or she relates to coworkers and customers on a daily basis. What personal qualities does the candidate use to influence, persuade, or convince coworkers and customers to see his or her point of view? Get the candidate to describe situations or interactions with other people that indicate whether he or she will interact effectively with your employees and customers.

Career Changers

2. What interests you the most about this new career path?

Sample Answer: As an industrial trainer in your change management division, I can use my teaching skills, especially patience and empathy, to help people overcome training barriers.

Advice: You should be looking for someone who is as good as or better than those applicants who come from the same industry. You must look for evidence that the applicant's past experiences will enrich your company. Why is the candidate interested in your organization at this time? What brings him or her to this industry?

• • •

3. Prove to me that your interest in changing to this new career is sincere.

Sample Answer: I've worked as a financial analyst at a bank, which gave me solid quantitative skills. But I'm interested in trading agricultural commodities. One thing you may not know is that I grew up on a wheat farm, so I understand the risks and impacts on crops.

Advice: Look for something unique that the candidate will bring to the table. Why should you believe that he or she will stay with your company? More important, what can he or she offer that candidates who are already in this field can't? Get the candidate to give you specific examples, from volunteer work, course work, or some other activity, that demonstrate a commitment to your industry.

4. Give me an example of how you can help my company.

Sample Answer: On my last teaching job my biggest contribution was my ability to measure student satisfaction accurately and to feed this information back to other teachers. I developed special questionnaires, conducted focus groups, and spent 10 percent of my time working with the students individually. I believe this attention to student satisfaction will transfer directly to your company in the form of customer satisfaction.

Advice: As the hiring manager, you should be looking for a unique skill or ability that does not exist currently in your company or department. What can this candidate do that no one else in your department can do at the present time? Is it a valuable enough skill to consider this candidate seriously for the opening? Is the candidate's story convincing enough?

• • •

5. Our other candidates for this position have industry-relevant skills and experience. How will you compensate for your lack of industry experience?

Sample Answer: I have already started my transition. I read all of the trade magazines for your industry, and I'm taking an evening telecommunications course at the local business school.

Advice: When hiring someone from outside your industry, you most likely will have to justify the hiring to your superiors. Therefore, the candidate must convince you that he or she can outshine and outperform other industry-savvy candidates. Don't forget: he or she may be a risky hire—you need a dose of skepticism and a great explanation from the candidate.

Career Changers

 6. *What concerns you the most about performing this new job in a new industry?*

Sample Answer: I have no concerns—I match up well with all of the qualifications you have described. And I believe that the ability to think and react quickly, which one develops in the classroom, is very relevant in your job.

Advice: The candidate's concerns about any obvious lack of industry experience should be accompanied by plans the candidate has for overcoming that lack of experience. Also, the candidate may be unfamiliar with certain technical aspects of the job, and you want evidence that he or she has thought through ways to compensate for this delivery.

• • •

 7. *What other types of jobs or companies are you considering at this time?*

Sample Answer: I interviewed yesterday with one of your direct competitors, but I would really prefer to work at your firm.

Advice: Find out if the candidate is approaching similar companies and applying for comparable positions. You want to make sure he or she is sincerely interested in this industry, and a good way to gauge this sincerity is to look for evidence that the candidate is interviewing with other companies in your field.

8. *By changing careers, do you believe you are sacrificing your advancement or your earnings potential?*

Sample Answer: Well, I was earning more as a teacher than I would expect to earn in this position, at least for a few years. But the school-age population is declining and teaching positions will be cut. In any event, I'm ready for a change.

Advice: There are always trade-offs in making career shifts. You need to find out if the candidate is willing to take a pay cut to work in your industry and for your company. Has the candidate researched pay scales in your industry, and is his or her salary expectation in line with what you have to offer? Will the candidate be looking for quick advancement to make up for the loss in income, if applicable?

Fired, Laid off, or Downsized

With references from previous employers harder and harder to obtain, you need to probe any fired or laid off situation as carefully as possible. Try not only to get to the root causes of the issue, but also to gauge the candidate's attitude towards the event. Is the candidate hostile toward his or her previous manager or company? Have his or her feelings become markedly more negative towards the corporate world as a whole? Or is the candidate ready to move forward positively without taking a bad experience to heart?

Should I hire someone who has been fired?

First, ascertain why the person was fired and determine the likelihood of a similar situation occurring within your work environment. Keep in mind that companies are much quicker to fire people today, despite the legal risks, than they were years ago. Don't rule out a candidate simply because of a previous firing.

On the other hand, if you have a choice between two candidates with roughly similar qualifications, and one has been fired from the last position but the other has not, chances are you should go with the one who has not been fired. It is often difficult to get to the truth of the matter in the case of firings. Previous managers are reluctant to divulge information about former employees, especially negative information. And often, even the job candidate doesn't fully comprehend exactly why he or she was fired. It is, after all, hard to admit that one's performance was unsatisfactory. Some people who are fired falsely claim that the firing was due to a personality conflict. These conflicts generally boil down to a difference in opinion regarding the employee's performance—the employee's opinion versus the supervisor's opinion.

Fired, Laid off, or Downsized

1. What were your failures in your last job?

Sample Answer: My boss wouldn't accept the reality that our time to market was too long, and we lost our competitive advantage to a number of alternatives. We never achieved our market share objectives. As a result, over 60 percent of our department was laid off.

Advice: Can the candidate realistically assess what went wrong in his or her last position? Could he or she have done something about it? If so, what could have been done differently? Were there external factors that caused the failure? How does he or she deal with failure? You want to make sure the candidate has worked through all problems associated with any letdowns before joining your company.

2. What do you think led to your company's downsizing?

Sample Answer: I could see our quality slipping over the past year. Our defects rose 2 percent. I was disappointed that my colleagues didn't take this seriously. During this period I intensified my efforts to reduce our department rejections to less than 1 percent.

Advice: You want to see if the candidate can honestly assess why the company decided to let him or her go. Was the problem fierce competitive pressure, internal politicking, or a bloated cost structure? The candidate should give a simple, straightforward answer that is basically unemotional and deals only with facts. Anything more indicates that the candidate may harbor resentment for individuals or the company as a whole, and you don't want to employ someone who is carrying that type of baggage.

Fired, Laid off, or Downsized

3. *When you look back on your past job, do you see anything you would have done differently to avoid the possibility of an ultimate termination?*

Sample Answer: The lesson I learned was never, never to sign off on a contract unless I personally double-checked all of the work of my staff. I thought I had competent employees whom I could depend upon; obviously, that was not the case. I believe I'm much better equipped today to assume project management responsibility.

Advice: You want to see if the candidate can focus on possible weaknesses or situations in which he or she did not use the best judgment. How did the candidate grow and become a stronger individual through this experience? Will the candidate be more valuable to you as a result of this experience? You want to see some initiative on the applicant's part to make the best of a tough situation. Did he or she take a proactive stance and attempt to improve performance and productivity?

• • •

4. *What do seek in your next job that was missing from your last one?*

Sample Answer: I hope my next job will include the rigor and leading-edge technology of my past job in the defense industry without the uncertainty of government contracts and congressional appropriations. I believe I'm qualified for the high-tech consumer industry because of my several years of varied technical projects. I also am excited about the future potential of consumer electronics.

Advice: What new responsibilities or input would the candidate like to have in his or her next position? Look for the candidate to describe specific skills, duties, or tasks that he or she would like to incorporate as part of a daily routine in this job. If the candidate describes responsibilities that seem mundane or repetitive, you should be concerned that he or she is not looking for new challenges or to acquire significant skills as part of his or her career development.

Fired, Laid off, or Downsized

5. *I notice from your resume that you've been out of work for several months. Why is it taking you so long to find a job, and what have you been doing?*

Sample Answer: My first reaction upon learning of the shutdown was to get another job, but it took me a while to realize that my entire industry was downsizing and that the opportunities within the industry were extremely limited. I now realize the unlimited opportunities in the wireless business for someone with my background, and I've completely redirected my search in the last month.

Advice: Does the candidate have a focus and a purpose that make sense given his or her background and experience? Was the candidate previously in an industry that is in a spiraling decline? You want to hear positive, enthusiastic responses and specific reasons why the candidate wants to work for your company and in your industry. Is the candidate realistic about what he or she can bring to your company, and likely to be an immediate contributor if offered the job tomorrow?

• • •

6. *Why were you fired?*

Sample Answer: Despite a strong showing early in the year, I missed my sales quotas for the last two months. I spent too much time trying to land a big account instead of paying attention to the company's monthly and quarterly results.

Advice: Look for an honest, direct response, and watch to see if the candidate looks straight at you or away, trying to duck the question. How did he or she react to being fired? What led to the firing? How has the candidate adjusted emotionally and psychologically to being let go from the company?

Fired, Laid off, or Downsized

7. Were you given a verbal warning before being fired?

Sample Answer: Yes, I was. Although I worked hard in the position, the product turned out to be very different from anything else I had previously worked on. I think my past successes blinded me to the differences in the new product line. I think I'm a much more seasoned manager now.

Advice: Ask the candidate to give you details about what led to his or her firing. Were there any warnings? If so, how many, and what kind? Were there any signs in performance reviews that should have tipped off the candidate that he or she was in trouble? Make sure you get as many details as possible to assess clearly if the candidate knew what was happening and has resolved any residual feelings about being fired.

• • •

8. What were the limitations in your past job, and what do you seek in a new one?

Sample Answer: My last position with a defense contractor was based strictly on federal budget allocations. I want my next job to be based upon my own creativity and ability to help a business grow. Most of my skills from my old job apply to this job.

Advice: If the candidate had the opportunity to rewrite his or her job description, what would be the top three duties or responsibilities on the list? Make sure the candidate does not dwell on aspects of his or her previous position that might be encountered in your opening. The candidate instead should reveal challenges and opportunities he or she expects to face in your opening, and also expanded duties and responsibilities over the long term.

Stress Questions

While some companies like to ask questions like these to a broad range of applicants, we suggest you use them sparingly, if at all. Stress questions can steer a strong candidate toward a competing job opening—or they might create a more negative, less trusting environment if the candidate is eventually hired for the position. The only situations you may want to use stress questions in are when interviewing for unusually stressful, more senior positions—for example, if you are hiring a manager to turn around a troubled product line.

1. How many piano tuners are there in the greater Chicago area?

Sample Answer: To answer that question, I would first have to estimate the population of greater Chicago at, let's say, six million, and assume that one in thirty houses has a piano. That gives you 200,000 pianos. I would then guess that the average piano is tuned every other year and that a piano tuner can complete an average of four jobs per day with 250 workdays per year. So I would estimate 100 piano tuners.

Advice: The answer to this question is not particularly important; you should be interested only in the process the candidate goes through to arrive at an answer, the way the answer is presented, and the soundness of the logic. If you are hiring for a sales or other high-pressure position, this question can be effective for determining how well the candidate can think on his or her feet and how well he or she can articulate thoughts in a stressful situation. Be careful about how you use this type of stress question, however, as some candidates may resent your asking it or question whether it is relevant to the job opening.

Stress Questions

2. *Your major client has an urgent need for you to be in Seattle tomorrow for a board meeting. That is also the day of your daughter's big dance recital. You promised her you would attend. How do you handle this situation?*

Sample Answer: I would call my client to see if there is any possible way the meeting can be delayed one day or if I could arrive late (or appear early to leave early). I would see what flexibility the dance instructor has to reschedule my daughter's performance. As a final compromise, I would consider hiring a service to videotape my daughter's performance and arrange for a dozen roses to be delivered at the conclusion of the recital.

Advice: Here you are testing the candidate's ability to prioritize and maintain a healthy balance between work and outside commitments. Can this candidate develop creative solutions to delicate problems on the fly? If so, how comfortable are you with the candidate's commitment to his or her job as opposed to outside obligations? How does the candidate strike an effective balance without hampering his or her effectiveness on the job, and what does this say about the candidate's overall priorities?

• • •

3. *Tell me about a time you didn't perform to your capabilities.*

Sample Answer: I was in charge of our employee newsletter. I was new to the publications business and failed to understand the importance of a press check. The printer ran the wrong color on our logo. I ended up having to pay for the rerun. After that I never signed off on anything I hadn't seen.

Advice: You want a concise example of a time the candidate failed to perform to expectations. By whose standards did the candidate fall short— a manager's or the candidate's own? What did he or she do in response to this situation? Did the candidate grow and learn from this experience? How will he or she contribute to your company tomorrow? Was this experience ever repeated? Why or why not?

• • •

4. Give an example of how you completed a project, despite major obstacles and disappointments.

Sample Answer: Our design engineer left to go to one of our competitors. We discovered that most of the work on our new product launch had remained in his head. We had to file a suit to get the information. In the meantime we hired a high-priced consultant capable of getting the work done on time. The costs were high, but in the long run that was the best solution because we still delivered product on time to our first customer sites.

Advice: Look for concrete examples of ways in which the candidate tackles projects and overcomes obstacles. The candidate should be able to relate several examples that show how he or she can manage and complete a project, despite problems or unforeseen developments.

• • •

5. An important report that required several weeks of your work has just been returned to you marked "rejected" with severe criticisms of your work. What is your first reaction when the boss hands it to you?

Sample Answer: I'd say, "I guess I was really off the mark, but let me spend the next twenty-four hours with this to see what I can do."

Advice: Determine whether the candidate can remain unemotional and respond objectively in the face of criticism. Can he or she handle rejection in a professional manner and work on the problem areas with a positive attitude? How sensitive is the candidate with respect to ownership of his or her work, and can he or she put emotions aside and rework the report? Listen to the candidate's tone of voice, and watch for body language clues as to how he or she might react to negative feedback.

• • •

6. Sell me this pencil.

Sample Answer: This is the oldest, most reliable, and most inexpensive writing instrument you can obtain. I normally sell them for fifty cents each, but today I'm offering you a special deal: two for 49 cents. I accept all major credit cards, and if you purchase them for business or personal use, you may be entitled to a tax deduction.

Advice: This statement can generate an array of responses. Can the candidate focus on product features and articulate benefits that would help you make a buying decision? Are you convinced to the point where you would actually buy the pencil? You should not look for an absolute correct answer; however, the candidate should be able to assess the situation or, in this case, evaluate the product on the spot and convince you to make an impulse buying decision. Look for some creativity in the sales pitch. Be careful about how you use this type of stress question, however, as some candidates may resent your asking it or question if it's relevant to the job opening.

7. Why are manhole covers round?

Sample Answer: Manhole covers are round because sewer pipes are round. Sewer pipes are round because round pipes are much stronger than any other shape. Pipes placed underground must endure a tremendous amount of stress—from earthquakes to frost.

Advice: You want to find out here if the candidate can think on his or her feet and give you an intelligent response that demonstrates a logical and rational thought process in a short amount of time. The answer should also demonstrate whether the candidate can handle the unexpected and respond quickly with a workable solution. Be careful about how you use this type of stress question, however, as some candidates may resent your asking it or question if it's relevant to the job opening.

• • •

8. You seem to have done very well in your past job. Why weren't you promoted?

Sample Answer: That's why I'm here talking to you now. My boss was very happy with my work, but there was only one opening on the next level during the entire time I was there, and that occurred only three months after I joined the company.

Advice: You want to see if the candidate will respond emotionally, in the belief that he or she was bypassed unfairly, or if there were concrete reasons for the situation, such as a general lack of upward mobility in the organization. Can the candidate reasonably assess his or her performance, given the realities of higher-level positions? What does this mean for the advisability of making an offer to this candidate?

9. Why didn't you complete your formal education?

Sample Answer: I decided to leave school because I was working thirty hours a week waiting tables to support myself. I just did not have enough time to devote to my schoolwork. When I do anything, I always give 150 percent.

Advice: You should determine if the candidate is someone who can commit to finishing what he or she has started or drifts from one experience to the next. Was there a good reason for the candidate to leave school? You must assess whether he or she was forced to leave for economic or other reasons beyond his or her control. Remember that it can be considered discrimination to require an educational degree if one is not necessary to perform the job satisfactorily.

College Graduates

With the typical recent college graduate spending about nine months in their first position, you want to do everything possible to weed out the grad who does not have a strong sense of purpose and direction. You want to hire a candidate who is realistic about career expectations for their first couple of years on the job. You also want a candidate who has not just the raw skills and ability, but also the maturity and confidence to quickly become a contributor in the workplace.

1. What did you learn during your most recent internship?

Sample Answer: Well, because I was deluged with projects from many different people, I learned how to prioritize and always check with my boss to make sure I was on track.

Advice: What aspects of an internship complemented the candidate's academic experience and opened his or her eyes to the day-to-day activities of working in that industry? What excited the candidate about the internship, and would he or she repeat the experience if given the chance? Look for the candidate to focus on one or two aspects of the internship that influenced work habits, discipline, or skill development.

• • •

2. How did you balance your part-time job and your academic requirements?

Sample Answer: It wasn't easy, but keeping a well-organized schedule and planning ahead kept me from overextending myself. This was particularly true around finals.

College Graduates

Advice: Is the candidate organized, and does he or she have some basic time management skills that led to success in the classroom and on the job? You don't necessarily care what type of job the candidate held during school; rather, you want to focus on the candidate's ability to schedule, prioritize, and manage multiple tasks while staying focused on a goal or set of goals.

• • •

3. Do you think that your grades are a good indication of how you would perform in this job?

Sample Answer: In school I always focused on learning the subject material steadily throughout the semester, and I never crammed before exams. I believe that consistent performance, along with strong interpersonal and communication skills, will ensure success on the job.

Advice: There are no guarantees that an individual's academic record will predict job performance; you want to see if the candidate can give you a broader indication that he or she will be an outstanding contributor to your department and company, academic record notwithstanding. What special skills, talents, or qualities does the candidate possess that are not reflected in his or her transcript? What is motivating the candidate to seek your opening?

• • •

4. Were you involved in any extracurricular activities while you were in school?

Sample Answer: Yes. During my junior and senior years I was the managing editor for my computer group's monthly newsletter. As managing editor, I got the opportunity to advance my team-building and communication skills. My editorial skills improved steadily as a result of reviewing the different writing styles of my staff reporters, and I also believe that I became a more decisive manager as a result of choosing what stories to print and to cut.

Advice: You want the candidate to discuss the importance of any activities not directly related to classes that had an impact on his or her overall collegiate experience. What specifically drew the candidate to this extracurricular activity, and what did he or she gain from participating in a student- or college-sponsored organization or team? Does he or she see the value of this participation translating into a first full-time position after college, and if so, how and why?

• • •

 5. *Tell me about a course you either failed or did poorly in relative to your other course work.*

Sample Answer: I had trouble with French, especially the second semester when we had to speak it in class. I've never had a good ear for languages, so I bought a set of conversational French tapes and played them over and over until I picked up the natural rhythm and intonation of the language.

Advice: A recent graduate may hesitate to openly discuss academic failures, and try to soften the issue by offering excuses that may or may not have anything to do with classroom performance. The candidate may also attempt to explain a poor or failing grade by emphasizing that even though he or she did not have a facility for that particular subject matter, the course topic was interesting, or the professor had a good reputation.

College Graduates

6. Why did you choose your major?

Sample Answer: I chose English because I love to write and communicate my thoughts on a variety of subjects to various audiences. English teaches you not only how to write but to think and analyze events, issues, and people's emotions—all of which play a significant role in creating an advertising message.

Advice: Was the candidate's choice of a field of concentration influenced by a plan to work eventually in a specific industry? Encourage the candidate to discuss any courses he or she was particularly strong in. Was the candidate influenced by a professor or a fellow student in his or her choice of a major? What was it about this field of study that convinced the candidate that taking courses in the subject for four years would be an interesting and pleasurable endeavor?

• • •

7. Why did you choose this particular career path?

Sample Answer: I chose advertising because I have always been a strong communicator with a good eye for design. I have a particular interest in creating dynamic, eye-catching pieces that support a new product being introduced to the market. I also like the fast-paced, high-energy environment that seems to be commonplace in the advertising industry.

Advice: Get the candidate to outline several aspects of your opening, company, and industry that are appealing and would hold the candidate's interest for at least a few years. What skills or abilities does the applicant possess that will translate into a successful career in your industry? Ask the candidate how he or she will effectively contribute to the company in this type of position.

8. *What concerns do you have about entering the workplace full-time?*

Sample Answer: I'm looking forward to the challenges of working in a dynamic industry such as advertising. I know there will be a period when I will need to adjust to the fast-paced demands of your company, but given the fact that I balanced a full course load with a part-time job, I'm quite certain I will make the transition successfully.

Advice: The candidate will most likely express concerns about needing time to adjust to the working world. Ideally, the candidate should try to allay your concerns by expressing confidence in his or her ability to learn quickly on the job. There should be no indication that the candidate has any deep-seated reservations about tasks or responsibilities associated with the position.

• • •

9. *Which of your part-time positions did you like most, and which did you like least?*

Sample Answer: I really enjoyed my summer job at Smith Advertising last year. I learned how to work as part of a team, improved my writing and design skills, and, most of all, conquered my fear of delivering presentations, as I was required to stand before senior ad executives and pitch ideas for accounts on a weekly basis. I believe that experience will prepare me for any assignment in advertising.

Advice: Although none of the candidate's part-time positions may have anything to do with your position, department, or industry, the candidate should be able to specify those people, tasks, or responsibilities that contributed either positively or negatively to the candidate's professional development. What particular aspects of the positions had a significant impact on the candidate's overall learning experience?

College Graduates

10. Have you ever visited the city where our corporate office is located?

Sample Answer: No, but I have several friends who live there, so I would be excited to have an opportunity to live and work in your city. I actually prefer to live in a larger city as opposed to an outlying rural area.

Advice: You want to see if the candidate has any reservations about relocating if that is an issue, or if he or she feels comfortable living and working where your headquarters are located. Encourage the candidate to discuss his or her favorite activities and interests outside of work to see if your corporate location will offer the candidate a chance to fulfill those interests and activities. It doesn't make much sense to consider a candidate who takes windsurfing seriously if your company headquarters are located near an arid desert—unless, of course, the candidate shows a strong desire and commitment to the position and your company, despite the location.

• • •

11. What will you bring to this job that other candidates with similar academic backgrounds may not offer?

Sample Answer: I have strong written and verbal communication skills, a natural ability to sell, above-average presentations skills, and a thirst for success. I want to bring these skills to your company and help your company continue to grow and expand.

Advice: What skills or abilities does the candidate have that would make you look great for bringing this person aboard tomorrow? What separates this candidate from others you are considering, and why would his or her academic experience make an immediate impact?

ACCOUNTING MANAGER

Growing auto repair shop seeking top-flight Accountant with aggressive, hands-on accounting management skills including AP/AR. Knowledge of auto repair industry and Quick-books a +. Fax resume and salary requirements to 508

Accountant: Accounts Receivable

National automobile rental agency seeks organized, detail-oriented entry level individual to coordinate accounting for credit card transactions and associated receivables related to business in its busy Hartford aeroplex office. Motivated individual with demonstrated ability to juggle multi-tasks must have BA in accounting. Interested applicants are invited to submit resumes to Car-4-A-Day, 120 Airport Way, West Hartford, CT 06107.

BANK TELLERS

IMMEDIATE OPENINGS!

Immediate openings in all branches of AtlantaBank for experienced Bank Tellers. Growth potential. for the motivated. Fax resume to Business Resources at 404-555-6778.

BOOKKEEPING/ ACCOUNTING

Small medical office requires the services of savvy bookkeeping/ accounting professional to oversee financial responsibilities for two busy family practice physicians. Experienced required in receivables, payables, and aggressive, but gracious, bill collections. 5+ years experience necessary with medical office background a definite +. Qualified applicants should fax resume and salary requirements to 514-555-3467.

Computer Technician

Chicago's largest electronic imaging service bureau is expanding rapidly with new branches opening in seven metro locations. Full-time experienced graphics output wiz with hands-on laser printer, digital printer, Iris Imaging, flatbed and drum scanning, Linotronic, Macintosh, and PC troubleshooting capabilities sought immediately to travel locations as required to keep us up and running and number one. Fax resume to 312-555-9999.

CUSTOMER SERVICE REPRESENTATIVE

Residential Interior Decorator pursuing creative individual with an avid interest in home decor to assist interior designers in servicing clientele. A background in design or demonstrated applied arts skills required. If you are also energetic, intuitive, wild about color and texture, eager to learn the trade, and flow with the trends, send us your resume today. TrendSetter Interiors, P.O. Box 950, Miami, FL 03111.

Electrical Engineer

Westerlund Ambitronics is searching for an electrical engineer with ten+ years in the home lighting system design and installation field. Excellent communication skills required to work closely with owners, architects and building contractors. management and marketing skills a definite plus. Excellent salary, company car and great benefits package. Please forward resume and salary expectations to N.K. Westerlund, Westerlund Ambitronics, 151 Razor Back Road, Rutland, Vermont 05701.

EVENT DIRECTOR

Centre Dome North desperately seeking a energetic, organized, multi-talented events coordinator to oversee planning and execution of sports, convention, trade show, fund-raising, and other events held at the dome. Must be able to prepare and target budgets, source and contract vendors, and manage time schedules. Outgoing. diplomatic personality required for close work with clients. Ten years experience corporate or facility events planning experience a must. Business background or education a +. Fax or send resume and salary requirements to Human Resources, Dept. C, Centre Dome North, 1045 Highland Street, Redlands, CA 00000, Fax: 804-555-5566. Equal Opportunity Employer

Field Recruiter

Fast paced personnel placement agency seeks well organized, charismatic communicator with strong networking skills to recruit and place professionals in high level positions at prestigious firms. Travel required. Fax resume to 617-555-8989.

Graphic Designer

Highly creative graphic designer sought to develop business communication, presentation, internet presence, and direct mail pieces for American Crafter's Catalogue Company..We represent internationally recognized artisans and require collateral and multimedia materials that reflect elegance and quality. The ideal candidate will be skilled in QuarkXpress, Director, Photoshop and Illustrator. He or she will have a minimum of five years retail/direct marketing design experience; will be capable of producing CD-ROM and Web Site graphics. If your portfolio is exceptional, your attitude dedicated, your imagination beyond limits—send three non-returnable samples, your resume and salary requirements to ACCC, P.O. Box 45, Charlotte, NC 28201. All submittals will be acknowledged. ACCC is an equal opportunity employer.

IMPORT CLERK

International freight forwarder has immediate opening for Ocean Import Clerk. One year experience required. Full time position with excellent benefits. EOE. Please call 212-555-5656 for appointment.

Legal Secretary

Part time legal secretary sought for busy law firm. Flexible hours—mother's, evenings, weekends OK with potential for full time in the future. Excellent Word Perfect 5.2 skills and experience required. Fax resume to 617-555-8900. EOE. .

LEGAL SECRETARY

Experienced legal secretary sought by Waltham firm. Top pay for top skills and credentials. Mr. Walters 617-555-9350. .

Marketing Coordinator

Leading construction management company seeking organized, motivated individual with excellent administrative, interpersonal and communication skills to support marketing management team. Work includes PR implementation, media contact, event and presentation coordination and database management. WP and ACT! required. Writing and design skills a definite plus. Excellent entry position with advancement potential. Degree preferred. Fax resume 518-555-9900.

MARKETING DIRECTOR

West Coast Gourmet Coffee purveyor with chain of trendy coffee bars and catalog mail order service conducting a search for a savvy, proven marketing director to position our company for success along the Northeast Corridor—Maine to Florida. This is a start-up opportunity integrating West Coast marketing resources with your own team development. Your resume must demonstrate extensive knowledge of the gourmet food industry, proven market development and penetration skills and fast track results. If you think you can place our name on the public's palette in six months—you're the key player we're looking for. Forward resume in confidence to Dept. G, The Daily Hemisphere, P.O. Box 780, 99 Planet Drive, Portland, OR 97201

Medical Receptionist/Secretary

Full time medical receptionist/secretary sought for busy four physician office in Troy. Knowledge of managed care procedures, familiarity with national and local medical plans, computer billing using Medi-Bill 3.1. appointment scheduling, and diplomatic, caring attitude all necessary. References required. Salary negotiable dependent upon experience. Benefits. Equal Opportunity Employer. Send resume to 45 East Main Street, Troy, NY 12180.

NURSING SUPERVISOR Psychiatric Home Care

Home care organization seeks Master's prepared psychiatric nurse with seven years acute experience and a minimum of two years home care experience. Demonstrated management skills required to schedule and oversee activities of ten visiting nurses and associated staff. Must have excellent communication and organizational abilities. Full benefits package. Send resume in confidence to HCS, Department PY, Code 3456, P.O. Box 78, Omaha, NB 68112.

SUNDAY CLASSIFIEDS GET RESULTS!

More regional companies, large and small rely on the Sunday Sphere Classifieds to attract the top candidates for their job openings than any other search vehicle. Searching for the right applicant? Have your query in by Wednesday.

BUILDING AN INTERVIEW

SPECIFIC CAREER QUESTIONS

To develop the strongest list of interview questions possible, you should carefully select questions from the first section of general questions. If appropriate, you should also choose questions from the special situation questions, as well as from this section of career-specific questions.

Even if the specific job you are interviewing for does not fall under one of the career categories in this chapter, you will probably get some solid ideas for questions by skimming through some of the interviews for other careers.

Accountant, General

1. What qualifications do you have that will help you as an accountant?

Sample Answer: I have three years' experience as an accountant for a small public firm, where I did everything from generating income statements and balance sheets to assisting the controller with the preparation of financial statements. I also have a degree in accounting from the state university, and I am a certified public accountant.

Advice: What areas of accounting expertise does the candidate offer to your company? The response can range from degrees and certificates to practical experience at a Big Six or other accounting firm. Why does the candidate believe that his or her qualifications are best suited for your position? Are you convinced that the candidate has a good understanding of your needs and what the position calls for, and can more than meet those needs with his or her level of education and experience?

2. How did you become interested in accounting?

Sample Answer: I've always been really interested in numbers. I remember budgeting my weekly allowance as a kid and convincing my parents to let me open my own savings account when I was eleven. In college I was immediately attracted to accounting classes; they seemed like a perfect match for my interests.

Advice: Look for someone who enjoys numbers and can use them logically. You should also look for someone who is detail oriented and comfortable handling a variety of tasks that are numbers intensive. The candidate should be able to give you an example of how to take raw data and turn it into a management decision tool.

• • •

3. What spreadsheets are you familiar with?

Sample Answer: I have extensive experience with both Lotus 1-2-3 and Microsoft Excel for Windows. In my current position I use Lotus 1-2-3 for all of my budget analyses. I also use Excel at home to keep track of my personal finances.

Advice: What application does the candidate prefer to use, and what specific tasks, such as budgeting or cash flow analysis, does the candidate perform on a regular basis using his or her preferred application? What level of spreadsheet expertise does the candidate possess? For instance, does he or she know how to use the application's macro language to automate certain tasks for improved efficiency and increased productivity?

Accountant, General

4. ## What experience have you had with credit and collection?

Sample Answer: A few months back my company experienced a temporary cash flow problem. It was my responsibility to talk to our creditors and explain our financial situation; I arranged to send minimum payments to our creditors every month until our crisis was resolved, at which time they'd receive all their money. I also had to lean on our customers to collect some past-due funds. I managed to get some money in, and the crisis passed without any real damage to the company.

Advice: You are looking for someone who can make credit decisions as far as determining creditworthiness and reading financial statements and credit references. You also want someone who can determine when accounts are past due and delegate someone to call the delinquent accounts, or make the calls him- or herself. The candidate should know how to read a balance sheet, when to grant credit, and how to pick up the phone and chase a delinquent account until it's paid.

• • •

5. ## Tell me about your experience in dealing with cash flows and variance analyses.

Sample Answer: I've prepared cash flow analyses on a monthly basis for senior management. I also was responsible for producing monthly variance analyses and explaining why the actual performance was different from the projections. I worked with the appropriate department manager to correct and/or improve the negative variances.

Advice: Look for someone who can do a fair amount of detail work using the knowledge of how cash is collected against standard credit terms and how funds are dispersed against normal vendor terms. Are the candidate's analytical skills up to par in terms of statement presentation? Can he or she explain to nonfinancial people the rationale behind the preparation of the statements?

6. *Have you ever been involved with the actual preparation of financial statements?*

Sample Answer: In my previous position as a controller I prepared the financial statements, including all journal entries, reconciliations, and comparisons of actual versus budget variances.

Advice: You should get at least one or two examples of the depth of the candidate's experience in preparing financial statements and the level of responsibility he or she has had in signing off on the statements. Has the candidate done all of the entry work right through the final statement, including all detail and subsidiary ledgers? Do you need someone who has done actual preparation, as opposed to just a review, of the statements?

• • •

7. *What type of general ledger system have you worked with?*

Sample Answer: At my last company I used McCormack and Dodge General Ledger Plus, which ran on an IBM mainframe. When I was with Small Office Print Shop, I used RealWorld and Peachtree software, which ran on our local area network and was better suited for small, emerging growth companies.

Advice: Has the candidate worked on systems similar to yours? If not, what kind of learning curve will be involved in getting the candidate up to speed on your system? Does the candidate display other qualities or skills that would allow him or her to grasp the fundamentals of your system quickly while contributing to your department or company in other areas?

Accountant, General

8. *Tell me about the type of costing systems you're familiar with.*

Sample Answer: I've worked with many different types, from standard to job cost. As most of my experience has been with manufacturing companies, I was specifically involved in the design and implementation of standard cost systems and have had to accumulate information and develop it into a readable and usable form for other managers.

Advice: For many accounting positions at manufacturing companies, you will require candidates with strong skills in cost accounting. Inquire about how the candidate's previous costing methods differ from yours. What method does the candidate feel most comfortable with, and how quickly could he or she adjust to your methods?

• • •

9. *Do you have experience preparing budgets?*

Sample Answer: I have prepared budgets at the corporate and department level. I was responsible for coordinating the information with each department and converting it into a readable and consistent form for upper management to use as a decision-making tool.

Advice: You want someone who has prepared operational budgets and departmental budgets. A candidate with experience doing operational budgets will have an understanding of the company as a whole rather than of a specific department only. You want someone who has interacted with other levels of management and who can extract information to put together a financial picture of the company.

Accountant, General

10. What is your level of tax experience?

Sample Answer: I have experience in preparing federal and state corporate returns for both C and S corporations, as well as sales tax returns. They were generally smaller companies with up to $2 million in sales.

Advice: Which direction to probe depends upon the position being filled. If you are looking for a payroll accountant, you need to emphasize payroll taxes. If you are looking for a controller for a small company that hires a payroll service, the knowledge of income taxes would be more important.

• • •

11. What is the yearly sales volume of your current company?

Sample Answer: Last year the company grossed about $8 million in sales, a 20 percent increase from the previous year. This year the company is probably looking at another 10 to 15 percent increase. Obviously, the company is still relatively small but is growing rapidly.

Advice: Expect the candidate to have some knowledge of what is happening in terms of

 sales volume with his or her company. This will tell you the level of experience the candidate has in working on problems associated with a $2 million company versus a $100 million company. You obviously should be concerned about bringing someone aboard who has little or no experience with companies of your size.

Accountant, General

12. *Do you have experience preparing documentation for accounting systems?*

Sample Answer: I prepared an accounting manual in my last position. The manual encompassed procedures, forms, and flowcharts as well as a detailed explanation of the nature of each general ledger account. It became the training manual for all new hires in accounting.

Advice: You would prefer someone who can look at the processes involved and put them in writing, be it a flowchart or narrative, to serve as a training vehicle for other employees. You are testing the communication skills of the candidate here, and his or her ability to articulate in writing all of the steps in a given process. Can the candidate put information into a form that nonaccountants can understand?

• • •

13. *Tell me about your auditing experience.*

Sample Answer: I worked for a year at a small public accounting firm, doing mainly review-type work of all the books and records for small service corporations. I was responsible for preparing all of the papers for those clients, determining the accuracy of the records prepared by the client companies, and drafting the financial statements and reports signed by the partner. I was also involved in drafting a management report for areas requiring improvement in internal control and other procedures, as well as working with the client to implement recommendations.

Advice: Although you should be prepared for some candidates to have little or no auditing experience, the ideal candidate will possess these skills and will be able to demonstrate them with several examples of times when he or she has performed an audit. Auditing experience teaches candidates to work on paper preparation and hones their analytical skills and deductive reasoning powers.

Accountant, General

14. *What experience have you had with accounts payable?*

Sample Answer: I had an internship during which I reviewed all invoices processed by the accounts payable department for verification of quantities received, pricing, and general ledger coding. I also was involved in negotiating prices with suppliers as well as resolving discrepancies that could not be solved by payable department personnel.

Advice: Look for a candidate who has gone through the entire process and preparation, including matching purchase orders and receiving reports, that verifies quantities received and prices paid against what was contracted for. Can the candidate assign the general ledger account numbers on the invoice? You should also look for someone who has done some batch entry.

• • •

15. *Tell me about your most difficult experience managing accounts receivable.*

Sample Answer: I was assigned the task of collecting the outstanding balances of our second-largest account. The account was six months past due, and the previous general manager had personally handled the account. I flew to the client's offices with copies of proofs of deliveries for all outstanding items and was able to resolve the communication problems as well as expedite collection by developing a payout plan agreeable to both parties.

Advice: Ask the candidate to describe instances in which he or she has dealt with major, or more problematic, accounts. The candidate should tell you how he or she resolved the problem—either by making a recommendation to someone higher up or resolving the issue with the vendor or clients. The answer should demonstrate the candidate's experience, resourcefulness, and ability to make sound decisions.

Accountant, General

 16. *Describe some specific accounting projects for which you had direct responsibility for the outcome.*

Sample Answer: I worked on a lease-versus-buy analysis for the acquisition of all our computer equipment. I had to do all of the research and analysis and make calls to financing sources. I also had to make recommendations to senior personnel once the analysis was completed.

Advice: Get the candidate to give you specific examples. Did these assignments add appreciably to his or her depth and breadth of experience? Would the experiences be of benefit to your firm? What did the candidate find most challenging about the assignments, and what new skills did he or she acquire as a direct result of working on these assignments?

• • •

 17. *What is the most difficult accounting experience you have ever had to face?*

Sample Answer: In my first job the company was faced with an IRS audit. I wasn't directly involved, because I wasn't working on any tax issues at that time, but we all had to go through our books and documentation to make sure everything was accurate. Luckily, the audit went well, so it actually turned out to be a good bonding experience.

Advice: The answer should reflect the candidate's background and experience and should be honest and forthright. Make sure the candidate understands that by "difficult" you mean "technically difficult" and are not looking for an example of a problem that required mere stamina—such as spending six hours entering fairly mundane and routine data.

18. *How do you cope when confronted with a stressful situation?*

Sample Answer: I usually take a deep breath, get up, and go on a five-minute walk around the building. If I am having a really bad day, I might take a short trip to the convenience store and buy a soda before returning to work.

Advice: Look for the candidate to demonstrate how he or she can walk away from a stressful environment and take time to de-stress before returning to the environment. The answer should involve more than just getting up and walking around the department; there should be some real commitment to take a break, even if it means leaving the building.

Accounts Payable Clerk

1. *Tell me about an average working day. Describe in detail your responsibilities and how you posted invoices to the accounting system.*

Sample Answer: I start by opening and sorting the prior day's mail. I match the incoming vendor invoices with the purchase orders and packing slips. I then verify the pricing against the purchase order for propriety, test the extensions, and test for invoice accuracy. Then, choosing the correct general ledger account, I post the transactions to the accounting system. In addition, I'm responsible for weekly computerized check runs, all manual check disbursements, and I summarize all journal entries and post them to the general ledger.

Advice: Here you're testing the candidate's organizational ability and his or her attention to detail. What system or method does the candidate believe is most efficient for posting invoices, and do you think that the candidate's experience with that system would allow him or her to work effectively in the same capacity in your department? Ask the candidate for the rationale behind his or her system of posting to the accounting system, and why it is effective.

2. *How would you handle the following situation: bills from a new vendor are received, and though a purchase order is referenced, the money due exceeds the amount authorized.*

Sample Answer: I would ask the person who originated the purchase order to explain the cost overage and why the invoice should be paid as submitted. I'd then request an authorization from the appropriate manager to exceed the amount authorized. I would also contact the vendor, advising them of the discrepancy and explaining that invoices in excess of the purchase order amounts must be approved in writing before any additional work is done or quantities billed.

Advice: What steps does the candidate believe are appropriate to take to identify where the problem originated and how it should be rectified? Is this an issue that the candidate thinks should be brought to the attention of his or her supervisor, or should such issues be resolved immediately without calling for help?

• • •

3. *What do you like most and least about doing this kind of work?*

Sample Answer: It is a steady and consistent job, and I have always enjoyed working with numbers. I like making things balance and tie out on a daily basis and at the end of the month. The pressure at month's end can be draining, but the satisfaction of contributing to the department is well worth the extra work.

Advice: You should be looking for specific tasks and responsibilities that the candidate looks forward to on a daily basis and what he or she truly enjoys accomplishing in an accounting position. What is it about the candidate's current position that is particularly motivating, and what aspects would the candidate prefer not to repeat in a new position?

Accounts Payable Clerk

4. How long does it take you to post an average daily batch?

Sample Answer: I usually post the bills once or twice a week. Sometimes it takes days to prepare a batch by verifying POs, checking with the receiving department, and getting approvals for cost overrides. But I can usually post a week's worth of payable in a day.

Advice: You should be testing the candidate's speed and efficiency here; you want to make sure that the candidate is responsible and aggressive in seeing that this process happens consistently and without any problems that would affect any other function of his or her department.

• • •

5. What do you think are the most important aspects of this job?

Sample Answer: Attention to detail is clearly the most important part of any job in accounting. Meeting deadlines and schedules is important, as well as being able to interact effectively with others in the company.

Advice: The candidate should give you two or three examples of what he or she considers the most important functional aspects of the position. You should also get a feel for the way the candidate prioritizes daily and weekly responsibilities, and how the candidate sees the job in relation to others within the department.

6. *Describe in detail the process you use when running a batch of checks.*

Sample Answer: I prepare a list of all invoices currently due by going into the accounts payable report module of the accounting system and selecting the open invoice report. My supervisor then selects the vendors that will be paid on this check run and returns the list to me. I then key the items to be paid into the accounts payable system and verify the totals per the batch run against my manual total. Once the two match, I print the checks, match them up with the corresponding invoices and POs, and present them for signature.

Advice: This question explores the candidate's understanding of the basic mechanics of this accounting position. Are you confident the candidate can handle this aspect of accounting, and do you approve of the process or methodology he or she employs? The candidate should demonstrate a working knowledge of all the basics, attention to detail, and a fundamental understanding of the process involved in running a batch of checks.

• • •

7. *What type of computer systems are you familiar with?*

Sample Answer: I'm familiar with PCs and local area network systems, as well as IBM minis like the '36 and the AS/400. I've worked with RealWorld, Solomon, Macola, Great Plains, and MAS90.

Advice: Determine the candidate's knowledge of hardware and software platforms and what experience the candidate has in executing various accounting functions using this hardware and software. You want to ensure that the candidate's technical knowledge and understanding of various computer systems is strong enough that little or no training will be required should you hire this person tomorrow.

Administrative Assistant

1. What is your typing speed?

Sample Answer: I'm usually accurate at about fifty words per minute.

Advice: This is a cut-and-dried question that requires a numerical response, measuring the candidate's ability to perform a certain job function at a high level. If the word count is somewhat lower than you require, is the candidate willing to improve through a class or exercises after hours? Of course, a test is the best indicator of typing speed, and you will usually find that the results are somewhat less impressive than a candidate's answer.

• • •

2. What word processing, spreadsheet, and database management programs are you familiar with?

Sample Answer: I'm very comfortable using Microsoft Word for Windows and Excel for Windows. I've also used ACT! from Symantec to do large-scale mailings of form letters.

Advice: How computer literate is the candidate, and which major application packages is he or she most familiar with? You want someone who can perform all of the basic functions in each application as well as demonstrate enough computer aptitude to pick up new skills using these packages.

3. *On a scale of one to ten, rate your proficiency with the word processing, spreadsheet, and database management programs you are familiar with.*

Sample Answer: I'd say I'm a nine with Microsoft Word, and a seven with Excel. In fact, I used both applications on a daily basis in my last position.

Advice: You want the candidate to be honest about his or her knowledge of basic application programs and give you a straightforward assessment of what he or she can accomplish using these programs. Of course, each candidate's "rating scale" will be unique, but this is a good device to get the candidate talking about different packages.

• • •

4. *What computer operating systems are you familiar with?*

Sample Answer: I am very proficient with Windows '95. I'm also comfortable using MS-DOS.

Advice: You want to feel comfortable with the candidate's ability to handle the computer's operating system and its basic function, and this is the most basic test of a candidate's computer knowledge.

Administrative Assistant

5. Do you have experience taking dictation?

Sample Answer: Yes. My last boss would often dictate long, detailed letters with a lot of technical jargon. He had a habit of speaking very quickly, so I had to learn to write and type very quickly. I would also transcribe his tape-recorded notes onto disk.

Advice: Taking dictation is a basic skill for candidates applying for this kind of position, and you should find out what types of dictation the candidate has had the most experience with. Basically, you want to ensure that if you have long, complicated letters or documents to transcribe, the candidate will be able to handle the task with ease.

• • •

6. Can you take shorthand?

Sample Answer: No, I can't. But as I mentioned earlier, I do have experience taking rapid dictation. My last boss never had to wait for me to catch up.

Advice: This is another common skill but one that the candidate may not possess. You should determine what skills the candidate has that might offset the lack of a knowledge of shorthand. How critical will it be for the candidate to take shorthand in the day-to-day execution of his or her duties?

7. ## Have you screened telephone calls?

Sample Answer: Yes. In my last job I fielded many calls from some pretty determined callers. If a caller became angry or upset at not being able to get through to my boss, I would say something like, "I'm sorry, Ms. Reynolds is not available this afternoon. If you'll leave your name and telephone number with me, I'll make sure she gets your message as soon as possible." I would politely restate this message until the caller finally realized that he or she was not going to get past my desk. I was always polite but firm.

Advice: You want to see that the candidate can exercise good judgment when deciding which calls to put through, and can sound pleasant and professional, though firm, when refusing to put through inappropriate calls. What communication techniques does the candidate believe work best in screening calls? Does he or she exhibit what you would describe as a professional manner, and would this candidate effectively represent the company and your best interests to outsiders?

• • •

8. ## Do you plan to further your education?

Sample Answer: I don't have any plans to go to school full-time in the near future, but I do like to take occasional night courses and weekend seminars to help keep my job skills up-to-date. Last year, for instance, I took a speed typing class and attended a seminar on international business protocol. I also make it a point to read *Business Week* magazine and several trade journals regularly to keep up with the latest business news.

Advice: This type of position can be subject to heavy turnover, so you want to determine if the candidate is using the job only as a brief transition to entering a full-time graduate program.

Administrative Assistant

9. *Tell me about your last boss.*

Sample Answer: Ms. Winters was a great motivator—she would push people to their limits, and she was a stickler for detail. But she was always fair, and she rewarded good, hard work. I would call her a tough boss but a good boss.

Advice: Listen carefully for anything negative the candidate may say about a previous boss. You will want to discover all you can here about the candidate's working relationship with his or her last supervisor, including any situations that may have been less than ideal.

• • •

10. *What type of person do you work with best?*

Sample Answer: I really get along well with almost everybody, but I work particularly well with other dedicated, hardworking people. The crew I worked with at my last job was made up of some really terrific people; everyone was completely professional, and we all considered ourselves part of a team.

Advice: Encourage the candidate to give you the most detailed picture possible of the qualities and types of individuals he or she is most comfortable working with on a daily basis. What traits does the candidate find particularly objectionable?

11. *What type of person do you find difficult to work with?*

Sample Answer: I really don't have any problems working with other people. My former colleagues would tell you that I'm actually quite easy to get along with.

Advice: Expect the candidate to try to sidestep this question by putting a positive spin on relations with both junior- and senior-level employees. You want the candidate to give you concrete examples of situations in which he or she has difficulty interacting with others. What qualities or characteristics does the candidate least admire in a coworker?

• • •

12. *How do you typically organize your work and plan your day?*

Sample Answer: I learned the value of good organizational skills when I worked for three different managers in a very hectic office. I had to juggle many different tasks at one time with a constant stream of contracts and paperwork crossing my desk. I decided to create a system whereby I would prioritize tasks for the next day before leaving work. I bought an electronic organizer to keep track of key phone numbers, appointments, and meetings. Finally, I physically reorganized my office to gain access to all important documents at a moment's notice.

Advice: Test the candidate's planning skills and ability to prioritize tasks, appointments, and meetings to perform at peak efficiency. What techniques does the candidate use to organize and manage the office and help the boss be an effective manager? Were there any extraordinary instances in which the candidate had to go the extra mile to make sure that all bases were covered and that every pressing deadline was met?

• • •

13. *We're a company that believes employee flexibility is crucial. How do you feel about that?*

Sample Answer: I consider myself very flexible and willing to do what it takes to get a job done. For instance, when my former boss at Sanders Chemical had a baby and was unable to put in long hours, I pitched in by taking over some of her responsibilities, including generating reports and interfacing with various departments. I also helped out by running personal errands for her. I think she appreciated my extra efforts.

Advice: Will the candidate go outside his or her job description to help others, while still managing to perform efficiently as an administrative assistant? Can he or she take on a task with little or no notice and complete it expeditiously, even if the assignment is outside the normal daily activities expected of the administrative assistant's position?

1. Tell me about a great idea you had.

Sample Answer: When I was president of the student government association in college, I had an idea to form a committee to volunteer at a local homeless shelter once a week. I also thought it would be great if every Thursday, the day we served food at the

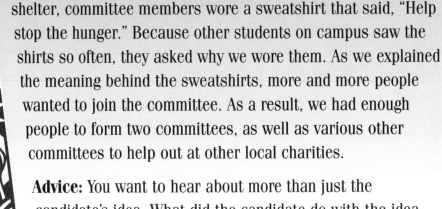

shelter, committee members wore a sweatshirt that said, "Help stop the hunger." Because other students on campus saw the shirts so often, they asked why we wore them. As we explained the meaning behind the sweatshirts, more and more people wanted to join the committee. As a result, we had enough people to form two committees, as well as various other committees to help out at other local charities.

Advice: You want to hear about more than just the candidate's idea. What did the candidate do with the idea, and what was the result of implementing the idea? Were others involved, and what steps did the candidate take to ensure the success of his or her idea? You are, in addition, testing the candidate's creative powers and innovative thinking, which should be an important factor in almost any advertising position you want to fill.

• • •

2. What's your favorite advertising campaign? How would you make that campaign better?

Sample Answer: The United Negro College Fund campaign is my favorite. I'm thinking of one TV commercial in particular, in which a young man is told by his parents that they just can't afford to send him to college. In response the young man's little brother donates his piggy bank to the cause. This commercial works because, although it's a tear jerker, it's still appropriate. It effectively expresses the point that the United Negro College Fund needs support so that highly qualified but financially needy African-Americans can attend college. I think the campaign could be improved by playing this particularly poignant commercial more frequently. Perhaps it could be aired during programs that draw a strong academic audience. Also, several new commercials similar in look and feel would be effective.

Advice: What is it about the campaign from a creative, technical, or design standpoint that makes it stand out from other campaigns? Does the copy, art design, delivery, imagery—or some other aspect of the campaign—deliver the message most effectively to the target audience? What does the candidate look for in a successful campaign, and what would he or she do to alter a campaign to make it more successful? Does the candidate demonstrate enthusiasm while discussing a favorite advertising campaign?

• • •

3. *What is your least favorite campaign? What would you do differently if you could change it?*

Sample Answer: I really dislike the Little Italy Pizza commercials with the flying monkeys. I get really annoyed when I see any of these commercials, and I always immediately change the channel. Any commercial that annoys viewers is ineffective. I think an approach like what Pizza Pizza has taken would be much more effective. I like the way it has variations on the old couple deciding how to spend a few bucks, because they're funny commercials and the couple always concludes at the end that they should have ordered a pizza. These commercials are a bit more avant garde and clever.

Advice: Get the candidate to critique an unsuccessful campaign and explain why the advertising fails to reach its intended audience. What did the ad agency overlook in putting the campaign together? If the candidate were in charge, what would he or she do differently to deliver the message? You want to measure the candidate's creativity, strategic thinking skills, and ability to pinpoint areas where ad campaigns traditionally fall short. Can the candidate make a distinction between attractive or award-winning advertising and advertising that builds sales?

• • •

4. What color is your brain?

Sample Answer: My brain is red because it's always hot. I'm always on fire with new plans and ideas.

Advice: You're not looking for a right or wrong answer here—just an indication of whether the candidate is a creative thinker. Does he or she have the imagination to develop ideas that might also be successful in developing your ad campaigns? This question is perfect to determine if the candidate can be spontaneous and respond to a far-out suggestion to stimulate his or her creative powers.

5. *If you got on an elevator and everyone else on it was facing the back, what would you do?*

Sample Answer: I think I would face the front and say aloud, "It's really much more comfortable facing forward, you know."

Advice: Here you're testing not only the candidate's imagination but his or her behavioral and emotional reactions to a specific extraordinary situation. This question affords you the opportunity to see if the candidate is independent-minded or tends to follow the crowd. Does the candidate march to the beat of a different drummer? Would he or she fit in with the culture of your firm? This question also tests the candidate's astuteness in predicting how other people may respond to stimulus.

• • •

6. *What would you do if a client asked you to design and significantly expose an advertisement on a very limited budget?*

Sample Answer: I designed an ad once for a ladies' auxiliary group in my hometown. The group's budget was extremely limited, but because we were publicizing its premiere event—a decorated Christmas tree show— we wanted to get the word out into the community. I designed a wonderful ad that I had put on the side of a building at the main intersection of town. I also had the newspaper run a full-page ad each Sunday. The first year was a hit, and the event has been repeated successfully for the past two years.

Advice: With this question, you're measuring the candidate's resourcefulness, aggressiveness, imagination, and ability to create successful ads with limited resources. What initial steps would the candidate take to begin putting together an ad under these circumstances, and what would he or she do if the client expressed dissatisfaction with the results? Is the candidate willing to work with limited resources on a regular basis, as opposed to having a blank checkbook and being limited only by his or her imagination?

• • •

7. What advertising media is best for making an impact on your buying habits?

Advice: The specific answer doesn't matter. You want to see how easily the candidate can articulate his or her viewpoint and evaluate the impact of various media. You also want to see how excited the candidate is about advertising in general.

• • •

8. What publications do you read regularly?

Sample Answer: I read the industry publications, including *Ad Age*, *Ad Week*, and *Brand Week*. I think *Ad Age* is the best, so I really study it carefully. I also read the local newspapers and the *Wall Street Journal*, because it helps me stay focused on what consumers want. Staying in tune with the trends and dynamics in our culture is important.

Advice: Beyond traditional advertising industry publications, does the candidate read journals or newsletters from other industries to stay on top of developments that could impact a client's advertising message? Ask the candidate to give you specific examples of articles or ads from journals, newspapers, or newsletters that contribute to his or her effectiveness as an advertising professional.

Advertising Account Executive

9. How did you become interested in advertising?

Sample Answer: I'm a very creative person, and I always knew that I wanted to make a career out of my creativity. But I also love the thrill of the deal, and I found that business really appealed to me as well. Advertising is the natural blending of the two, so it made perfect sense.

Advice: In this type of interview you should not be surprised to hear the candidate tell a story about an individual or an experience with an ad agency, or a story about a commercial that piqued his or her interest in the field. The more details you get, the more enthusiasm the candidate is likely to inject into his or her answer—and the more comfortable you should feel that the candidate is truly committed to advertising for the long haul.

• • •

10. What do you think your primary responsibilities would be as an account executive here?

Sample Answer: As an account executive, I'd work in the client service area, as opposed to the creative, research, or media divisions of the agency business. I would service my clients fully and would become an expert in their businesses. I'd also have to be an expert in our other service areas so that I could put everything to work for the client. Projects would probably be both executional, like creating TV and radio ads, and strategic, like writing the client's marketing plan for the next year.

Advice: Ask the candidate to explain how he or she envisions the position, including its daily responsibilities. What does the candidate think he or she can accomplish for you as an account executive? The answer here should not be a regurgitation of the job description; rather, the candidate should articulate what he or she can contribute in the role of the account executive and how those contributions can satisfy your own expectations of the position. Whom does the candidate expect to interact with on a regular basis, apart from the firm's clients?

• • •

11. *What skills do you think you'll need for this job, and do you have these skills?*

Sample Answer: I think I'll need strategic thinking skills, which I've developed from solving problems and approaching client problems analytically. I also think both formal and casual presentation skills are important. Actually, I've developed my casual communication skills just by being in the business. And I make a point of taking an occasional class at the local community college to learn the latest presentation software.

Advice: Assuming the candidate has a good handle on what the job entails, he or she should be able to articulate the talents and skills necessary to be successful in the position, and explain what he or she can offer immediately if hired tomorrow. Using examples from prior account executive positions, or any other work experience you consider relevant, the candidate should prove to you that he or she has the ability to handle the core responsibilities of the position.

Banking Officer

1. What types of customers do you lend to?

Sample Answer: I lend to middle market companies with sales ranging from $5 million to $50 million. I've had experience with several companies in different industries such as pharmaceuticals, high technology, and consumer goods.

Advice: You should expect the candidate to give you a profile of his or her customers that includes revenues and sales, numbers of employees, products, and so forth, as well as his or her history with those customers. Does the candidate have a broad range of experience in that he or she has worked with both small and large companies, both residential and commercial accounts? Why does the candidate prefer one type of customer over another, or one industry over another?

• • •

2. Are you a cash flow or balance sheet lender?

Sample Answer: A little of both, really. However, I'm primarily a cash flow lender because that's my loan's primary repayment source. I do look at the balance sheet to analyze my downside risk.

Advice: You want to measure the candidate's skill and ability to analyze these particular financial statements. Would he or she use one statement over another as a measuring tool to evaluate a company's prospects as a customer? What is the basis for the candidate's preference for either a cash flow statement or a balance sheet, and what specific elements of each statement tell the candidate that a prospective company is a good risk?

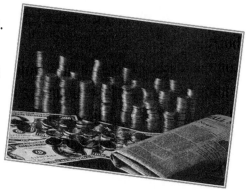

Banking Officer

3. *I notice on your resume that you worked for Mid-States Bank, which is considerably larger than our institution. How will you make the transition from a big bank to a smaller institution?*

Sample Answer: One of the primary qualities of a good loan officer is strong people skills—something I count as one of my best assets. No matter what size the organization you work for, it always comes down to people, and because of my strong skills in this area, I know that I can work for a bank of any size.

Advice: Working for a larger institution often provides a candidate with exposure to a different set of procedures or operational guidelines, type of customer, and internal resources, as well as opportunities for growth. Make sure a candidate going from a big bank to a smaller institution has a complete understanding of the type of customer you deal with on a regular basis, and of your bank's corporate culture and prospects for growth. What skills or abilities will the candidate bring to your bank that would make him or her an immediate value-added hire?

• • •

4. *Tell me about the new business you've developed.*

Sample Answer: Over the past twelve months I've developed $15 million in new loan commitments, resulting in average loans outstanding of $9.5 million. This business resulted in five new relationships for the bank, and in addition to the loan volume, these accounts will generate one hundred thousand dollars in new fee income for the bank.

Banking Officer

Advice: How comfortable is the candidate going after new business, and what has been the candidate's experience in the types of new business he or she has managed to attract for previous banks? What type of customer or industry does the candidate favor, and does this preference match your expectations of the type of new business you want to pursue for your bank?

• • •

5. How do you target and call on customers?

Sample Answer: I use various sources to target prospects, and employ several different calling methods, depending upon the situation. In my calling area the bank has a list of companies by sales size that I use as a starting point. I also use my contacts with accountants, lawyers, and the local chamber of commerce to come up with more prospects. In addition to cold-call visits, I often call ahead to prospects to get appointments. This can be especially effective if I've been referred by someone they know, like their accountant or attorney. I find that my current customers are the best source of prospects. They like the job I do for them and feel confident referring me to others.

Advice: What sources, including business associates, friends, and family members, does the candidate believe are most effective in helping him or her identify and pursue prospective clients? What criteria does the candidate use to evaluate the prospect? How does he or she make the first contact with the prospective client?

6. How do you sell your institution?

Sample Answer: I sell the bank as a financially sound, customer-responsive organization. Customers and prospects are interested in financial strength and excellent customer service. We don't just sell a commodity; we sell excellent service.

Advice: Put yourself in the role of a prospective customer and test the candidate's ability to convince you that his or her bank can meet your needs with a variety of products or services. How effective is the candidate in matching your needs with banking services that exceed anything you can currently obtain at another bank? Has the candidate done an effective job acquiring you as a potential customer for his or her bank?

• • •

7. Give me an example of one of your customer-service success stories.

Sample Answer: One story that stands out in my mind is the time I personally answered a credit reference request right away. It was a request that's usually handled by a central area of the bank within forty-eight hours. My quick response enabled my customer to get the items needed quickly and on the right terms from a new vendor. This allowed my client to obtain even more business from his own client in the future.

Advice: Ideally, the candidate will not only tell a story but will also describe concrete steps or actions that demonstrate a desire to go the extra mile to service a customer's needs at a moment's notice. What steps did the candidate take to make sure the customer's needs were completely taken care of as soon as possible? Was the candidate reactive or proactive in his or her approach? How complex, in your mind, was the customer's problem and do you agree with the candidate's final solution?

• • •

8. *Is there a new-business success story that stands out in your mind?*

Sample Answer: Yes, as a matter of fact, I'm most proud of the $3 million financing package we recently acquired. We were one of three bidders, and we won primarily because of our fast turnaround time, which impressed the prospect as much as did the content of our proposal. It conveyed the idea that we were serious about wanting the business.

Advice: Evaluate the candidate's accomplishment in terms of what you would define as an important accomplishment at your bank. Does the candidate's achievement measure up to your standards, and is he or she likely to duplicate this type of success at your bank? Candidates may try to bulk up the accomplishment to impress you; cut through the hype and determine what role the candidate played in creating new business. What extraordinary skills or ideas did the candidate use to help facilitate this success story?

9. *What is your approach to monitoring a portfolio? What do you watch for?*

Sample Answer: I firmly believe that the real work begins once a prospect becomes a customer. To do a good job monitoring an existing portfolio, you must be proactive, not reactive. You need to set up systems and procedures with the help of others in the commercial loan department to monitor the financial reporting requirements and the financial covenants as outlined in the loan approval documents. You watch to see that customers are keeping to projections. Monitoring deposit balances as opposed to historical or seasonal patterns is one sure way to uncover "red flags" early.

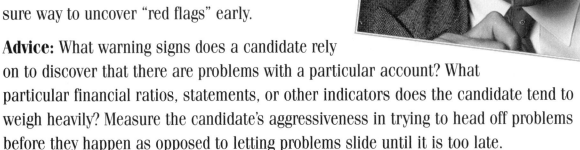

Advice: What warning signs does a candidate rely on to discover that there are problems with a particular account? What particular financial ratios, statements, or other indicators does the candidate tend to weigh heavily? Measure the candidate's aggressiveness in trying to head off problems before they happen as opposed to letting problems slide until it is too late.

• • •

10. *Tell me about a problem loan you helped turn around.*

Sample Answer: One of my customers, a residential construction company, experienced problems handling rapid growth when it decided to expand into commercial construction. I met with the company's senior management and convinced them that in order to resolve their loan problems, they should focus on their core business, namely residential construction. Taking my advice, they were able to turn around their delinquent payment schedule.

Advice: At what point did the candidate realize he or she was dealing with a customer who was having problems meeting a payment schedule? How aggressive was the candidate in approaching the customer, understanding the nature of the customer's difficulty in making payments, and devising a schedule to alleviate the problem? Did the candidate notify his or her supervisor, and if so, when? What recommendations did the candidate make to the customer to try to avoid these problems in the future?

• • •

 11. *In calling on new accounts, what is the main obstacle you encountered in selling your bank over your competition?*

Sample Answer: I found that many small businesses viewed my bank as generally being unresponsive, cold, and too large to care about their needs. I countered this problem by demonstrating a sincere interest in their business, and in problems that were unique to their business. When they requested more information about my bank's services, I made sure they received it within forty-eight hours.

Advice: What objections or concerns regarding the candidate's bank did the candidate find when he or she first met with prospective clients, and what did the candidate do to try to overcome those concerns? What was the competition doing to make it difficult for the candidate to acquire new business? You should focus on the candidate's ability to sell the client on his or her bank's services and reputation, and measure the candidate's understanding and awareness of how the competition is positioning itself in relation to the candidate's bank.

• • •

12. Is there a particular industry or firm you enjoy lending to?

Sample Answer: My experience as a lending officer has put me in touch with many different types of businesses, both large and small, and from a variety of industries. I really don't have a particular favorite, but I've found that working with small companies can be very rewarding because I get to know the people behind the business and work with them as they grow into a larger company.

Advice: What types of companies and industries does the candidate feel most comfortable dealing with and approaching for new business? Why is this industry or company so appealing to the candidate, and why does he or she claim success in working with these companies? Does the candidate's experience with these companies or industries fill a hole in your business portfolio?

• • •

13. Why are you interested in our bank specifically?

Sample Answer: I like your association with a larger national bank, despite the fact that you operate under a regional name here. One of your AVPs I spoke with explained that two transactions she managed recently were actually booked at the parent bank, which has been number one in loan syndications for years; I understand they're also well-known for agented deals and the high-yield market. The advantage for clients in this relationship is one-stop shopping. If the parent bank is better set up for a certain type of transaction, you can move the business up there. It seems to me that most banks are more segmented; they don't share business back and forth the way you do.

Advice: What does the candidate see that separates this bank from others in terms of opportunities for growth, clientele, corporate culture, or other bank operations? Test the candidate's knowledge about your bank, going beyond annual reports and marketing literature to see if he or she has a genuine interest in the type of business your bank conducts and the type of people who work for you.

• • •

14. What key skills would make you successful in syndication work?

Sample Answer: I have a good memory for quantitative information, which is important because you often have to recall quickly where you bought and sold something. My seasoned sales and negotiation skills are critical also, because once you have secured a large issue of stock, you want to sell it on the secondary market quickly. My relationships with the smaller banks you typically deal with are excellent.

Advice: The candidate should give you several examples of how he or she can apply key skills and abilities to this particular aspect of banking and produce immediate results. If you hired this candidate today, what specifically could the candidate do for you tomorrow that other candidates could not? Why does the candidate believe that this type of banking service is a good match for his or her background and experience?

15. *If the consumer price index is off this month, how does that impact our bank?*

Sample Answer: The CPI influences consumer confidence, so if you're holding a lot in, let's say, a retail portfolio, that's not good.

Advice: This question tests the candidate's ability to go beyond typical banking operations and evaluate economic factors that may influence how a bank performs in any given month. Does the candidate have the knowledge and financial awareness to study external economic factors and determine how they might affect a bank's income statement or balance sheet?

• • •

16. *If you wanted to look at how a company financed a large equipment purchase, where would you find that information?*

Sample Answer: I'd look at the company's statement of cash flows to examine capital expenditures.

Advice: This question should determine the candidate's accounting expertise and facility with various capital financing alternatives. Could he or she identify how a capital expenditure might impact a balance sheet, an income statement, or cash flow?

Banking Officer

17. *If you're an account officer and presented with a problem loan, what would you do?*

Sample Answer: I might increase the pricing to reflect the increased risk, or I might review loan and collateral documentation to see what other options might be available.

Advice: How does the candidate turn around a difficult situation, and what steps would he or she take to ensure that payments continue to be made while a solution is worked out between the bank and the customer? This question tests the candidate's problem-solving ability, as well as his or her listening and communication skills, to ensure that the customer understands the severity of the problem and how best to avoid it in the future.

• • •

18. *Lender liability claims might arise in what type of situation?*

Sample Answer: You might have a discretionary line of credit—a demand line—where the bank decides not to lend the money. The bank might do this if it sees large overuse of the line and hasn't seen a pay-down period anytime during the year. Or the bank might be concerned if it sees late interest payments or notices that a borrower is consistently not meeting collateral requirements of his or her receivable balances.

Advice: What red flags does the candidate look for that might negatively impact a bank's position regarding a lending situation? How does the candidate balance the bank's legal exposure with retaining a customer who has a large credit line? You are looking not only for analytical skills but for professional maturity and insight that will determine the candidate's ability to weigh different variables.

• • •

19. *So many deals in the corporate finance group take a long time to develop. Describe a situation when perseverance got you the desired result.*

Sample Answer: When I worked in sales of expensive industrial equipment, I usually had to help my customers arrange financing, sometimes including long-term lease arrangements. Often, after convincing them to buy, I had to do the legwork for financing. Sometimes, though, a company still might not buy right away, but most appreciated my diligence, and I stayed in touch. Many times I would earn the company's business one or two years later, even when the financing terms weren't as favorable as before, because I'd earned the customer's trust.

Advice: Does the candidate have sufficient depth of financing experience to handle complicated corporate deals, and the patience and maturity to stay with them, even when

it looks as if they will never reach fruition? Assuming the candidate has an understanding of the numbers, can he or she manage to coordinate all aspects of the deal, including the people and resources necessary to satisfy all concerned parties? It doesn't hurt to make sure the candidate has strong "selling" skills and the persistence that closing a deal often takes.

Banking Officer

 20. *What are appropriate actions to take after you've made a proposal to a potential banking customer? How would you follow up?*

Sample Answer: I would follow up within a week to see if the customer needed more information. I wouldn't pursue someone more quickly because, in the case of a corporate lender decision, the client has a big decision to make and shouldn't feel rushed. During the phone call I'd try to determine whether I'd really gotten to the decision maker.

Advice: How quickly will the candidate call or visit the prospective customer, and what will he or she say to convince the customer to sign on with the bank? The candidate's actions will also depend upon the type of customer, be it a consumer loan or a corporate account. Evaluate the candidate's judgment and communication and selling skills, as well as his or her determination to bring a customer into the bank.

Brand Manager

1. What do you see as the best new product opportunities in this market?

Sample Answer: The whole wave of wellness—like your new reduced-fat cheeseballs with 33 percent less fat and your cheese curls with 50 percent less fat. I understand you're coming out with a reduced-fat peanut line now.

Advice: This question addresses the candidate's awareness of changing trends and consumer preferences and measures how effectively the candidate can capitalize on those changes with new product ideas. How does this applicant track the market and come up with ideas about product development? Does he or she follow the lead of other companies by improving on existing brands, or does the candidate prefer to be a leader, a generator of innovative, marketable new concepts?

• • •

2. What would you say is different about working on new products as opposed to working on an established brand?

Sample Answer: When you work on an existing brand, your main worry is about how to squeeze more volume, because the product's positioning within the company's portfolio is already well established. New product introduction involves everything from brand management to coming up with an original idea and positioning it. The thinking is more strategic. You have to think about how the new product fits into the overall portfolio for the company.

Advice: Here you're testing the candidate's marketing acumen for rolling out a new product as opposed to supporting an established product. What marketing vehicles does the candidate think are crucial for each, and what are the special challenges involved in both tasks? Evaluate the candidate's strategic ability and his or her knowledge of the product life cycle.

Brand Manager

3. **What are the big challenges with your current brand?**

Sample Answer: My peanut products fall into the salty snack category. Our challenges in getting consumers to purchase our product are (1) awareness, because people think of baked chips rather than peanuts in this category; (2) health, because peanuts offer protein, folic acid, and other benefits not found in other salty snacks; and (3) price value, because peanuts aren't bulky like chips, and we have to work hard to show value per serving when the serving is visibly smaller than a typical serving of, say, chips.

Advice: Can the candidate quickly identify areas in which he or she believes marketing or product development has not addressed the needs of the market? This question goes beyond the traditional four P's of marketing, and you should expect the candidate to list all areas wherein either the product fails to meet market expectations or marketing programs have not addressed consumer needs.

• • •

4. **What would you say you learned in your various marketing positions that will help you in new product development?**

Sample Answer: One of my product manager roles was on our flagship brand, peanuts. Therefore, a lot more cash flowed into it. We look at our company name as a franchise with one brand identity, so the peanut brand person does the big promos. Basically, whatever peanuts do affects the rest of the trade calendar. I learned to make decisions and feel confident about them. I also learned a lot from working in retail, especially about how customers in different store locations go for different things. That's helped in my decisions about regional promotional adjustments.

Advice: You want to know how past job experiences are most relevant to the job under consideration. How has the candidate learned to make decisions and move ahead? What analytical skills and knowledge about market segmentation and consumer behavior does the candidate believe would be critical in working with new products?

• • •

5. *If you had to define brand management as more creative or more financial, which would you say it is?*

Sample Answer: In a company like yours, which is more performance driven, it's definitely financial. With long-established brands less creativity is needed to support the business because awareness is established and habits keep the business alive. With new products more creativity is needed to build initial interest and to create a new behavior pattern with consumers.

Advice: You want to be sure that the candidate is realistic about the challenges of the job and has a good sense for the balance between the financial and creative aspects of brand management. The candidate's answer should reflect experience handling the financial ramifications of marketing as well as the creative ideas, which may or may not have been costly to implement but were needed to support and enhance the brand.

Brand Manager

6. *Here are some packaging changes we implemented. Take a look and give me your opinion on what we wanted to accomplish.*

Sample Answer: This is obviously a special pack in a convenient one-serving size. I think you were trying to get people to think of a reduced-fat item in reasonable quantity as a healthy snack they can carry with them. Peanuts are compact. I think carrying a bag of peanuts is much more convenient than carrying around a bag of chips, but you have to remind people of that. It seems as if the packaging is helping to establish the healthy characteristics of peanuts as opposed to other salty snacks like chips, but you're also suggesting that the peanuts are just as convenient as a candy bar for quick energy. That's my impression. Do you mind if I ask how close my answer was to your actual goals?

Advice: You are testing not only the candidate's skill for design and visual sense but his or her ability to pick out key elements of packaging from a consumer's standpoint as well as from a marketing standpoint. The candidate's answer should be detailed and give a point-by-point description of what the packaging says about the product and how it communicates benefits to match consumer needs. Above all else, you are looking for a strong opinion from this candidate one way or the other.

• • •

7. *Tell me about a time you test-marketed a product.*

Sample Answer: Last month we tested a different package size in several major markets. The special pack did work as we had hoped—mostly to remind people that peanuts can be a healthy snack. But, of course, special packs aren't really money makers like our regular-size containers, so building awareness was our primary goal.

Advice: What is the depth of the candidate's experience in product testing, and what methodology does he or she prefer to use in testing a product? You want to find out what has worked for the candidate and why: What are the specific steps the candidate takes to test a product? Before a test is implemented, what does the candidate consider from a timing, resources, consumer profile, and test market standpoint?

• • •

8. *In the context of brand management, what do you think are the differences between a leader and a manager?*

Sample Answer: A leader is a visionary person, whereas a manager is a coordinator. A good brand manager has qualities of both. I don't think you coordinate people effectively unless they have a good idea of where their contributions will make a difference and what the possibilities are.

Advice: Determine the candidate's management philosophy and personality on the job. How does the candidate see him- or herself in relation to others in the department and the company? Should a brand manager be a category champion outside the company as well as within the company? How visible does the candidate need to be within the company to market his or her product effectively?

Brand Manager

9. *Tell me what you've learned in trade marketing.*

Sample Answer: I held a trade marketing position involving a six-month assignment as liaison between marketing and sales. It helped me understand where salespeople are coming from, especially when they have a bizarre request. I took the job because I thought I needed some perspectives I didn't have. It definitely helped me learn to be more diplomatic and more thorough in getting everybody's buy-in to my decisions. I suppose it helped me be a little more visionary.

Advice: This question targets a specific type of marketing and calls for the candidate to draw from past experiences, and from skills acquired during those experiences. What did he or she learn that would prove valuable in your opening? Would the candidate repeat these experiences, given the chance? You want to see that the candidate makes career decisions based on the opportunity to acquire new skills that will round out his or her experience and lead to a successful, long-term career in brand management.

• • •

10. *Which of your personality characteristics is a weakness in brand management?*

Sample Answer: My lack of diplomacy. I didn't always understand why you need everyone else's buy-in on decisions that are rightly your own to make. Now I'd say I'm very careful about it. I've learned how to wait before coming forward with my reasoning for something, rather than just making a quick conclusion on my own.

Advice: You want to see if the candidate can be honest and direct in assessing his or her characteristics and abilities and what he or she thinks may be a possible liability in brand management. Do you agree with the candidate's assessment, and does he or she have a solid understanding of what it takes to succeed in brand management?

Brand Manager

11. *What growth opportunities do you see in this product category?*

Sample Answer: Health consciousness is here to stay. But, then, when you remember the movement away from red meat in the eighties, you realize how quickly steak has regained popularity. The real opportunity is to take advantage of the fact that consumers are more educated and more disciplined about what they eat. Providing more information like nutrition facts on menus is an example.

Advice: You want the candidate to demonstrate creativity and leadership through an understanding of the marketplace and the industry. What trends or opportunities does the candidate foresee in the near future that would benefit the current product offerings, and what marketing vehicles would the candidate pursue to reposition the product for a different target market?

• • •

12. *What personal qualities are important to brand management?*

Sample Answer: The ability to link together pieces to see the big picture that moves your brand along, the ability to juggle and reprioritize a number of responsibilities, and the ability to get the teamwork going to support your brand throughout the departments that affect it.

Advice: This is a straightforward question that asks the candidate to enumerate the qualities and skills that lead to successful brand management. You also want to know why the candidate chose these qualities and skills and how he or she has developed them through past experiences. Can the candidate bring these skills to your opening?

Brand Manager

13. *How is your management style suited to product management?*

Sample Answer: Somehow I learned how to link everything together to see the big picture, which is why I think I make good judgments for my brand and why I anticipate problems before they arise. So I work hard to make sure people who work with me see the big picture too. And I'm a big believer of getting everybody who's involved in a project together every other week to talk about problems that exist or are likely to arise.

Advice: Why does the candidate believe he or she is well suited to be a product manager, given his or her abilities and preferred method of managing people and resources? Does the candidate understand what it takes to manage a product successfully through its life cycle while at the same time managing other aspects, such as relationships with the PR firms, industry analysts, and inside management?

• • •

14. *How do you use in-store promotions?*

Sample Answer: I rely on in-store promotions to help me with several things: promoting new products, introducing a new package size or complementary marketing with another product, or advertising seasonal promotions. In general, in-store promotions help us get the consumers' attention for something we think they may otherwise not know or notice.

Advice: This question determines the candidate's depth of knowledge and experience in using promotions either to jump-start a brand or to maintain position in the market. You are also looking for a strong opinion rather than a textbook response. Would you use the candidate's example of an in-store promotion for one of your products?

15. *Describe how you can use the off-season to expand a seasonal product's use.*

Sample Answer: One example I've always considered as a missed opportunity is barbecue sauce. If barbecue sauce were my brand, I'd be concerned about how to increase use when people are no longer outside using their grills. For example, in the winter I might advertise recipes that use barbecue sauce as a base for holiday appetizers.

Advice: You are testing the candidate's creativity, promotional skills, and ability to think outside the box to keep a seasonal product in the consumer's mind during the off-season. What are some of the more offbeat marketing ploys used by the candidate to get consumers to buy his or her product out of season? Encourage the candidate to think beyond outrageous sale prices, or one-shot blowout price reductions, to lay out a step-by-step plan that would hold the consumer's interest year-round.

• • •

16. *If you had to recall a product, what might you do?*

Sample Answer: Well, that's certainly happened to a number of good companies with good products. The nature of the recall would affect my action. For example, with a safety concern I'd immediately recall and replace products with some sort of assurance campaign to follow. I might establish an 800 number for people to call with questions or concerns. One manufacturer of a baby product actually had a press release on an 800 number. That was a very effective way to reach consumers without using a lot of manpower.

Advice: This question goes beyond problem-solving ability. You want to see how quickly the candidate would respond to the problem and focus on a solution without dwelling on what caused the recall. Ask the candidate for the specific steps he or she would take to get the product off the shelves and maintain consumer confidence in your product or company.

Brand Manager

17. *This is your thirty-second commercial. What else do you want to tell me?*

Sample Answer: I would say that nothing beats an unending curiosity for the brand business. That means when I go to a store, I never go just to shop for myself. I constantly watch what people are putting in their shopping carts, how long it takes them to pick something off the shelf, and what they say if they are shopping with someone else; I learn something every time. I also notice what people are eating at the park, what people bring to work for lunch, and what my friends and family have at home. I don't think you can teach someone to be curious. They either are or aren't, and curious people are good at this business. That's what you'll get, in addition to everything else, if you hire me.

Advice: This question tests the candidate's ability to home in on just two or three qualities or skills that set him or her apart from the competition. This question is not just about passion for the job or company. You want someone with true marketing acumen. If the candidate has trouble marketing him- or herself, would you really want to hire that person to market your products?

1. ### Why are you interested in our firm and in this particular practice?

Sample Answer: I look at the quality and quantity of projects you are working with here, and that's the attraction for me. Among Big Six firms that have developed strong manufacturing consulting reputations, this office was one of the early ones to develop a unique reputation without relying on leads from the audit side. I think that audit and strategy work need to remain separate in terms of the images being different. What you're selling to a client is very different. You look at the past in audit/tax work; you look at the future in strategy work.

Advice: The candidate should give solid reasons why your consulting firm, as opposed to others, offers the candidate an opportunity to develop his or her own unique set of skills. What is it about your firm, and the types of clients or industries you focus on, that is especially appealing to the candidate? You want to cut through any hype or canned response and get the candidate to give you concrete examples of why your organization makes the most sense given this candidate's background, experience, and interests.

• • •

2. ### Why do you want to continue a career in consulting?

Sample Answer: When I first started consulting, I wanted the intellectual variety of working with a lot of different clients, industries, and project teams. Second, I wanted an accelerated pace of learning, and nothing throws you into that at a faster rate than consulting. Third, I wanted to be involved in proactive business decisions. Now I don't want to leave because of the respect I have for consulting professionals in general and because I'm surrounded by peers who are so intelligent that they push me to my limits. In a client's corporate environment you find that level of intensity with some of the employees, but not with the majority.

Advice: You must be convinced that the candidate has long-term aspirations in consulting and isn't merely looking for consulting assignments as a way to leverage a corporate opportunity. You should press the candidate to give you examples of consulting assignments that excite and motivate him or her. Do these assignments parallel your firm's business? The candidate should at least give you a logical career path that is consistent with what you can offer in your firm.

• • •

3. *What is your biggest concern about a consulting career?*

Sample Answer: For any consultant who thrives on the quality of projects, I think the real fear is that you'll either get stuck on the beach—not assigned to a project—or that you'll get a project that isn't going to be challenging enough. I'd like there to be as little downtime or in-office time as possible and more time with clients. That's why I'm interested in your firm and this office in particular—because of the projects you have secured and reassurances from consultants who work here that they're always busy.

Advice: Determine if there are any aspects, such as travel or long hours, that the consultant would feel uncomfortable committing to. Does the candidate display the flexibility and adaptability necessary to work with a variety of clients and provide them with a high level of service? Any hesitation on the part of the candidate concerning responsibilities, accountability, or managing projects, should raise a red flag about the candidate's true commitment to consulting.

• • •

4. *As an engagement manager, how would you motivate a team under the pressure of aggressive deadlines?*

Sample Answer: I've learned a lot about managing project teams, including the fact that if you hire good people or select the best people for your team, you can delegate easily and leave them alone to do their work. I remember one team that I did not have

much time to devote to because I was managing another team that really needed my knowledge and skills on a steady basis. What I learned to do with the first team was simply make lunch and dinner appointments to get caught up on their progress and find out if they needed any help from me. That worked out great because they didn't feel abandoned, and we all had to eat anyway. I found that talking about stressful issues over a meal helps people to open up, but also to keep things in perspective. And the casual environment helped me communicate that I was there as a resource, not as someone checking over their shoulders—they knew I trusted their work.

Consultant/Manager, Senior

Advice: You're measuring not only the candidate's management style but also his or her ability to organize and prioritize tasks, delegate to team members, and adhere to a rigid schedule while keeping team members enthusiastic and on track. What techniques does the candidate use to keep his or her team focused and on track to meet tight deadlines? How does the candidate balance rigid deadlines with the necessary sensitivity to the team's ongoing dynamics?

• • •

5. In what ways are your personality and skills suited to consulting?

Sample Answer: Well, one thing that anyone in consulting needs to be comfortable with is dealing with ambiguity. There is always more you could do or more data you might collect, but you have to make progress. This underscores everything and explains why you have to stay focused on your deliverable or end product. That's something I learned to do. With experience behind me I see how often the same types of problems are shared among companies in different industries. So my strength is the ability never to seem lost, the ability to establish confidence with the client and move the project forward.

Advice: You want to determine personality on the job and compatibility with the consulting environment culture. Would the candidate be better suited for a corporate position than a consulting position? You want to see if the candidate is more suited to moving from project to project and adapting quickly to different corporate environments than to working for one company and one supervisor.

6. What do you find the most difficult aspect of consulting?

Sample Answer: I would say that I wasn't always as good as I am now at making quick decisions. A quick decision is better than a decision that's made too late; you simply have to collect information fast, count to ten, and think. You also have to bring to the table everything you've seen from other engagements; it's amazing how often different companies have similar core problems.

Advice: You should try to uncover any weaknesses in the candidate's background or skills that would prove to be a liability to your firm. Expect the candidate to turn this question into a positive by emphasizing a minor obstacle that he or she has overcome, perhaps early in his or her career. You should also expect the candidate to focus more on positive achievements and accomplishments and on what he or she can do for you tomorrow. Don't hesitate to ask for a more substantive example

• • •

7. What new opportunities do you see in the consulting business?

Sample Answer: I see all the firms moving toward specialization. In other words, they are collecting a group of consultants with detailed functional knowledge in an industry or type of business process. Clients are less and less willing to deal with young, smart people; they want to see a track record. So the big firms like the Big Six are moving toward industry specialization in terms of their internal divisions, and boutique firms that play to one or two specializations are springing up. As far as my own interests,

I want to be able to say that people think of me when they have an issue regarding international business development.

Advice: What future opportunities does the candidate see in corporate consulting, and what industries, technologies, or products will provide consulting assignments for him or her in the short term? Where does the consultant see opportunities that will sharpen and broaden his or her experience within your firm? You want to ensure that the candidate is committed to being a consultant as opposed to using consulting merely to land a corporate position.

• • •

8. Would you be willing to do an extended assignment overseas?

Sample Answer: Yes, I would. In fact, my wife and I have discussed it, and she is trilingual, so she could easily find employment abroad if the project was more than a few months. I spent six months at a manufacturing plant in Spain with my current job. Unfortunately, she wasn't able to accompany me at the time because she had just started a new job, and we've always regretted that.

Advice: This is an extension of asking the candidate if traveling is a problem, because you want to find out how committed the candidate is to a consulting career and whether he or she can balance outside interests with an international assignment. You also want to make sure the candidate has no qualms about adjusting to a foreign country and its customs while continuing to deliver the results you expect from the project.

9. *Describe a business process that you determined was not value added.*

Sample Answer: I had a manufacturing client whose warranty program had led to skyrocketing administrative costs and time. I looked into the problem and found that 90 percent of administrative time was spent investigating claims of less than thirty dollars. So I instituted a policy of paying those warranty claims automatically, which created goodwill with customers and allowed the company to reduce administrative staff drastically in the customer service department.

Advice: How tough will this candidate be in assessing, for efficiency's sake, whether a client should dump a division or business, thereby laying off employees? Consultants are not hired to rubber-stamp existing operations—they are hired to fix or improve a situation. You need to measure not only the candidate's analytical skills but also his or her ability to "deliver the news" to a client about any aspect of the business that clearly does not contribute to the bottom line.

• • •

10. *Describe your project management skills.*

Sample Answer: I've learned how to treat members of my client team differently from members of my consulting team to help move a project along. In general consultants are highly motivated and self-directed—you can point them in a direction and go. Members of the client team generally have more of an eight-to-five mentality, so I spend more time interacting with them, and even doing a little bit of hand holding. That way information is ready when my consultant team needs it.

Advice: Try to determine the strength of the candidate's ability to get along with and motivate a client's senior management team in an effort to strive for project excellence. How does the candidate lay out a project, assign tasks and deadlines, and monitor progress? Does the candidate balance his or her mandate to push a project to completion against the need to "win over" the client's management team, who may or may not share the same commitment or vision?

• • •

11. *Tell me how you might employ best practices in a new engagement.*

Sample Answer: Well, for example, there might be a sales incentive program created by a player in the telecom industry that's been very effective. Perhaps I've read about it in a *Forbes* article. If my new engagement at an insurance company involves problems motivating the sales force, I would look for ways to modify the telecom sales incentive program to fit the insurance sales reps.

Advice: What new methodologies or consulting techniques does the candidate believe are cutting edge and give him or her an advantage in assisting a client company to solve a problem? You want to feel confident that this candidate is aggressive and eager to remain current on new technologies or consulting concepts that could help a client company become more productive and efficient.

Consultant/Manager, Senior

12. *Describe a business process re-engineering engagement you've worked on.*

Sample Answer: I did a project for a billion-dollar health care company. We re-engineered the entire supply chain for one business unit. The core problem was the manufacturing infrastructure strategy.

Advice: How much experience does the candidate have in this particular type of consulting practice, and what is the level and depth of that experience? Ask the candidate for a specific example of a re-engineering project and his or her role on the project. What did the candidate take away from this experience, and how would it benefit other clients in the same or different industries?

• • •

13. *What are the most critical success factors in domestic manufacturing?*

Sample Answer: Today's manufacturers need flexible manufacturing to be more consumer driven. As the U.S. has become more consumer oriented, part of being "closer to the customer" has meant being physically closer—that is, putting plants near product demand points. The alternative is flexible manufacturing, whereby manufacturing line changeovers are easy, and numerous products can be produced efficiently in one plant.

Advice: Determine the depth and scope of the candidate's experience in manufacturing, and what specifically makes the candidate well equipped to consult to your manufacturing clients. What changes in manufacturing have led to unusual or complex consulting assignments for this candidate, and what were the critical elements for success on these projects? What obstacles did the candidate encounter, and, based on the experience, would he or she do anything different for a similar project with a new client?

Consultant/Manager, Senior

14. *What are the most critical success factors in international manufacturing?*

Sample Answer: Multinational corporations, or MNCs, are aggressively establishing global sourcing policies. To maintain competitive prices, they buy parts all over the world. The move toward global quality standards is important in making that happen effectively. And we have to work toward reducing isolationist policies and trade barriers among countries.

Advice: You are not looking for a European history lesson here; rather, you want to find out what types of international projects the candidate has worked on and what he or she did to effect a successful conclusion of each project. What problems or barriers did the candidate have to overcome to manage an international manufacturing project successfully? How has this experience enhanced the candidate's understanding of the ways new methods of manufacturing can be implemented to resolve problems both in this country and abroad?

• • •

15. *What advice would you give to a consumer products company having trouble with distribution in certain regions of the country?*

Sample Answer: I'd first examine demographics in various locations around the country to determine different demand levels for the company's various products. Then I would examine where its manufacturing sites were as well as what was being produced at each site. The goal is to

produce the products in greatest local demand. This is especially critical if shipping costs are a major component of total cost, such as in the case of bottled soft drinks.

Advice: Here you're testing the candidate's problem-solving skills and ability to think creatively to overcome a problem getting product onto store shelves. You also want to go beyond the candidate's experience in consumer products to see if he or she can quickly identify why certain problems exist in regional distribution and what steps will result in a winning solution. What aspects of the marketing mix does the candidate believe are overlooked when it comes to distribution trouble spots?

• • •

16. *If you could work with someone (or a particular client) who you think exhibits best practices in a lot of ways, who would that be?*

Sample Answer: I would work with Herb Kelleher of Southwest Airlines. I would want to study him to learn firsthand how he motivates his employees with things other than cash. What I learned from him would help me deal with any clients who have people-motivation problems—and most do.

Advice: Look for stories or examples of companies or leaders whom the candidate considers exemplary in managing to stay out in front of the competition. Why does the candidate think this example stands out, and what specific business practices does he or she believe translate effectively to other companies and other industries? You want to ensure that this candidate has stayed on top of current management consulting trends and techniques and can apply them to a variety of situations.

• • •

17. How might you advise a client to speed product development cycles?

Sample Answer: First of all, I would advise the client not to rush the phase of determining customer requirements. I would put a lot of time and people resources into making sure the up-front assumptions are valid. That way we could avoid costly redesigns. I would then advise the client to create a lean development team. What I have found is that companies tend to throw more people into a project when they want something done quickly; ironically, more often the greater the size of the group, the more you lose in cohesiveness and in assigning responsibility.

Advice: Here you're testing the candidate's depth of knowledge of different product development models and of methods he or she believes work best within different industries. What types of experiences in product development does the candidate think would help him or her to advise clients on the best processes to decrease time to market? What are the key factors according to the candidate in improving time to market performance?

18. *How do you keep up with cutting-edge business practices?*

Sample Answer: I read the *Harvard Business Review,* the *Economist, Forbes, Business Week,* and the *Wall Street Journal.* I also read various trade publications in my specialty. For example, I read the American Production and Inventory Control Society (APICS) magazine.

Advice: Any consultant who is not up on the latest trends in management consulting and cannot cite examples of new managerial consulting techniques should be a concern to you. You should evaluate this candidate not only on past engagements but also on what he or she is doing to improve skills and broaden knowledge, which ultimately makes a person more valuable to clients.

Customer Service Representative

1. Do you believe that the customer is always right?

Sample Answer: Yes, we do whatever it takes to see that the customer is satisfied and continues to buy from us. There *are* limits. If the customer is clearly taking advantage of us, we may draw the line. But if there is any doubt, we side with the customer.

Advice: Does the candidate have the ability to distinguish between a customer who is justified in his or her request and a customer who simply wants to get something for nothing? Can the candidate determine the real motivation behind a complaint? What are the consequences if the candidate denies the customer's request, and how does the candidate weigh those consequences when making his or her decision? Can the candidate treat a customer with respect even when the customer's demand is way out of line?

• • •

2. How do you handle unruly or demanding customers?

Sample Answer: I try to talk in a calm, even voice, to get the person to respond in the same businesslike manner and not vent his or her anger.

Advice: What communication skills and personal qualities does the candidate use to deal successfully with irate customers? At what point would the candidate consider referring the customer to his or her supervisor? You are looking for the candidate's personality traits here, as well as character, common sense, and the self-confidence necessary to minimize a confrontation quickly and resolve a problem.

3. *What level of decision-making authority have you had in your last two positions?*

Sample Answer: I was able to make decisions up to one thousand dollars in value. This included issuing credits, replacing merchandise, and offering price adjustments.

Advice: Has the candidate demonstrated increasing responsibility and a willingness to make decisions without supervisory guidance? What has the candidate done in previous positions to merit more decision-making authority? You also should weigh the types of decisions the candidate has made in prior positions and whether the candidate should have consulted a supervisor before making them.

• • •

4. *How did you handle a situation when the customer was totally wrong?*

Sample Answer: I recently had a situation in which a customer returned merchandise for credit, and the item was not purchased from our company. I explained that the merchandise was not ours and that probably someone in the other company's shipping department had put the wrong label on the box.

Advice: You want to test the candidate's ability to stand firm with a customer and not to shift responsibility. What communications skills does the candidate believe are most effective in this type of situation? Do you agree with the candidate's methods and final solution? What was the end result of the candidate's actions, and would he or she handle it differently a second time around?

Customer Service Representative

5. *Why did you go into the customer service department of your company as opposed to sales?*

Sample Answer: I like the challenge and satisfaction of dealing with customers and resolving problems. I also like the fact that every day is different. In reality, most of the job is sales.

Advice: What duties or responsibilities does the candidate believe make customer service an attractive career choice? Are the candidate's personal qualities better suited to handling customer inquiries and complaints after the sale, or trying to pursue leads and close sales? What is it about customer service that the candidate thinks will hold his or her interest for the long haul?

• • •

6. *After a difficult day, how do you handle stress?*

Sample Answer: I usually go for a ten-minute walk. This allows me to relax, unwind, and forget about the day.

Advice: You want to see how the candidate deals with the day-to-day demands of meeting customer needs without letting the pressure affect his or her performance. How is the candidate able to cope with the pressure, and what techniques does he or she use to eliminate stress from the job? You should make sure that the candidate has the character to withstand the daily grind and still perform at peak efficiency when servicing your customers.

Customer Service Representative

7. What was the most difficult customer service problem you had to face at your last company?

Sample Answer: I had to recommend that we stop doing business with one of our oldest customers. The company claimed there was a problem with every shipment, even though we triple-checked each order and had signatures on all of the shipping documents. Apparently, the customer was belligerent with every one of its suppliers and used complaints to get additional price concessions.

Advice: Get the candidate to outline the problem and give you his or her methodology for attacking and resolving it successfully. Evaluate the problem based on its difficulty. Do you think the candidate's solution was the best alternative? Do you feel comfortable with this candidate's problem-solving ability and willingness to tackle tough issues when there may be no clear-cut answer?

• • •

8. In what type of industry do you prefer to work?

Sample Answer: I prefer to work with a consumer-oriented type of product. The exact nature of the industry is not that important.

Advice: Why is the candidate attracted to your industry and, by extension, your company? Is there a particular product or service you provide that the candidate is excited about? Does the candidate have prior experience dealing with customers in your industry? If the candidate's past experience is in a different industry, decide if he or she will be a successful customer service representative in your industry, and define the qualities or prior experience that substantiates your answer.

Customer Service Representative

9. *When you are going into a new company or industry, what do you do to get a firm grasp on the organization and its products?*

Sample Answer: The first thing I generally do is get a copy of the most recent catalog, order forms, pricing lists, and any other marketing literature. I also try to look at the company's sales reports and/or receivable aging in order to find out what the products are and to whom they are sold. Additionally, I speak with the sales manager to learn what the concerns are in handling any given account.

Advice: The candidate should demonstrate how he or she, from the first day on the job, would go about getting to know your products inside and out. How much training will be required, and what type of learning curve should you expect from this candidate? How much does the candidate already know about your company and products, and could he or she hit the ground running tomorrow if hired today?

•   •   •

10. *What was the pace at your last company?*

Sample Answer: We were extremely fast-paced. In a multimillion-dollar consumer-oriented company, there were constant demands and issues to resolve each day.

Advice: If your company is a dynamic, fast-paced organization that is in a growth mode, you need to make sure that this candidate has the experience and the personality to grow with you and handle the demands of your corporate culture. You should be wary of candidates who are used to the slower-paced environment of a large company if your company is small, flexible, and constantly changing.

11. *How have you been able to interact effectively with others on a variety of levels in your most recent job?*

Sample Answer: I'm an even-tempered individual who believes in treating everyone professionally. I believe that I am a good listener and can work well with everyone to resolve the problem at hand. I don't worry about who gets credit for a decision.

Advice: Does the candidate seek out coworkers to share information with, or get advice from, when solving a customer service problem? Determine how often the candidate approaches his or her supervisor and other senior managers, and, in general, how the candidate's company operates at different management levels.

• • •

 12. *What do you think are the personal qualities necessary to be successful as a customer service representative?*

Sample Answer: The ability to listen to the customer's complaint. The ability to deal with people on a professional and reasonably sympathetic level. The ability to talk to people. And the ability to make decisions that satisfy all parties.

Advice: What characteristics, personality traits, or communication techniques does the candidate use to resolve customer problems successfully? Why does he or she believe that these tools are more effective than others in handling day-to-day customer problems? Do you agree with the candidate's assessment, and is it consistent with your own ideas about what makes a successful customer service representative in your organization?

Customer Service Representative

13. *What types of decisions are difficult for you?*

Sample Answer: The ones for which there are no formal guidelines or policies in place and on which I have to spend a lot of time trying to figure out what has happened and what should have happened.

Advice: Determine what problems are most likely to prevent the candidate from making a decision, and assess the level of the candidate's difficulty with the problems. Was time lost in the past as the candidate struggled to reach a decision? Are these types of decisions too emotional for the candidate to handle, or is the complexity of the problems what causes the difficulty? You are testing the candidate's maturity level here, as well as his or her ability to see the consequences of failing to make a decision.

• • •

14. *In your current job, what are some of the things that you spend most of your time working on?*

Sample Answer: Researching paperwork for bills of lading, invoices, and credits; obtaining proofs of delivery; mailing out customer statements; handling correspondence; and making phone calls.

Advice: How much time does the candidate spend on the phone with customers compared to performing other duties, such as learning more about your company's products and services, testing products, or writing reports for upper management? How does the candidate prioritize responsibilities, and can he or she focus on the two or three duties that you consider critical for success in your opening?

Customer Service Representative

15. *If you were head of the customer service department with authority to effect changes, what three things would you change?*

Sample Answer: I would get a new computer system that would allow us to call up all relevant information on the screen without having to dig through files for the data. I would hire an additional person to help with the workload. I would clearly state our returns and claims policies in our catalog, on our order form, and on our invoices. These steps would eliminate two-thirds of the calls from customers who claim they don't know our policies.

Advice: Here you are testing the candidate's overall knowledge of customer service as well as his or her ability to identify areas where improvement could lead to greater efficiency. Does the candidate have experience in effecting change within prior customer service operations, and if so, what were they? Do the candidate's ideas make sense and demonstrate awareness of problems that can hamper the effectiveness of a customer service organization? How ambitious is the candidate, and do you think he or she wants to rise to a position of authority in a customer service organization such as yours?

Engineer

1. Have you been involved in new business development?

Sample Answer: Yes. In response to a formal request for proposals, I participated in the development of a proposal for engineering design services for a water treatment plant upgrade. I was responsible for writing those sections of the proposal relating to the existing water treatment facilities, and I also participated in the presentation of the proposal to the town's selection committee.

Advice: What new projects has the candidate personally developed—from proposal to project completion? What was the level of involvement, and what specific steps did the candidate take to bring new business into his or her firm? You want to see if the candidate enjoys soliciting new clients, and to discover the types of projects he or she is most successful at procuring for his or her firm.

• • •

2. Do you have experience using personal computers for engineering and general office functions?

Sample Answer: I have used personal computers for a number of years, primarily in report writing with word-processing programs such as Word and WordPerfect, and in performing engineering calculations and analysis with spreadsheet programs such as Excel and Lotus 1-2-3. More recently, I have started to use Access, a database management program, to create an inventory of storm-water inflow sources for a sewer separation project that I'm working on. I use AutoCAD for computer-aided design and drafting work. I also attended two training

courses in the past year, and I'm investigating the use of geographic information system technology for use on a landfill sitting project.

Advice: Since the personal computer has become a staple in the office environment, you want to determine the candidate's range of experience and familiarity with their use for general office applications and also for the more technical applications that are increasingly found in consulting engineering offices. Try to get the candidate to discuss specific applications and to explain how he or she has used those applications to improve productivity or to solve a problem for his or her company or client.

• • •

3. How do you envision the development of your engineering career over the next few years?

Sample Answer: For the past four years I have worked mainly in a technical capacity and have gained solid technical expertise in the water and wastewater treatment areas. I'm confident of my technical skills, but I also realize that these skills will need constant updating. I feel ready to complement those skills with a greater project management role. I have had some project management responsibility, setting budgets and monitoring costs for a number of projects on which I have worked, and would like to become more involved in this aspect of the business. Ultimately, I see myself in a management role rather than in a purely technical one.

Advice: Has the candidate thought through possible career options in engineering and about skills or new experiences that he or she would like to acquire in the next few years? You want to see if the candidate has taken the time to flesh out what he or she really wants to accomplish as an engineer, be it in research, design, or some specialized field. Can your company provide the opportunities to satisfy the candidate's career aspirations?

Engineer

 4. *Tell me about the most interesting project you successfully completed.*

Sample Answer: While in engineering school, I did a project in which I reorganized the factory floor for a company. I worked on the project for an entire semester, relaying out the tools so they had a better flow. I did all the engineering drawings for the factory floor and presented it to management. They were impressed and ended up using my plan.

Advice: Test the candidate's depth of engineering knowledge and his or her experience with various engineering projects. What specifically did the candidate accomplish on the project, and what new skills or insights did he or she acquire as a result of working on this project? What new projects does the candidate want to tackle as a result of working on this past project?

• • •

 5. *Have you had any co-op engineering assignments? Which assignments did you prefer, and why?*

Sample Answer: I was put to work helping on a manufacturing line. The purpose of the project was to determine how many operators could run an automated tool using a man-machine analysis. I automated the man-machine analysis technique by putting it on my PC. It was a challenging project that involved not only a lot of engineering know-how but also computer expertise. It was exciting putting to work in the real world all the skills I had learned in school.

Advice: In lieu of any professional work, what types of experience does the candidate believe make him or her a strong contender for your opening? Ask the candidate to describe in detail any co-op assignments, with emphasis on accomplishments, skills, and knowledge acquired and obstacles met and overcome. Why was the experience a positive one for the candidate, and was it beneficial in terms of his or her education?

• • •

6. *Which do you prefer and why: projects in which your individual accomplishments are apparent, or projects that are team oriented?*

Sample Answer: I really like to work on teams. I find that a project tends to be more successful if there is input from many different people with many different areas of expertise. I was lucky in that my university's engineering program placed a lot of emphasis on teamwork, and I was able to work on many different engineering projects and assignments in groups.

Advice: Here you are going squarely after the candidate's personality and preferred working environment and determining whether he or she is a team player or needs to be the star of the department. Can the candidate put aside his or her ego and raise the team above the candidate's own need to be recognized for contributions made to a project?

7. What software programs are you familiar with?

Sample Answer: I've done a lot of work on Microsoft Excel and Word for Windows. I'm also proficient in Corel Flow.

Advice: You want to find out what programs the candidate is familiar with and what level of expertise he or she has with each program. Does the candidate know the industry standard applications and the tasks or projects that require the use of these programs on a regular basis? If not, how quickly can he or she get up to speed?

• • •

8. What computer design experience do you have, and at what level of application?

Sample Answer: I have experience with AutoCad and CAD/CAM and have used them in product and process redesign.

Advice: You should be testing the candidate's knowledge of specific applications, and projects or assignments for which he or she has used those applications. To what degree did the candidate use the application to solve an engineering problem that otherwise would have slowed progress on a particular project? What expertise did the candidate have using these applications going into the project, and what did he or she acquire in the way of enhanced computer or applications skills when the project was finished?

9. Do you have experience with quality programs?

Sample Answer: I have experience working in an ISO-9000 environment. My responsibilities included documenting manufacturing procedures to ensure consistent processing on three manufacturing shifts.

Advice: What is the candidate's depth of experience in using quality programs, and what does he or she consider to be a top-flight program? What was the nature of the experience with the quality program, and how did the candidate first come into contact with the program? In addition to measuring the candidate's expertise with quality programs, you want an opinion as to why he or she believes one program excels over another.

• • •

10. Have you had any experience in process optimization?

Sample Answer: In my last position I had to increase production in a stamping machine by 10 percent. I redesigned the equipment to combine two functions and increased production by 15 percent.

Advice: Determine the candidate's problem-solving ability and the way he or she used a particular methodology to achieve measurable results on an engineering project. What was the nature of the problem that required the candidate to use this particular methodology over another process, and what skills did the candidate learn as a result of this experience?

11. *Tell me about a time when you had to take a shortcut or a less-than-optimal approach due to time or financial constraints.*

Sample Answer: When helping to convert an accounting package to a new platform, a rushed schedule prohibited me from thoroughly testing the module I was working on. Our testing department was understaffed at the time, and the product hit the market with too many bugs in it.

Advice: You want to test the candidate's understanding that the business world is always demanding tradeoffs between quality, time, and money. Does the candidate demonstrate an appreciation of this? Will the candidate exercise appropriate judgement in making tradeoff decisions?

• • •

12. *Why did you choose mechanical engineering over other engineering disciplines?*

Sample Answer: I have always enjoyed working with my hands, and a mechanical engineering curriculum has enabled me to enhance my innate skills.

Advice: What initially attracted the candidate to this discipline, and what skills or abilities does the candidate believe make him or her an ideal candidate for a mechanical engineering position? Why would this discipline hold the candidate's interest for a long period of time? You want some indication that the candidate has thought through all issues that are relevant to a career in this engineering discipline.

13. **Have you been involved with any direct customer-related issues?**

Sample Answer: I have experience in responding to and resolving customer issues on a front-line basis. Customers feel comfortable talking with me directly about design issues, and I respond in a timely fashion.

Advice: Determine how comfortable the candidate feels when dealing with customers. What sort of customer problems did the candidate tackle, and how did the experience affect his or her communications skills? Is handling customer inquiries or problems something the candidate would like to do as part of a future position, and if so, what level of involvement does he or she prefer?

• • •

14. **Have you facilitated any systems training?**

Sample Answer: Yes, I have trained employees in various process control systems, including SPC (or statistical process control), as well as material testing and maintaining production control sheets.

Advice: You want to measure the candidate's initiative in taking a leadership role when deploying department- or companywide training on various systems. What is the depth of the candidate's experience in various systems and processes, and how easy or difficult is it for the candidate to train employees who have different technical capabilities?

15. Are you certified as a professional engineer?

Sample Answer: Yes, I am a fully certified ME and have testified in court on engineering issues.

Advice: Certification not only measures technical competence in a particular engineering discipline but also is indicative of the candidate's aggressiveness in pursuing the best education and training available in his or her engineering discipline.

• • •

16. Have you been involved with patenting a product or process?

Sample Answer: I have been a team leader of two patented products that went to market ahead of schedule. Both products have proceeded to gain solid market shares.

Advice: This question goes to the heart of the candidate's desire and initiative to develop new products and understand the process that is involved in securing a patent for a product or process. Did the candidate take a leadership role in this experience, and what, if any, were the obstacles he or she had to overcome to reach a successful conclusion?

17. Have you had any experience supervising other engineers?

Sample Answer: In my last position I had two entry-level mechanical engineers and ten machine operators report to me. I was responsible for hiring, training, evaluating performance, and handling discipline issues.

Advice: How does the candidate relate to other engineers he or she oversees, and what techniques does the candidate use to motivate them to produce high-quality work? Has the candidate had any problems when managing a group of engineers, and under what circumstances? If your position calls for an engineer with strong leadership and communication skills, you cannot afford to treat this issue lightly.

Financial Analyst

1. Do you have an M.B.A.?

Sample Answer: Yes, I do. I graduated last May with an M.B.A. from New York University. I took two or three classes at night for the past three years.

Advice: You should be interested in more than just the candidate's degree here; the candidate should be prepared to discuss particular courses, projects, or assignments he or she participated in during school that served to enhance the benefits of receiving an advanced degree.

• • •

2. What are your qualifications?

Sample Answer: I have a B.S. in finance as well as an M.B.A. I also have three years' work experience in finance with a Fortune 500 company, and two years' additional financial experience in another major company.

Advice: What skills and experiences does the candidate bring to this job that will add value to your company or department? You want to see if the candidate can go beyond the job requirements to give you a list of unique qualities, skills, or credentials that will position him or her as a solid contender for your opening.

Financial Analyst

3. **What class have you taken that has helped you the most in the workplace?**

Sample Answer: One class that I took in business school that was not required as part of my finance concentration was Cost Accounting. It has probably helped me more than any other course.

Advice: How has the candidate applied his or her course work to real-world business problems, and what information, specifically, has he or she used from a course to solve a business problem or create a solution for a client? Has the candidate recently taken a course that helped him or her get ahead, either at a company or within a chosen industry?

• • •

4. **How could you determine if your costs were too high or too low for a manufacturing plant you were assigned to analyze?**

Sample Answer: I would compare benchmarking within the company at my division as well as at other manufacturing sites. I would also benchmark outside the company with any industry data available for that type of manufacturing process.

Advice: You are testing the candidate's analytical ability and knowledge of financial modeling techniques to determine the appropriate cost structure for a plant in this industry. You want to see how the candidate approaches the problem and methodically and rationally breaks it down to arrive at a final figure. If you require someone with significant cost analysis experience, you should make sure the candidate can give you a detailed plan for attacking this problem quickly and efficiently.

Financial Analyst

5. What software application packages do you use?

Sample Answer: I'm equally comfortable on a Macintosh and a PC. Although I'm very familiar with Lotus 1-2-3, I prefer Microsoft Excel, Microsoft Word, and Microsoft PowerPoint.

Advice: How much does the candidate know about computer software, and how proficient is he or she with standard applications such as word processing, spreadsheets, and presentation programs? The candidate should feel totally comfortable with financial applications and have a positive attitude toward learning new applications as required by your opening.

• • •

6. What do you think being a financial analyst really means?

Sample Answer: It means putting the numbers together and seeing if they work. If they don't work, the financial analyst must uncover the problem and decide why things aren't working.

Advice: What does the candidate consider crucial to effective performance as a financial analyst, and what are some of the key skills that make an analyst successful on a daily basis? What contributions does a financial analyst make to a company or industry, and how would the candidate describe this position to someone unfamiliar with the term "financial analyst"?

• • •

7. What are the best tracking methods?

Sample Answer: It absolutely depends on the situation and what the problem points to. When I did some tracking for accounts payable, I looked at inputs, approvals, and deletions. I compared the number removed from the outstanding.

Financial Analyst

Advice: Determine the depth of the candidate's knowledge and experience using various methods. How does he or she think these methods should be applied to everyday business problems when alerting company management to potential problems? Has the candidate found one method more effective than others, and if so, which method, and why? What signals should the candidate receive from these methods, and when does the candidate believe it's appropriate to alert management?

• • •

8. How good are your writing abilities?

Sample Answer: I really concentrated on further developing my writing skills while working on my M.B.A. I took an entrepreneurial class in which the chief assignment was developing, writing, and continually rewriting a very involved business plan.

Advice: Ask the candidate for writing samples as proof of his or her ability to communicate ideas or critical information verbally. What types of writing does the candidate prefer—short memos or more lengthy treatises? Does the candidate plan to take writing courses in the near future, and if so, what style of writing will the class emphasize? How confident is the candidate in his or her ability to communicate technical terminology in writing to a nontechnical audience?

• • •

9. How good a communicator are you?

Sample Answer: While working toward my M.B.A., I further honed an existing set of solid communication skills. For example, before starting business school, I could deliver a presentation to a group just fine, but I didn't necessarily feel comfortable. I was a bit nervous, and I couldn't relax and enjoy myself. By the end of business school, I had given so many group presentations that they no longer fazed me.

Financial Analyst

Advice: You want examples here of how the candidate prefers to communicate with external clients or internal employees, and, ultimately, how he or she will communicate with you on a daily basis. Will the candidate immediately inform you of a problem, or will he or she try to dance around an issue to avoid a direct confrontation? With external clients you must make sure the candidate's mode of communicating ensures that he or she will always act in a professional manner and consistently articulate company messages without massaging the truth.

• • •

10. Tell me about something you analyzed.

Sample Answer: I incorporated many accounts payable records into one account. To do this, I looked at what was outstanding in each account. By using the consolidated report that I was able to prepare, the financial officers determined some significant benchmarking.

Advice: Get a feel for the types of projects the candidate has had success in analyzing and the steps he or she took to prepare the analysis for review by upper management. What approach did the candidate take to break a problem down into component parts, and how did he or she arrive at a conclusion? You should test the depth and breadth of the candidate's answer to determine the strength of the candidate's analytical skills.

• • •

11. Tell me about a particularly difficult project you handled.

Sample Answer: My company knew that the consulting firm it hired had not done the work that was proposed and paid for. The problem was that we didn't know where the holes were. To discover the discrepancies, I divided all of the information into quantitative material, which included the budget and the cost, and the time and hours spent. I also divided it into qualitative material, which encompassed all of the memos and correspondence. I lined everything up and discovered that the consulting firm had done only a third of what it had promised. I made a presentation to my supervisor and the key financial people of the company. From there we decided how to handle the consulting firm, which we couldn't have done without getting the whole picture.

Advice: Ask the candidate for details about a project in which he or she had to overcome obstacles or resolve particularly difficult problems that had no readily apparent solution. How did the candidate reach a solution, and what in particular did he or she find frustrating in trying to reach that solution?

• • •

12. How do you structure presentations?

Sample Answer: For the consulting firm project I discussed, I made bar graphs. On one chart I made a bar in one color to show the projected time the consulting firm should have spent. The second bar on the same chart showed the actual time spent, so the discrepancy in proposed versus actual time was very clear. On another chart I presented the disparity in the actual money charged versus the proposed charges by again using a bar graph.

Advice: How does the candidate go about delivering information to his or her audience? What steps does he or she take to ensure that the message of the presentation is clearly articulated? Does the candidate believe in a formal agenda, or does he or she prefer to wing it with an informal presentation that includes interaction and questions from the audience?

Financial Analyst

 13. How important do you think qualitative concerns are to financial analysis?

Sample Answer: I think it certainly depends on the individual case. I have found, however, that qualitative issues often raise the right questions. They can help you determine where the problem started. For example, in the consulting firm issue, nobody in my company had anything positive to say about the firm. These negative feelings may have led to my supervisor's suspicion that things were not right on the books.

Advice: You first want to determine what qualitative issues the candidate believes can impact an analysis, then get the candidate to outline his or her reasons for the critical nature of qualitative issues. How should these issues be presented as part of a complete analysis of a problem, and how does the candidate weight them in relation to the numbers?

• • •

14. What publications do you read on a regular basis?

Sample Answer: I read the *Wall Street Journal* and the *Harvard Business Review* for general business. I also like to read *Forbes* and *Business Week*.

Advice: The candidate should display a strong interest in business publications and magazines as well as any business books that he or she has found helpful in assisting with client problems or imparting other useful knowledge. You might also want to find out what books or magazines the candidate reads for enjoyment or self-improvement.

Financial Analyst

15. How did you become interested in financial analysis?

Sample Answer: I'm very prudent with personal finances, and I really enjoy solving difficult situations, so I majored in finance in college. I complemented my major with a minor in English to develop my writing and communications skills. I also concentrated in finance when I got my M.B.A., which I really enjoyed. Starting my career as a financial analyst seemed like a natural progression.

Advice: Determine if an event, class, seminar, experience, or individual first sparked the candidate's interest in financial analysis. What is so compelling about financial analysis as a career option, and what does the candidate see as important applications of financial analysis techniques to everyday business problems?

• • •

16. What are your primary financial responsibilities in your current job?

Sample Answer: I manage the company's monthly and annual costs forecast. I go through an annual budgeting forecast, which feeds our profit forecast, with my supervisor.

Advice: What are the two or three most important functions that the candidate performs on a daily basis, and what would the candidate like to do in his or her next position as a financial analyst? Try to determine what it is that excites the candidate about this type of position and what the candidate believes have been his or her primary contributions in previous jobs.

General Manager

1. What were the principal products at your last company?

Sample Answer: Our largest revenue line was computerized conveyor systems. We also made a large variety of less sophisticated items such as weigh stations, loading systems, semiautomated packing equipment, and shrink-wrap machinery.

Advice: You want to learn about more than just the products here; you should look for the candidate's level of responsibility in overseeing some aspect of either creating the product or delivering it to the marketplace. Has the candidate had significant experience with your product category, and if so, what kind of experience and at what level?

• • •

2. What do you see as the key factors behind your group's financial performance over the last several years?

Sample Answer: Our firm has had a tradition of anticipating changing market demands; this mind-set played a key role in the early and substantial funding commitment to develop our computerized conveyor systems, which have been a cornerstone of our growth. At the same time, by retaining our lower-tech lines, we have become a one-stop source for our customer's warehouse equipment needs.

Advice: Does the candidate have a good grasp of the overall success factors and financial performance of his or her firm? How astute is his or her analysis? What specific actions did the candidate take to help his or her former company? The candidate should provide several examples of how he or she made a positive impact on the company's performance.

General Manager

3. *How do you think the challenges of managing people in this environment would differ from your current position?*

Sample Answer: Here the work force is much more highly motivated and more sophisticated than the one I managed at the Warehouse Systems Group. Issuing commands to sophisticated, dedicated professionals doesn't work. I've found that a work force of this caliber first needs to understand to their own satisfaction why they are being asked to do something. But if you do succeed in winning their trust, they can accomplish just about anything.

Advice: This question addresses the candidate's knowledge of your industry, company, and, specifically, your company's management style and corporate culture. For example, if the candidate's background is based on matrix management and your company is more top-down oriented, can he or she adjust to your company's management style and be an effective producer? You should be concerned not only about industry but also about the size of the candidate's prior company and the number of employees the candidate is used to managing on a regular basis.

• • •

4. *How closely do you tend to monitor the people who report to you?*

Sample Answer: Generally, I meet privately with each person for a progress report once a week. Unless a serious ongoing problem, such as a key project running behind schedule, emerges, I like each manager to keep me up-to-date. I find this builds trust and inspires extra effort. I have also found that more frequent or less formal meetings tend to become superficial.

General Manager

Advice: Does the candidate prefer to micromanage his or her people or give them free reign to do their jobs with minimal supervision? Much will depend upon the candidate's prior work experience and the management style at those companies. What type of professional relationship does the candidate prefer to foster with employees, and would he or she consider altering the style of that relationship to suit your needs? Flexibility is a key issue here, especially if the candidate is coming from a different industry.

• • •

5. What qualities do you tend to look for in hiring people?

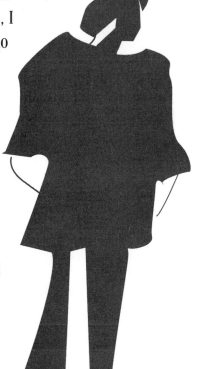

Sample Answer: I look for people who are driven to succeed but who also have 360-degree vision. In other words, I want an engineer who's going to drive his work ahead but who will make engineering changes to satisfy marketing and manufacturing demands—not because he is told to, but because he appreciates that such factors are important.

Advice: To some extent senior employees tend to look for certain characteristics in job seekers that remind them of themselves. What does this candidate value above all else in hiring people for key positions? The answer here should tell you something worth knowing: how the candidate evaluates his or her own strengths, and what value he or she can bring to your company.

6. *How do you handle a professional employee whose work is unsatisfactory?*

Sample Answer: I have found that by clearly identifying the problem areas and, if necessary, working closely with an employee, his or her work can almost always be turned around.

Advice: How much will the candidate tolerate before deciding to reprimand or even terminate an employee whose work falls below standards set by the department or company? How does the candidate interpret unsatisfactory work, and what measures does he or she take to ensure that an employee gets back on track and improves the quality of his or her work? You need to ensure that the candidate's views on handling and improving an employee's substandard work mesh with your standards of quality and the measures you would take to rectify an employee's poor performance.

• • •

7. *Do you try to avoid terminating underperformers?*

Sample Answer: I see termination as a last resort. In addition to believing that most people's performances can be turned around, I find that terminations are bad for everyone's morale. But a successful company can't tolerate underachievers, especially in key positions. If a person is clearly not going to work out, then the sooner he or she leaves, the better for everyone.

Advice: You want to see whether the candidate has a problem confronting and firing weak or mediocre employees. Ask about the style or method he or she uses to terminate an employee. If the candidate has had an extensive history of firing employees, this could indicate less than stellar hiring techniques or an inability to motivate and work with employees to improve performance.

8. ***What work habits or traits do you find most annoying in people who work for you?***

Sample Answer: I'm most concerned about problems that can influence the group as a whole—for example, a negative attitude or lack of dedication to one's work or to the company.

Advice: How does the candidate relate negative work traits—such as tardiness, absenteeism, overt socializing during work hours, and gossiping—to company performance? How strict are the candidate's standards in this area, and how closely do they match those at your company?"

• • •

9. ***What do you do about attitude problems with employees who report to you?***

Sample Answer: I try to get to the heart of the matter. If the employee is disgruntled about a particular work issue, I try to confront and resolve it. Sometimes I find the employee simply wants more recognition and attention. Other times it may be a personal problem, and with my key employees I make the time to discuss any personal issue they want. I care about them, and they know it.

Advice: Rarely will a senior manager applying for a high-level corporate position be a stranger to some kind of difficulty with employee attitudes. How did the candidate confront the situation, and what communication techniques did he or she use in working with the employee to improve his or her attitude?

10. When do you believe meetings are an important use of time, and why?

Sample Answer: I have found that long meetings are to be avoided, except when facing major issues; people tend to get weary, attention lags, and the discussion begins to go in circles. Short, highly focused meetings, however, can help bring a group together. I have found meetings to be particularly effective for making decisions on new products and new marketing campaigns and for resolving problems. Ideally, I like to reach a consensus at a meeting—but even if we don't, it's important to let everyone know he or she had a chance to air a view.

Advice: Does the candidate believe in few meetings or in a lot of meetings? Does the candidate emphasize decision-making meetings? Brainstorming meetings? Problem-solving meetings? Or information dissemination meetings? What do these opinions about meetings tell you about the candidate's leadership style?

• • •

11. What have been your keys to success as a manager?

Sample Answer: I think many managers tend to be either results driven or people driven. I've tried to find a balance between both extremes. I make time to be available for my key people, to "sell" them on key decisions (not just tell them what to do), to listen to their input, and to take into consideration their perspectives. But at the same time I give plenty of focus to driving the company ahead.

Advice: What personal qualities or professional skills does the candidate believe contribute to his or her success as a manager? What separates this candidate from other managers— style, certain methods that achieve above-average results, or an attitude that carries the candidate through good and bad times? From each managerial position, what has the candidate learned that has honed his or her skills as an effective leader and manager?

12. *What is it about this company that caused you to apply for this position?*

Sample Answer: I've seen your Polarfleece products in the marketplace, and I have been advised that this company wants to grow. I believe that my own desire to help a company expand and improve will also give me a personal opportunity to excel.

Advice: What is the candidate's level of familiarity with your company? How aggressive has he or she been in trying to get to know your company beyond marketing literature and 10K reports? Has the candidate had firsthand experience with your products or services? You want an answer that goes beyond the standard "Your company is a market leader," and so forth, and pinpoints one or two substantive reasons why the candidate is attracted to your firm.

• • •

 13. *What is your management "style"? By that I mean your overall management technique in the guidance of and contact with those people who report to you.*

Sample Answer: The most effective management technique, I believe, is to establish mutually agreed-upon goals for each person who reports to me in his or her area of authority and to describe how those goals fit into the overall goals of the department. The formal monitoring of progress toward those goals will be on a periodic schedule, assisting when required. At the same time, I would be able to advise my superiors of my progress toward my department's goals.

Advice: What type of approach does the candidate feel most comfortable with in dealing with employees, and why is that approach effective in the candidate's mind? How does the candidate prefer to interact with different levels of management? You want to get a sense here of the candidate's communication skills, leadership ability, and views on what criteria are important in getting the most out of his or her employees. What techniques have been successful for the candidate in developing entry- and junior-level employees?

• • •

 14. *Upon taking over the management functions of this area, what is the first thing you will look for, or put in place if not in existence?*

Sample Answer: I would immediately track the decision-making chain to determine if the process is centralized or is disseminated throughout the manufacturing operation. Extending the decision-making process to the lowest level in the organization brings all  employees together in the decisions that will affect their workplace and, at the same time, gives me a chance to discover employees who may have potential for promotions.

Advice: You should be concerned not only with the candidate's ability to micromanage day-to-day details but also with his or her ideas about how to improve existing processes over the long term. How quickly can the candidate assess a situation and implement a lasting solution? What factors does the candidate take into consideration when he or she looks to make a change?

15. *What comments do you have regarding the International Standards Organization (ISO)?*

Sample Answer: ISO-9000 is the wave of this country's quality future. It was started just after World War II, in order to provide common standards and dependable quality to all European nations as they rebuilt after the devastation of the war. Essentially, it provides eighteen elements that not only must be followed, but also documented, to assure that customer expectations are met for every product shipped. ISO-9000 does not tell a company how to run its business—it merely requires that the eighteen elements be satisfied. The businesses of the United States are just beginning to achieve ISO certification. It will be critical for U.S. companies that want to do business in Europe in the next century because certification will be required by these potential customers.

Advice: Here you are testing the candidate's knowledge of an industry standard and its relevance to future technology development. The candidate may or may not be a champion of this standard, but you at least want an opinion of the merits of using this standard and the way it impacts product development now and down the road. The candidate's answer should also reflect some interest in future standards and the ways they will affect businesses such as yours in the future.

Graphic Artist

1. Which software programs are you familiar with?

Sample Answer: I've worked primarily on Macintosh computers but have some experience with the Windows environment. I'm familiar with most major software programs and consider myself to be expert in QuarkXpress, Pagemaker, Photoshop, Illustrator, and Freehand. I'm also familiar with many word processing programs.

Advice: You should be interested primarily in the candidate's experience with graphic software packages, although any knowledge of software applications and platforms will enhance the value the candidate will bring to your company. What projects or assignments has the candidate been involved with that required his or her knowledge of and skill with these applications?

• • •

2. What makes you an "expert" in QuarkXpress?

Sample Answer: I've used it daily for the past three years. I've designed and produced everything from business cards to catalogs to album covers on it. I know the strengths and weaknesses of the program. I know what it can and can't do. I know the shortcuts and extensions.

Advice: The candidate should give you several examples of how he or she used this application to complete demanding tasks as part of a complex project. You are testing the computer skill level of this candidate and how much he or she knows about the program's capabilities and how it can solve graphic design problems and add to the creativity of a project.

Graphic Artist

3. *What is the difference between RGB and CMYK colors?*

Sample Answer: RGB stands for red, green, and blue and is the usual standard by which images are displayed on screen. CMYK stands for cyan, magenta, yellow, and black and is the process by which images are printed on conventional presses.

Advice: This question tests the candidate's understanding of how color functions in display as opposed to output. This knowledge is fundamental to any designer's ability to use color when creating displays, brochures, or artwork used in printed material. Beyond an explanation of what RGB and CMYK stand for, you should expect the candidate to describe how each color set factors into the design process.

• • •

4. *Suppose I gave you a piece of artwork and told you to scan it and that it was going to be used in a printed brochure and as part of a disk-based presentation. What would you do?*

Sample Answer: I'd make one high-resolution scan, correct it if necessary, and then save it in separate files: high resolution for the printed piece, and a lower resolution for the disk-based presentation. The reason I'd do that is because the disk-based presentation doesn't need the high resolution (or large file size) of the printed piece.

Advice: You want to see if the candidate can intelligently determine how to solve the problem so that both print and disk will have appropriate material for display. Does the candidate have a strong grasp of proper resolutions for display as opposed to printed material? How would he or she approach the problem so that quality does not suffer for either medium?

5. **Which are your favorite serif and sans-serif fonts?**

Sample Answer: My favorite serif font is Garamond. My favorite sans-serif font is Futura.

Advice: You want to know two things here: whether or not the candidate can distinguish between the two categories of fonts and whether the candidate chooses a font that is considered "current" or in fashion in each category, as opposed to an older font that is not widely used in graphic design.

• • •

6. **Suppose you were setting type at 12/14 and had a 3 3/4-inch column to fill. How would you figure the number of lines that would fit?**

Sample Answer: First I'd convert the inch measurement to points by multiplying by 72. Then I'd divide that number by the leading of 14.

Advice: The candidate's understanding of how different measurements are used in graphic design is tested here. You want the candidate to give you a logical, rational method for calculating how many lines can fit the space and why the method makes the most sense. What are the important considerations for the designer when initiating this type of calculation?

Graphic Artist

7. Describe a trap and why it's important.

Sample Answer: A trap is an area where two different colors of ink butt. The two different colors need to overlap slightly in order to prevent a white edge between them.

Advice: The candidate should not only know what a trap is but be able to discuss its significance in the printing process. What are the ramifications for the designer, as well as for the printer, of failing to trap, and at what point in the process should this be an issue? What would happen to the project if the printer received output that was not trapped properly?

• • •

8. Suppose I gave you two sets of specifications, one on Monday and another on Wednesday, for the same piece, and they were different. What would you do?

Sample Answer: I'd bring the discrepancy to your attention and ask you which set of specifications I should use.

Advice: You want to see if the candidate will act responsibly to alert you to the two specifications or try to determine which one should be applied to the project. Any candidate seeking a position in graphic arts should have enough common sense to double-check all specifications that cross his or her desk before committing them to print or disk.

9. How fast can you produce a thirty-two-page catalog?

Sample Answer: That really depends on the nature of the piece. Certainly, a thirty-two-page catalog of one-color straight text with two head levels would be much easier to produce than a thirty-two-page catalog with four-color images, multiple page designs, runarounds, and so on. I could probably give an estimate if you give me more information.

Advice: You want to see how the candidate interprets the complexity of the job and weighs that against how fast he or she can complete the job. In order of importance, what factors does the candidate consider crucial in determining the complexity of the job, and how quickly can the candidate deliver a finished product? Given the nature of the job, could the candidate pick up the pace and hand you a finished product that was 100 percent error free?

• • •

10. Have you ever missed a deadline?

Sample Answer: I've worked late into the night many times to meet deadlines.

Advice: How aggressive is the candidate in meeting deadlines, and how willing is he or she to go the extra mile to make sure that a project finishes on time? If the candidate has indeed missed a deadline, by how much and what did he or she do to quickly turn a bad situation into a positive situation? How did the client or company react to the missed deadline?

Graphic Artist

11. *How do you feel when someone finds an error in a finished piece?*

Sample Answer: Horrible. I work very hard to avoid mistakes. I realize the impact they can have.

Advice: No one enjoys having his or her mistakes paraded in front of others, and you want to see how the candidate reacts to a failure to catch a mistake. A good graphic designer learns from his or her mistakes and sets up systems to ensure that they don't happen again, such as additional rounds of proofreading, color proofs, or mock-ups. What did the candidate do to prevent the same mistakes from happening again in future projects?

• • •

12. *How many times will you redo a piece?*

Sample Answer: I try not to keep count. I look at it this way: I'll redo a piece until you tell me it's done. I realize that many people might have input.

Advice: How flexible and adaptable is the candidate, and is he or she willing to accept criticism and suggestions from multiple sources even if the source does not have the design experience of the candidate? How does the candidate measure the usefulness of the input, and does he or she insist upon imposing a cutoff date at the expense of the client's or company's wishes? You want to see whether or not the candidate can stick with a job through multiple changes without losing patience or becoming frustrated.

Graphic Artist

13. How often do you back up your work?

Sample Answer: Daily. I have a good system, and it usually takes less than half an hour to back up all my work. I've gotten into a routine, and it's rescued me several times.

Advice: You want to make sure that the candidate is responsible and thorough in archiving and storing important files and information in case of an accident or destruction of property. Does the candidate have a system in place whereby he or she can easily retrieve ongoing work and not lose any time with a project that might be approaching a deadline?

• • •

14. How would you deal with freelancers?

Sample Answer: I've found that when dealing with freelancers it's important to establish certain ground rules such as payment, schedule, copyrights, and so on. Once those are established, it's much easier to focus on the creative aspects. I've also found that clear instructions are essential to define a project.

Advice: Can the candidate evaluate and work with artists who are self-employed and who may not share the same standards as the candidate? How does he or she get outside help to apply the same rigorous standards to a design project as the candidate would if working solo on the project.

Human Resources Director

1. In your current position, in which area have you concentrated the most effort?

Sample Answer: When I took my current position, I was not familiar with the state's labor laws or federal mandates such as the Family Medical Leave Act and COBRA. Although knowing these regulations inside and out was not the most exciting part of the position, becoming very familiar with them was an absolutely necessity for succeeding in this job. For a year I attended every course I could find related to labor laws and took manuals home to study at night. The knowledge I now have in this area is one of the strengths I could bring to your company.

Advice: Expect the candidate to discuss one or two areas that he or she is not totally familiar with, or that require additional training to master completely. Why does the candidate believe these areas require extra attention, and are you concerned that the answer indicates the candidate may not be able to handle the responsibilities of your position?

• • •

2. Do you think the human resources field utilizes your abilities well?

Sample Answer: Definitely. When I was hired for my current position, I did not have the extensive background of many of the other applicants. What earned me the position was a broad knowledge of both our company and competitive companies; I believe this separated me from other applicants. As people both inside and outside the department have come to realize the value of this broader perspective, the number of decision-making opportunities in which I am involved has increased.

Advice: What is it about human resources that brings out the best of the candidate's abilities and strengths, and how might the candidate's skills impact your company? What attracted the candidate to this field in the first place, and what particular aspects, duties, or responsibilities in human resources showcase the candidate's intelligence and talent?

• • •

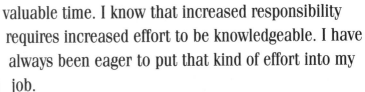

3. *How has being in this field prepared you to accept increased responsibility?*

Sample Answer: The very nature of human resources gives an individual a great deal of exposure to employees at all levels. I have observed that people who hold positions of high responsibility seem to have certain traits in common. They are typically well prepared and, as a result, have confidence in their opinions. When I communicate concisely and convincingly, I am respected. When I am ill prepared, I sense that I am wasting people's

valuable time. I know that increased responsibility requires increased effort to be knowledgeable. I have always been eager to put that kind of effort into my job.

Advice: Ask the candidate for concrete examples of how his or her position in human resources continually provides opportunities for additional responsibilities. Has the candidate been aggressive in going after new assignments or responsibilities, and what new duties has the candidate assumed in the past year that would add to his or her effectiveness in your opening?

4. *What do you particularly enjoy about your current position in human resources?*

Sample Answer: In human resources, I interact more with other departments than does any other department head in the company. This is particularly true if I'm involved in the interviewing process and have to understand the position for which I'm interviewing. I really enjoy learning about my company's new products and services, and I think this makes me a more effective recruiter for the company.

Advice: What aspects of the candidate's current position, such as interviewing, screening resumes, or designing benefit programs, give him or her the most satisfaction? How much enthusiasm does the candidate show for the day-to-day work of the position?

• • •

5. *Tell me about the person to whom you report. What do you like or dislike about this person?*

Sample Answer: Mary is very comfortable with herself, more concerned with respect than with popularity. Rather than being threatened by the success of those who report to her, she views the success of each person in her department as a shared success. Because of this attitude she always strives to educate me and others in the department and to share the spotlight. Not only have I learned a lot about the human resources field from her, but she is also the inspiration for the management philosophy on which I intend to base my future.

Advice: Have the candidate assess his or her manager's character, management style, personality, and temperament. Compare the candidate's response with your own preferences for interacting with your employees. Does the candidate paint a picture of a manager who is similar to you in terms of managerial style, personality, and leadership? Are you concerned about any aspect of the candidate's answer that might not be overwhelmingly positive?

• • •

6. What areas does your boss believe you excel in on a daily basis?

Sample Answer: Mary has complimented me several times on my contagious enthusiasm. She also values my writing ability, usually coming to me first when she needs some assistance in editing or writing business memos or letters.

Advice: If you were to call the candidate's supervisor, what would he or she say are the candidate's strong points, and in what areas does the candidate shine outside the job description? What does the candidate do exceptionally well, and what aspects of human resources would he or she make an immediate impact on if you hired this candidate tomorrow?

7. ## What are you criticized for most often on the job?

Sample Answer: Mary often expresses concern that I become too involved in my job. She is a real advocate of separating one's work from one's personal life. When I shared with her that I had not done my usual amount of reading lately because I was spending my spare time familiarizing myself with labor laws, I was surprised at the degree of anger she expressed in my having chosen work over pleasure.

Advice: Expect the criticisms that the candidate mentions to be light and not to carry much substance. You will probably have to pursue the issue to find out what tasks the candidate has problems completing, and how the candidate responds to criticism. Does he or she take responsibility for correcting mistakes, or offer excuses and blame external factors?

• • •

8. ## What books or publications do you read on a regular basis that help you with your job?

Sample Answer: I always read the current event capsules on the front page of the *Wall Street Journal*; they give me a quick idea of what's going on in the country and the world. I look forward to reading the Sunday business section of the *New York Times*, saving it for during the week if Sundays are too frantic. And though I don't always read it as thoroughly as I'd like to, I enjoy *Time* magazine.

Advice: You should expect an answer that includes several business and trade publications demonstrating a knowledge of and interest in your industry and company. Has the candidate gleaned anything from these publications that significantly impacted his or her job, and if so, what was the outcome?

Human Resources Director

9. Why is this job important to you at this time?

Sample Answer: I want to affect the lives of the people with whom I work. Though I have enjoyed other jobs I have held, I just was not as satisfied as I am in human resources, where I know I impact people's lives. I felt a true sense of satisfaction several weeks ago when I helped an employee who was having problems with another employee resolve those problems quickly and to everyone's satisfaction.

Advice: You should be looking for the candidate to emphasize a commitment to your department and the position, and to give you solid reasons why this position would fulfill his or her goals at this time. What does the candidate want to accomplish at this point in his or her career, and are you convinced that there is a good "match" between what you have to offer and what the candidate is seeking?

• • •

10. How does your company treat its employees?

Sample Answer: In recent years management has really been dedicated to having a satisfied work force. Their efforts, however, often rekindle past upheavals where employees made sacrifices for the company and received little in return. In human resources we spend a lot of money trying to break down the walls between exempt and nonexempt employees. If "the company" is management, I would have to say management is making a conscious effort to mend fences and do right by our employees.

Advice: You want to see if the candidate can walk the fine line between upholding an obligation to management and the company and retaining concern for the employees. Can the candidate avoid being biased and comment objectively on the company's attitude toward its employees? What examples does the candidate offer to support his or her opinion?

11. *This job may occasionally require weekend work with little notice. Can you vary your schedule as the job requires?*

Sample Answer: Not a problem. I often come in on weekends to make sure I stay on top of all pending and future projects so that my work week proceeds as smoothly as possible.

Advice: In answering this question some candidates may give you an affirmative response even if they are not sure they can work weekends, so as not to be eliminated from consideration. You need to make sure the candidate has no reservations about working weekends and, in fact, has the kind of proactive attitude about the job that would lead to working on weekends without being asked.

• • •

 12. *Because this job involves responsibility for both of the company's locations, there will be a considerable amount of travel required. Do you have any problem being away from home a couple of nights each week?*

Sample Answer: Not at all. My family has various commitments during the weekday evenings, and I would probably not see them anyway, so working weeknights is not a problem.

Advice: Travel is always a hot button for candidates, so you should make sure that this candidate has no reservations about being out of town during the week. Some candidates may respond favorably to weekday travel even if they are not crazy about doing it on a regular basis, so you should make sure that the candidate will, in fact, travel on short notice and will not raise this as an issue if you decide to extend an offer of employment.

13. *Frankly, we have received many impressive resumes. What is unique about you that makes you the best candidate for this opening?*

Sample Answer: My background includes working for small, midsize, and Fortune 500 companies in a variety of jobs where I have gained insight and knowledge about the company's products and services. I have been able to use that knowledge to good effect when charged with the responsibility of bringing in new talent. My communications experience includes writing articles for newsletters, position statement speeches, and interdepartmental communications. Finally, I have an innate ability to recognize how individuals from different backgrounds and experience can make a significant contribution to the overall success of a company.

Advice: You want the candidate to give reasons why he or she would be a more valuable hire than anyone else you are considering—and not only because the candidate happens to fulfill all the job requirements. Encourage the candidate to give you examples of special skills that he or she can bring to your company that would make an immediate impact.

Human Resources Manager

1. What kind of organizational structure do you believe is effective?

Sample Answer: Actually, one of the reasons your company appeals to me is the fast-paced, informal structure in general. My work in executive search was fast and furious, so I think that background matches well with the culture here. As I have dealt with HR generalists over the years, one thing they've seemed to agree on is that the job is as boring or exciting as the pace of the group you work with. I wouldn't be interested if the division I worked in was out of the mainstream, or off the priority list, of the company.

Advice: Determine whether the candidate has the range of experience suitable for your organization; in other words, is the candidate used to the pace and demands of your organization, and does he or she have the experience and flexibility to adapt to rapid change, and to quickly evaluate and target candidates that are appropriate for your company? Is the candidate more comfortable operating in a top-down approach or a flat organizational structure? Which one does the candidate believe contributes to greater organizational efficiency?

• • •

2. What prompted your initial interest in HR management?

Sample Answer: Part of the intrigue for me was having the information first in terms of knowing what group was going to grow or downsize. Although something like downsizing can be unpopular, I'd rather be the person with knowledge than the person without it. The pulse of the company is always up front in your work priorities. That would be hard to walk away from. And I love knowing that when the business is thriving, I had something to do with making sure the best people were hired for the right jobs and had the right incentives to perform so well.

Advice: Encourage the candidate to be specific about the aspects of HR management that he or she finds particularly attractive in terms of a career choice. Is it the people, the duties and responsibilities, the day-to-day activities, or some other aspect that suits the candidate's personality or temperament? You want to know that the candidate is truly committed to this field and to developing a career in human resources management at your company.

• • •

3. What is your approach to managing costs per hire?

Sample Answer: Well, I would not sacrifice quality—quality comes before cost. The goal is to hire the best if the company wants to stay number one in the industry. I try to foster positive employee referrals and things that are relatively low cost, or no cost. I also believe in staying current with what's going on in the industry. If a major competitor changes its benefits plans, and its employees revolt, you can use that fact to your advantage to point out the quality of your own benefits plans; that way you might pick up some employees with solid industry experience. I use all angles, and overlap and integrate all of my approaches: advertising, college relations, affirmative action, creative relocation strategies, and so on.

Advice: In determining how the candidate approaches problem solving, you want to test his or her methodology and analytical ability. Encourage the candidate to give you real numbers. How does he or she apply the numbers to each hiring situation? Do you agree with the candidate's analysis? If not, is the analysis so weak that you would deny the candidate this opening? How strongly does the candidate feel about the efficacy of his or her approach?

4.

When you have an opening, do you tend to search for a candidate within the industry, or outside of it?

Sample Answer: I've never believed our competition was within our industry, but outside. So I ask myself where I can find the best people who could thrive in a relatively unstructured, fast-paced company. I've learned how to go out and find new sources for candidates—I go to top business schools, for instance. And I find out where the best companies are hiring people regardless of the industry. Our growth means that our business is changing fast enough that prior industry experience isn't that critical; having the right job skill, like sales instincts for a PR job, is critical.

Advice: This question tests the candidate's ability to go beyond the norm or "safe" hire and identify individuals whose skills and talents could benefit the organization despite the fact that they come from outside the industry. Is the candidate willing to take risks to help his or her company grow and diversify with employees who bring to problem solving unique experiences and mind-sets that may not exist within the company currently?

• • •

5.

You could do staffing at any type of organization. What appeals to you about this industry?

Sample Answer: The hierarchy within the high-tech field and the demand it places on staffing creative people make the job more interesting. Also, my engineering background gives me validity in this business. To some degree people in HR are still fighting the "personnel" image. In this company, when I talk to engineering groups or development groups, I'll be able to talk their language and so better understand what they need in prospective job candidates in terms of technical skills. And I'll be more effective at screening candidates because I have that technical orientation.

Advice: What does the candidate find particularly appealing about your industry? Has the candidate had experience in hiring individuals from your industry, or does the interest stem from personal experience or a curiosity about the people who work in your industry? Try to determine if the candidate's interest is superficial or grounded in experience, be it personal or professional.

• • •

6. *Suppose you had a new PC delivered to your office. How would you learn to use it?*

Sample Answer: I've always been a self-starter. When I don't know something, the first thing I do is jump in and give it a try. Then I figure out who the experts are within my company, and I get their advice or get a dialogue going so I have someone to share things with, like neat features of a software application I might discover, or they might discover.

Advice: Regardless of the industry, you want to measure not so much the candidate's technical skills as his or her willingness to learn a new piece of equipment necessary to

perform his or her job. Is the candidate's approach highly systematic or unstructured? To what lengths would the candidate go in setting up a training schedule, and would he or she ensure that others in the department were also familiar with the PC?

Human Resources Manager

7. What differentiates you from all the other staffing people out there?

Sample Answer: I'm more resourceful than most people. I use all sources simultaneously when searching for a particular type of candidate. I also make it a point to know my business, industry, and competitors. And although I know what I'm looking for, I keep my mind open about where I'm going to find the person with the right background. Here's an example: I know that you are trying to improve your market position in the government, and I know that no one in the PC industry is doing a particularly good job at that. I know that you've been searching unsuccessfully to fill a top position as VP of government and education. If you hired me in staffing, I'd start looking at retired officers from the U.S. military. What you really need is someone who knows Washington, who is a leader, and who knows business. There are ex-military people out there who have run military commissaries all over the world. So if you hire me, you won't get a "me, too" approach to staffing; you'll get someone who helps you break the mold.

Advice: What qualities, characteristics, or special talents will this candidate bring to your company that other candidates cannot offer? What is it about your opening that the candidate finds particularly attractive, and why does the candidate believe he or she will make a greater immediate impact than other candidates you are considering?

• • •

8. Suppose you really have to find a candidate and you aren't having success. What would you do?

Sample Answer: I'd do two things. First, I'd reexamine the skills I'm looking for to make sure my expectations were realistic. Assuming they were, I'd expand my search geographically. I'd also tap into resources such as schools or trade associations to see if I could find candidates through word of mouth. A last resort, if the job is senior enough in level, is to turn to an executive search firm that specializes in that type of placement.

Advice: How creative and aggressive is the candidate in coming up with suggestions for trying to find good people to fill your openings? What resources, contacts, or other ideas does the candidate have to help rectify an unpromising situation? You want to feel confident that the candidate will not give up but will doggedly pursue a well-thought-out course of action resulting in the hiring of a talented individual.

• • •

9. What is your interviewing style?

Sample Answer: I've always believed in the behavioral interviewing style. In other words, I begin by identifying how the question I want to ask will help me evaluate some important aspect or behavior, of the candidate—like teamwork or leadership or management style. That approach alone keeps inappropriate questions out of the interview. I also believe that this method, in which you insist on examples of each behavior, helps you weed out people who can't support the buzzwords they've used. The candidates must be able to offer proof.

Advice: How does this candidate approach the first meeting with an interviewee, and what types of questions does he or she prefer to ask on this and subsequent interviews? Does the candidate stick with a standard list of questions, or will he or she modify the interview based on an applicant's responses? Does the candidate need to have complete control during an interview, or can he or she conduct an interview as if it were a casual conversation?

10. *Describe a situation in which you were involved in recruiting and had to use outside search firms.*

Sample Answer: At my last company we often hired scientists with business experience for our R-and-D management. I turned to a search firm for directors and vice presidents. I thought the important thing was to find an organization specializing in natural science candidates and to let that firm know everything about my company. I spent a lot of time early on helping my contacts at the search firm understand our company and the type of person we were looking for. This organization ended up helping us locate numerous people.

Advice: How often has the candidate had to go outside the company to use an executive search firm, and under what circumstances did he or she believe it necessary to do so? You want to make sure the candidate has the ability and is resourceful enough to attract the right candidates for each opening without using a search firm on a regular basis. If the candidate regularly goes outside for positions other than those at the most senior level, this might be a source of concern for you.

• • •

11. *How have you used salary benchmarking?*

Sample Answer: I've always believed in benchmarking. At my current company I prefer to look outside our industry rather than within it. I'm more interested in what financial analysts with x years of experience in a lot of different industries are making. In our low-tech industry we tend to employ people with higher levels of education than do many of our competitors; we're known as the premium employer. That, again, is a reason I believe I'd be effective working for your PC division; you are known for hiring the best people regardless of prior industry experience, as long as they are PC junkies at heart.

Advice: Determine how knowledgeable the candidate is about salary structures within your industry. Can the candidate give you a comparison of salaries across several industries, and if so, how accurate do you believe the comparison to be? The candidate should also be able to tell you how this type of knowledge can be an advantage in evaluating a candidate's suitability for a particular position.

• • •

12. *Suppose several job candidates you made offers to turned you down. How would you react?*

Sample Answer: Handling rejection is something you have to get used to in this business. At the same time, you want to make sure you are doing an effective job. I always follow up to find out why someone didn't accept. I want to make sure, as a PR representative for my company, that candidates come out of interviews with a good impression of the organization I work for. This often can help at a later time—I've had candidates become customers or refer other candidates to me.

Advice: Beyond handling rejection, you want to see how effective the candidate is in representing his or her organization. You should measure the candidate's ability not only to size up applicants but also to promote and sell the benefits of working for the hiring company. If the candidate seems to have a problem selling his or her organization to good candidates, who end up turning down the position, what steps is the candidate willing to take to improve his or her recruiting skills?

13. *Describe a time when a staffing situation required confidentiality.*

Sample Answer: Confidentiality is always the rule in our business. For example, I'm always careful never to leave things out on my desk when I'm gone. Sometimes employees will come in to complain about a manager. Rather than tell that manager, I'll follow the case carefully to see if anyone else makes the same complaint, or if the manager's boss mentions a related problem during the manager's performance review. Then what I do is offer the employee practical suggestions on ways to try to improve his or her position without alienating the manager.

Advice: With this question you are testing the candidate's integrity when it comes to the protection of proprietary information. What steps does the candidate believe are appropriate to take to protect both the company and the applicant from the disclosure of confidential information? How does the candidate handle controversial situations—for example, an interview in which a job applicant reveals proprietary information about his or her previous company, which happens to be a competitor of the candidate's company?

• • •

14. *Suppose you were trying to attract a candidate to a small town. What would you do?*

Sample Answer: First of all, I'd never use enormous pressure because people have to make these kinds of decisions on their own; otherwise, you'll end up sorry if their misgivings later turn out to be justified. However, these are some practical steps I've taken in the past: show cost of living adjustments to demonstrate their increased buying power in a small town; arrange one or two visits with their families to learn about housing, schools, and the town's social life; and provide names of several employees—who have also relocated to the town—as contacts for questions and any concerns they may have.

Advice: What techniques would the candidate use to attract applicants to an area considerably smaller than what they are used to? How persuasive is the candidate, and are you convinced by his or her methodology of attracting applicants? How much emphasis does the candidate place on company culture, benefits, and people, as opposed to what the town may offer? To what lengths would the candidate go when selling an applicant on moving to an out-of-the-way location?

• • •

15. *How would you plan and organize a campus recruiting program?*

Sample Answer: Assuming I'm starting from scratch, I'd first determine an entry-level salary benchmark, and I'd call similar companies to see where they recruit; then I'd look at starting salaries suggested by the various schools. That would give me a long list of schools. Then I'd pick schools in areas where we have regional needs, and I'd visit. I'd want to meet some students by floating around, perhaps at a career event like a speakers series, to determine if the school's culture seemed compatible with our company's. Then I'd set up interviewing schedules at schools I thought would be appropriate. Long term, I'd use alumni to help me recruit and maintain a presence at each school.

Advice: This question measures the candidate's ability to strategize, plan, and execute a major recruitment campaign. Does he or she approach this issue logically, starting with the broader strategic issues such as establishing needs and determining objectives, then shifting focus to tactical issues?

16. *How do you calculate your annual salary plans and projections?*

Sample Answer: I look at past years' data primarily, because my current company has had steady growth for four straight years. For any high-level openings we anticipate—for example, setting up a new division—I plan to use search firms, which will cost 25 to 33 percent of the first year's salary. For attrition openings I expect to bring in people at the salary midpoint for that position classification. For general raises I believe that average performers should simply get cost of living adjustments at the rate of inflation; so I generally set the total adjustment for the year at that rate and ask each department manager to hold to that, so they can determine who outperformed and who underperformed—as long as the total departmental increase doesn't exceed that percentage.

Advice: What methodology does the candidate use to determine salaries for different levels of an organization, and to project for an employee's review increase? How does the candidate set salary ranges and steps for yearly increases? You want to evaluate the candidate's logic, and his or her ability to create a salary standard for entry-level to senior positions.

Loan Administrator

1. *Have you had any formal credit training?*

Sample Answer: Yes, I've taken Omega lending courses and other courses from the American Institute of Banking and the New England Banking Institute.

Advice: You should be looking here for prior training experience, as well as for any current or future plans to learn more about this particular aspect of banking. How thorough is the candidate's knowledge in this area, and do you feel comfortable that he or she could handle any type of credit problem, regardless of the situation?

• • •

2. *What are the five C's of credit, which is the most important, and why?*

Sample Answer: Credit, character, capacity, collateral, and capital. Credit is the most important. If customers have a history of paying their debts, they will continue to do so.

Advice: This should be an answer that rolls off the candidate's tongue right away, with an explanation of the importance of each *C* in credit decisions. How does the candidate determine what criteria to use when establishing a credit line with a customer?

Loan Administrator

3. *If a customer requesting a loan was undecided between your bank and a competitor's, what would you do to convince him or her you are the one?*

Sample Answer: I would stress our bank's and my own ability to provide prompt and personal service. I'd also stress our commitment to our customers in general, and our intention to be around for the long run.

Advice: How far will the candidate go to ensure that a fence-sitter will choose your bank over a competitor's? What strategy has the candidate used in the past to lure an indecisive customer to a commitment? Are there particular selling techniques that work better than others? How does the candidate weigh the competitive need to obtain someone's business against the need to provide personable, professional service?

• • •

4. *Have you ever had a situation in which you had to set your own rate on a loan in order to save a deal?*

Sample Answer: Yes, in order to remain competitive; but I did not put the bank at risk, as the margin was still profitable.

Advice: Determine the candidate's ability to weigh the importance of a customer's business against the interests of the bank. To what lengths will the candidate go to secure business, and at what point will the candidate conclude that the rate must be set or the customer lost? Do you agree with the candidate's approach, and was the rate acceptable considering your bank's normal lending practices?

Loan Administrator

5. *How would you go about increasing the size of your loan portfolio?*

Sample Answer: I find it most helpful to become involved in community organizations such as Rotary, chamber of commerce, YMCA, Boys & Girls Clubs, and so on. I also foster professional contacts such as attorneys and accountants.

Advice: You should be focusing here on the candidate's ability to sell your bank's services and his or her commitment to the customer, as well as any creative approaches the candidate has used to bring in new business. How does the candidate go about seeking leads for new business? What resources or personal contacts have proved valuable in finding the candidate new customers?

• • •

6. *If you presented a loan to a supervisor for approval and were denied, what would you do?*

Sample Answer: If I thought it was a request that had merit and would be profitable for the bank with minimal risk, I would find out what my supervisor did not like and try to get additional information to reverse his or her decision.

Advice: How does the candidate react to rejection? Can the candidate accept a decision that he or she doesn't necessarily agree with? Further, can the candidate make logical and viable arguments about the validity of the application, keeping in mind the supervisor's argument for turning it down?

Loan Administrator

7. *How would you describe your thinking, and does it affect your ability to tell someone no?*

Sample Answer: I consider myself a moderate. The ability to tell someone no is something I have developed through experience over the years.

Advice: What goes into the candidate's thought process in evaluating a potential customer for his or her bank? How difficult is it for the candidate to reject a customer? How does the candidate justify a negative response to a customer's request and get the customer to accept the rationale? Make sure the candidate has no qualms about turning down a customer for any reason and can justify the action without hesitation.

• • •

8. *What sort of lending authority and portfolio size have you had in the past?*

Sample Answer: I have had a great deal of experience presenting large loans to senior management and loan committees.

Advice: You should be convinced that the candidate has the experience and ability to handle any size portfolio, and that he or she is able to handle increasing responsibility for making loan recommendations. You're testing the candidate's analytical ability here, and his or her self-confidence in managing the loans for businesses of any size without requiring intervention from a supervisor.

Management Consultant

1. Describe projects you have run or managed. What role did you play?

Sample Answer: I was the lead consultant on a systems integration project for a major Midwest banking firm. The bank had just acquired a competitor and was in the process of combining its computer systems to process transactions across a six-state region. My role entailed design specification, process analysis, end-user needs analysis, and working with the software developers to finalize interface requirements and implement the new client-server system.

Advice: You are looking for examples of leadership, if applicable, and of contributions the consultant made as a true team player. You want to see if the consultant can take direction from your senior management team, and lead junior members of your department or company through a project cycle. What did the candidate attack first on the project, and how did he or she delegate tasks and assign parts of the project to other team members?

• • •

2. What specific experiences helped you improve your team-building skills?

Sample Answer: The last company I worked for decided to switch from a traditional hierarchical management approach to a team-based management approach. At first it was difficult for me to make the switch because I was so focused on getting my work done that I overlooked the dynamics of getting people to work together as a team. Then I specifically focused on getting my team to interact and work together as a unit. Although it took time and patience to build a smoothly functioning group, the payoffs have been tremendous.

Advice: The candidate should describe assignments for which he or she started out as an individual contributor but over time transitioned into a key member of a departmental team that solved a company problem. How was the candidate able to put aside his or her own methodologies and work with the team to effect a positive solution? Dig into the candidate's answer to discover concrete skills and determine if he or she is a committed team player and can work effectively with your employees and managers.

• • •

3. *Have you ever had a conflict on a project with a client? How did you handle it?*

Sample Answer: One of my clients disagreed with our findings after a rather lengthy needs assessment. He wanted a complete, immediate overhaul of his computer system instead of migrating to a new client-server system over a period of eighteen months. I showed him three case studies of companies similar to his that had made the transition to client-server at half the cost with a minimal amount of disruption. He still was not convinced, so I brought in a senior consultant who had worked with him before to persuade him to adopt our conclusions. He eventually came around.

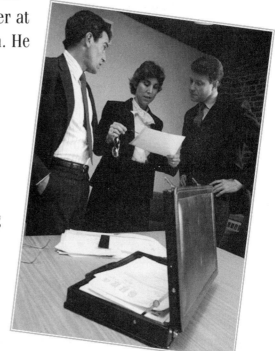

Advice: Determine the nature of the conflict and what steps the candidate took to eliminate any problems that he or she might cause by continuing to be affiliated with the client's project. When did the candidate realize there might be a problem, and did he or she approach the client, or did the client bring it to the candidate's attention? Did the conflict ever impair the candidate's judgment or ability to deliver accurate monthly reports?

Management Consultant

4. Tell me about a time you interacted with senior management at a client company.

Sample Answer: One of my clients asked me to conduct a site survey for his corporate headquarters. I recognized early on that I needed input from the senior executives as to what they would find acceptable in a new site. To do this, I developed a questionnaire and polled the executives in private one-on-one meetings. I compiled the results and presented my findings to my client with three acceptable sites that met everyone's criteria.

Advice: How comfortable is the consultant working closely with senior managers to see a project through from start to finish? How does the candidate go about creating a favorable impression with senior managers and getting them to share information and provide input on a daily basis? What techniques does the candidate use to get these managers to cooperate from day one and work with the candidate to complete projects successfully and benefit the company?

• • •

5. What role do you usually take within a work group?

Sample Answer: On recent projects I've been assigned the leadership role. But I'm comfortable in just about any role, including a supportive role to senior executives, and the role of a peer member of a self-directed team. My satisfaction comes more from being part of a group that successfully serves a client's needs than having any particular role within the group.

Advice: Does the candidate feel comfortable only when leading a group, or can he or she successfully integrate ego into a team situation? You want evidence of the consultant's best; if that means leading rather than following, you must evaluate your internal projects and decide if you need a leader or someone who can more successfully lend his or her expertise and experience as a team player. Listen for a description not only of the role but also of the types of situations and responsibilities that motivate this candidate to perform at peak efficiency.

• • •

6. What opportunities do you see in the consulting business?

Sample Answer: Companies will continue to go through enormous changes in the way they do business—evolving to more mobile work forces as well as continuing to decentralize information systems. I believe that, to keep up with these changes, companies will be looking to consultants who have not only technical savvy but also the experience and sensitivity necessary to make these difficult transitions.

Advice: Is the candidate aware of emerging technological or market trends that would provide opportunities in the industry sector? What types of companies or industries will emerge as prime candidates to take advantage of what the candidate can offer? Are there specific types of projects, such as programming, marketing consulting, graphic design, or systems integration, that excite and motivate the candidate and from which the candidate will benefit?

Management Consultant

7. *Give me an example of a time something you read about another company helped sell your idea to a client.*

Sample Answer: The *Wall Street Journal* did an article not too long ago on a fast-growing company that hit a roadblock and had to refocus its strategy in a completely new technology area. I found the strategy and execution intriguing and shared the information with a potential client, who eventually hired me to help refocus his own company's strategy and implement changes.

Advice: You want to test the candidate's awareness of what companies are doing in a variety of industries to improve their prospects and expand their markets. Does the candidate continually try to improve his or her knowledge and experience by exploring what other consultants and companies are doing to solve business problems? How does the candidate exploit that knowledge to sell his or her services to a potential client?

• • •

8. *Have you ever developed a plan that failed to meet your client's needs? How did you remedy this?*

Sample Answer: I created a three-tiered channel marketing plan that I thought would effectively help promote and sell a new product line for my client. Unfortunately, I didn't realize until the plan was completed that senior management was totally committed to focusing the sales effort through its current direct sales force. I reworked the plan to use the other sales channels, primarily as a complement to the company's direct sales efforts.

Advice: How does the candidate deal with falling short of a client's expectations, and what does he or she do to rescue a failed effort? You want to measure not only the candidate's persistence in achieving positive results but also how quickly he or she can analyze a problem and create a solution that satisfies everyone involved. You should also consider the complexity of the project and the validity of the solution based on resources available to the consultant.

• • •

9. I'm a potential client. Why should I hire you?

Sample Answer: Mr. Baines, let me see if I understand your needs. You require someone who can effectively lead a transition team to ensure that your migration to client-server is accomplished within six months and that all training materials, manuals, and software are thoroughly tested and documented. In addition to having seven years of technical client-server experience, I've been part of the consulting team aiding migration to client-server at six Fortune 500 companies. I was the team leader for the last four projects I worked on.

Advice: The candidate should have a better than average understanding of your needs and of the necessary buttons to push to land your business. You should not be swayed by the consultant's marketing material or ability to drop names; rather, you want concrete proof that this consultant has the experience and skills necessary to analyze your company's problem and implement a cost-effective solution.

Marketing Manager

1. *It can be challenging to work with field sales reps who manage their own time and have home offices. How might you motivate a group of reps to push your product line?*

Sample Answer: You need to use technology to its fullest—for example, e-mail and other efficient, time-saving tools. You have to hire people capable of being their own secretaries. People at home offices often work seven days a week, especially with so much traveling to stores in their territory during the week. So you also need to recognize that, and reward it by offering aggressive upside commission potential.

Advice: What ideas does the candidate have to motivate and lead a mobile sales force in your industry? You want to hear two or three factors that the candidate considers critical to success for a sales force that is on the road most of each month. What selling strategies would the candidate use to encourage the sales force to go beyond quotas each month? You're testing not only managerial style but also the ability to think creatively and develop winning formulas for sales success.

• • •

2. *What has been the greatest challenge for you in this industry?*

Sample Answer: For most people in our business, knowledge comes through experience, starting from the ground up. Sometimes I wish I had the business theory to back up those decisions I intuitively know how to call after ten years in the business. Where the lack of formal business training hurts is in strategic planning and finance, but I've made a commitment to attend seminars to learn those things. And I'd consider any executive education that doesn't interfere with my travel schedule.

Advice: Expect the candidate to discuss a "safe" weakness or a challenge that could be readily met given his or her set of experiences. You want to see how the candidate deals with a situation or problem that requires extra training, more schooling, or mentoring from a coworker. Assess the candidate's creativity and aggressiveness in tackling this obstacle and how he or she manages to turn it into a positive.

• • •

3. Why do you want to work here?

Sample Answer: As a serious runner, I'd like to work for a company with a technology commitment to running shoes. Now, with the market and technology mature, I think athletic footwear companies will have to go back to operational excellence. This company never abandoned that concept because it focused on running technology all along, while others went after fashion trends. Consistent product quality is critical now, as there are fewer instances of technology revolutions.

Advice: How familiar is the candidate with your product line and your company? Does he or she have a strong understanding of your company's reputation and position in the marketplace? How would he or she sell your products to distributors or corporate customers? What would the candidate emphasize in a marketing campaign for your products that best represents your company and product line?

Marketing Manager

4. *What internal structure is necessary to achieve operational or technological excellence in this industry?*

Sample Answer: The flat structure at your company is one of the things I like. It makes sense because you are lean and can respond faster to demand shifts. Larger, more bureaucratic organizations will take longer responding to feedback from the sales force. And if you take too long, customers will have shifted to a new product.

Advice: A candidate for a marketing position may think that you are after a technical answer involving manufacturing or some process efficiency. What you really want here is to measure the candidate's ability to assess an organization's strength in delivering product to market in the most efficient manner, given organizational resources. What does the candidate believe is necessary to achieve a premium position in the industry as a market leader, and what resources, people, or methods can get your company to that position?

• • •

5. *What has your experience been gaining marketing insights from your sales reps?*

Sample Answer: These reps are as critical as the corporate salespeople, but you have to make sure they're giving your brands a fair shake. Earlier in my career as a manager, I fired an independent rep for good reasons, but I almost ended up in court. I learned that there is a statute in that specific state that gives special protection to independent sales reps. An experience like that teaches you to ask a bunch of questions before you proceed with certain actions, even if the actions are warranted. There's a safe, thorough way to do everything. I've just learned to take the extra time to figure out that safe way, but I won't tolerate unproductive people in my organization.

Advice: How have field reps helped the candidate better understand his or her customers, and what marketing vehicles are best suited to reach this market? What techniques or incentives has the candidate used to work with sales reps to get them to feed back information on a regular basis? What value does the information have for the candidate when making decisions about allocating spending for marketing budgets?

• • •

6. *What industry contacts are invaluable to you that could help in this job?*

Sample Answer: I've made efforts to get to know the editors of the major sports magazines; I try to take them to dinner when I can. Also, I know many independent sales reps who have a lot of crossover in terms of people they get to know in noncompeting sporting goods lines. That helps me stay current on the larger retail industry we operate in. Some of my biggest customers are my current company's oldest customers. Some of them have told me they buy from me because of my service level, not because of which shoe I represent.

Advice: Determine what benefits the candidate brings to the table beyond his or her ability simply to execute daily responsibilities. Measure the candidate's ability and aggressiveness in staying in touch with a network while cultivating new contacts. What environment does the candidate believe is optimal for meeting industry insiders? Does he or she feel as comfortable networking on the golf course as at industry functions such as trade shows or seminars?

7. Tell me how you conduct market research.

Sample Answer: Here's an example that comes immediately to mind. I'm doing consumer research about kids playing basketball. So I play basketball with the kids. I pick up games all over town in my spare time. Then I ask myself, "How can what I heard today fit into the picture and bring our marketing to the next level?"

Advice: What techniques does the candidate use to determine customer preferences for his or her product? Does the candidate believe in conducting in-house research using focus groups, or does he or she prefer to use independent testing firms? How much faith does the candidate place in the results, and has there ever been a time when research results wound up skewing actual consumer preferences for his or her product?

• • •

8. The cultures of various firms in this industry are vastly different, from loose to conservative. What environment is right for you?

Sample Answer: I'm a very spontaneous person by nature, which is why I believe I'm a good fit with this company. I understand your presentations here are very MTV oriented.

I've also noted that you use basic overheads, not fancy graphics. That suits my personal style; I tend to believe that paperwork is best used to record historical information and that productive time is time spent on action. That seems consistent with what various managers at your company have said to me.

Marketing Manager

Advice: Your concern here should be the candidate's preferred working conditions as they compare to your own—that is, are you talking about a structured or a nonstructured personality here? What does the candidate know about your company and its culture? Does he or she see an immediate compatibility based on the people, dress code, day-to-day demands of the job, and overall camaraderie? The candidate's answer should give you substantial evidence of familiarity with your company's culture and a potential to blend in easily with your people.

• • •

9. *What marketing shifts do you think the leading firms in this industry will go through in the next few years?*

Sample Answer: Women and men who grew up with our company are now forty to fifty years old. We're trying to get to twelve- to seventeen-year-olds. We must figure out what our forty- to fifty-year-olds like and how to make it appeal to the younger group. So we're weaving a thread through our advertising, and our product, that we're a family brand.

Advice: This is a question of perception and, to some extent, vision. As the population ages, what does the candidate think companies should be doing to attract the young consumer? You should be looking for problem solving, planning, and trend awareness as well as an ability to see how a company and its product mix need to change to maintain or, if necessary, take over significant market share with a well-focused marketing program.

Marketing Manager

10. How can Household Panels from Nielsen be useful in this industry?

Sample Answer: One way is through cross promotions with a product like a popular cereal brand. You can then recontact end users and learn about their likes.

Advice: This is a question that obviously requires knowledge of a specific research technique. You want to see not only how familiar the candidate is with this particular research methodology but also how he or she would apply the methodology to guide companies in formulating their marketing programs.

• • •

11. How do you manage the creative nature of people who are predominant in this business?

Sample Answer: I can complement someone else's creative goals by quantitatively backing up what they are trying to do. I have a lot more accounting and financial modeling skills than many of my peers. When they have a good idea, I say, "Let me run some numbers based on that idea." Then I can give them real ammunition to get the idea approved. So my answer to your question is that I look for a way to balance their creativity with my own skills.

Advice: You want to see if the candidate can work with different types of people on a regular basis and get them to provide the information he or she needs to be effective on the job. You don't want to apply a personality test here; just determine whether the candidate can recognize the special contributions of creative individuals and whether he or she can draw from their experience and talents to be an effective contributor.

Marketing Manager

12. *In your experience, what are the typical wholesale and retail price markups in this industry?*

Sample Answer: On average, for products in this industry, the markup can range from 50 to 100 percent by the time the product reaches the retailer. It also depends on whether the product is a brand name as opposed to a house label.

Advice: This is a nuts-and-bolts type of question to see if the candidate understands how pricing is determined through the channel. Does the candidate have a complete understanding of all the elements that go into the pricing structure for the products in this industry? Such knowledge is critical for marketing professionals, and a weak answer should be a red flag in your evaluation of the candidate.

Multimedia Project Manager

1. How did you become interested in interactive multimedia?

Sample Answer: My father has always been interested in the possibilities of interactive multimedia, and I guess that excitement rubbed off on me. I think it's a phenomenon that's here to stay and that will dramatically change the way we live as a society.

Advice: Determine if an event, class, seminar, or multimedia application first got the candidate excited about working in multimedia. What is so compelling about this particular area of technology, and what role does the candidate see him- or herself assuming as part of a company or group project in interactive multimedia?

• • •

2. What are your qualifications for being an interactive multimedia project manager?

Sample Answer: I've worked as an associate for an interactive multimedia company for nearly three years. For two years before that I worked as a development junior executive for a television production company in Hollywood.

Advice: Because multimedia projects require a broad range of skills, the industry tends to attract candidates from various fields. The candidate should be prepared to list skills and experiences that enhance a project involving interactive multimedia, and to demonstrate the technical acumen necessary to keep up with the fast pace of this area of computer technology.

Multimedia Project Manager

 3. *How did you decide what your role within an interactive multimedia team should be?*

Sample Answer: My biggest strength is my organizational ability, so being a project manager made sense. I'm also very creative, and this role allows me to use both these skills.

Advice: What strengths or skills does the candidate possess that are ideally suited for a particular role within a project team, and why does the candidate believe that he or she is best suited for that role? Does the candidate have enough experience with these projects to understand how he or she can best contribute to future projects?

• • •

4. *What do you think makes the ideal interactive multimedia team?*

Sample Answer: I definitely think it varies from project to project, but in general, it first takes someone to come up with an idea. This is often the producer, who might also provide funding for the project. Then you need at least one writer as well as a computer programmer. You also need a marketing person to sell the finished product. And, of course, you need a project manager to keep everything organized, on time, and within the budget.

Advice: Here you are testing the candidate's ability to determine what individual specialties or expertise is required to produce an interactive multimedia product successfully. What experience does the candidate have working with specialists in interactive multimedia programming, design, content, and marketing? How has he or she been able to persuade these individuals to pool their talents and efficiently produce an interactive multimedia project?

Multimedia Project Manager

5. Did you take any college courses on interactive multimedia?

Sample Answer: I took a class called Interactive Multimedia: Design and Research Issues. It emphasized design, application, and evaluation. I did my first interactive multimedia project in that class.

Advice: If the candidate is a recent graduate, you should determine if he or she had the opportunity to take classes focusing on a particular aspect of interactive multimedia. Did the candidate's academic pursuits in this area feature any project work in which he or she developed and produced an interactive multimedia project for credit? What skills or abilities did the candidate acquire as a result of taking an interactive multimedia course?

• • •

6. Have you attended any interactive multimedia training seminars?

Sample Answer: I go biannually to the SALT, or Society for Applied Learning Technology, seminar. It's a good way to keep up with what is going on in the industry. I also find it interesting to see what my colleagues have been creating.

Advice: How aggressive is the candidate in pursuing opportunities to increase his or her knowledge in interactive multimedia outside of his or her own daily responsibilities? What value has the candidate gained by participating in classes or seminars, and how would he or she rate classroom training as opposed to teaching oneself various applications and programming languages?

Multimedia Project Manager

7. **What interactive multimedia industry publications do you read on a regular basis?**

Sample Answer: There are many interactive multimedia publications. I read *Wired*, *Multimedia Week*, *New Media*, *Technology Review*, *CD-ROM Today*, *Internet World*, *Electronic Entertainment*, and *Multimedia* on a regular basis.

Advice: How committed is the candidate to keeping up with industry news and technological developments on a weekly or monthly basis? What does the candidate learn from these publications that helps him or her perform more effectively in interactive multimedia? What publications would the candidate recommend to people interested in learning more about what really happens in interactive multimedia?

• • •

8. **What interactive multimedia programs have you created?**

Sample Answer: I developed an interior design aid that helps users visualize what the different rooms of their houses will look like after they decorate them. It's been very well received in the designing circles in my town.

Advice: You're looking for not only technical aptitude but also overall design expertise and the ability to take a project from the concept or storyboard stage to delivery. Get the candidate to provide details of how he or she built the product, including artwork, scripting, interface design, and actual programming. What aspects of building interactive multimedia programs does the candidate enjoy the most?

9. *What do you think are the most difficult aspects of creating an interactive multimedia product?*

Sample Answer: In my experience getting to the end product without going tremendously over budget is the most difficult aspect of the project. It takes many resources to create an interactive multimedia program, and most programs end up costing much more than originally expected or budgeted for.

Advice: You want to discover what challenges or obstacles the candidate has had to deal with in creating a program. How did he or she resolve these issues and complete the project? How persistent is the candidate when it comes to confronting and overcoming problems in project development? The candidate's answer should give you certain clues about what he or she does not enjoy doing when it comes to creating an interactive multimedia project.

• • •

 10. *What would you like your next interactive multimedia program creation to be?*

Sample Answer: Because the interior design program I created was so successful, I'd like to expand that idea a bit further. I'd like to develop a program that will enable people to see what their house renovations will look like when completed.

Advice: Ask the candidate to explain why a certain idea or concept will make a great interactive title or project. What type of material does the candidate think will transfer easily to this medium, and why? Are certain businesses and industries particularly well situated to take advantage of this medium? For instance, could interactive multimedia make a significant difference to productivity within the service industries? Within manufacturing? Within medicine and health care?

Multimedia Project Manager

11. What is your favorite interactive multimedia program?

Sample Answer: I really think Myst is a great interactive multimedia software program. I've used it over and over in my spare time. I also have really enjoyed From Alice to Ocean.

Advice: You want the candidate to give you more than just a title, or a comment that the program has great video or graphics. What is it about the program that sets it apart from other interactive titles? Is the candidate impressed by design techniques, functionality, or some other technical aspect that suggests a strong understanding of how such a product is conceived and built?

• • •

12. Whom do you see as industry leaders?

Sample Answer: Although there are many brilliant minds in interactive multimedia, in some ways Nicholas Negroponte is the guru of information technology. What is particularly impressive about his book, *Being Digital,* is that it speaks to both the layperson as well as the interactive multimedia professional.

Advice: Beyond the popular names in high technology, is the candidate familiar with people doing groundbreaking work in the industry? Who does the candidate believe best exemplifies leadership, vision, or the establishing of important technological trends in interactive multimedia?

Multimedia Project Manager

13. Do you work better in project- or task-oriented situations?

Sample Answer: I'd say that I lean more toward the project-oriented side of things. I tend to look at the big picture, then work from there toward a conclusion.

Advice: What you're really asking here is whether the candidate fancies him- or herself someone who enjoys doing task-centric work as opposed to managing an entire project, which includes only some detail- or task-oriented work. Does the candidate prefer to take on a project task by task, or oversee a project and delegate tasks to others?

• • •

14. Do you work better in a conservative corporate office or a casual office?

Sample Answer: I'm much more comfortable and productive in a casual office. Further, I find I can spend more time at the office when I'm wearing "business casual," or even jeans, than a formal suit.

Advice: You want to determine the individual's corporate cultural preferences and what he or she believes is an optimally productive environment. Ask the candidate to describe the type of company atmosphere and dress that he or she thinks is conducive to increased productivity and employee satisfaction.

Multimedia Project Manager

15. *Are you on the Internet?*

Sample Answer: Of course! I've been on it for some time now. In fact, I have to be careful that I don't spend too much time surfing the Net. I can easily spend hours in one sitting during evenings or weekends.

Advice: Multimedia is fast becoming a staple on the World Wide Web, and you should make sure that the candidate regularly visits the Web for both business and personal interests. What types of activities does he or she like to engage in on the Internet, and what multimedia tools does the candidate believe will become prevalent on the Internet in the coming year?

• • •

16. *What do you see as Hollywood's role in the interactive multimedia revolution?*

Sample Answer: I think it's a bit early to tell what the long-term outcome will be. However, we're seeing an increasingly larger number of computer-animated films. I think that in some ways interactive multimedia could be called the next Hollywood.

Advice: The entertainment industry is fast becoming a major player in interactive multimedia, and the candidate should be aware of what companies and individuals from film and television have staked a claim in this arena. The candidate should discuss how interactive multimedia will affect the future of filmmaking and television production, as well as how computer technology will merge with entertainment to redefine standards and methods of delivering content to users.

17. *What other industries do you think will be affected by interactive multimedia?*

Sample Answer: I think every industry will be affected by interactive multimedia. Right now I'd say the most pronounced changes due to interactive multimedia are occurring in public relations. I think education will change dramatically, but I also think it will take time, because this kind of technology will continue to be resisted in educational environments for a while.

Advice: Does the candidate have experience working with interactive multimedia for companies in different industries, and if so, what was the nature of the projects he or she worked on? How will companies or industries use interactive multimedia now and in the future to enhance productivity, develop new products, or improve current processes?

• • •

18. *What platform do you feel most comfortable with?*

Sample Answer: I really prefer working on a Macintosh, although I am just as proficient on a PC.

Advice: This is an either/or type of question, but you want to see if the candidate has taken the initiative to understand how different platforms operate and coexist. Because many applications today are built for multiple platforms, you should measure the candidate's willingness to learn how different platforms handle interactive multimedia.

Multimedia Project Manager

19. *What books on information technology do you think are particularly insightful?*

Sample Answer: There are many. In terms of manifestos about the direction and scope of technology, I found Stanley M. Davis's *2020 Vision* quite interesting, as is Paul Kennedy's *The Rise and Fall of Great Powers.*

Advice: How much time does the candidate spend reading books on technology, and who does the candidate believe best addresses the role information technology plays in our society today? Has he or she read anything lately that's been helpful in understanding how information can be used to make one's job more interesting and powerful?

• • •

20. *What direction do you see interactive multimedia taking?*

Sample Answer: I think it's difficult to predict fully at this point. I believe it will become a part of everyone's daily life sometime in the near future. One area I think will greatly benefit from an increased use of interactive multimedia is education. In fact, I think we'll see a lot more interactive multimedia programs in schools in the future.

Advice: Determine if the candidate has the vision and understanding to appreciate future implications of interactive multimedia in the marketplace. Ask the candidate to cite at least two or three areas in which multimedia will impact sectors of our society, including business and nonbusiness applications.

Product Marketing Manager

1. *Tell me about a product positioning strategy that worked for you.*

Sample Answer: As a product manager with Comptree Toys, I was responsible for the K-to-twelve market for educational games. Our first offering in this market was an interactive CD-ROM tour of the Grand Canyon. To position this product successfully, I focused on three key selling points that I thought would appeal to third-graders: the short, quick tours of specific parts of the canyon, the "tour" guide that was created in conjunction with a local kids' program and was featured on the front of the package, and the opportunity for kids to orchestrate their own adventure in the canyon. Within the first three months we outsold our competition two to one.

Advice: Get the candidate to provide a step-by-step analysis of how he or she positioned a product in the marketplace against that of a competitor. What factors did the candidate consider to be crucial in developing a successful strategy? Do you agree with his or her thought process and methodology for maneuvering the product against the competition? Did the strategy take into account any countermoves by the competition to combat the strategy?

• • •

2. *What are three keys to successfully rolling out a new product in a niche market?*

Sample Answer: Well, first make sure, through a carefully constructed advertising and PR program, that the customer fully understands the benefits inherent in the product and what separates it from the competition. Second, ensure top-quality support and service for the first ninety days, or even beyond, with a money-back guarantee. Third, make sure that it's simple to purchase the product either directly from the company or from retail outlets located within a five-mile area of the target market.

Product Marketing Manager

Advice: Can the candidate quickly give you at least three crucial avenues to pursue that will help ensure success in a niche market? What experiences have led the candidate to decide that these key issues determine success in a particular market? You should not only look for substantive examples that support the candidate's key points but also test his or her conclusions based on your experience in niche product marketing.

• • •

3. If you had complete control of our marketing budget, how might you reallocate our spending?

Sample Answer: I would place the emphasis on local advertising, as much as 60 percent for local ad buys on radio and television programs that air during morning and evening drive time. I would also buy more print advertising in the metro section of the daily and Sunday editions of the local newspaper. I would continue to use the other 40 percent for national advertising, focusing on magazines and cable television.

Advice: Does the candidate have enough familiarity with your product line to discuss intelligently how he or she would spend your marketing dollars for maximum effectiveness? In addition to asking about the amounts this candidate would spend on various ad mediums, you should also probe the reasoning behind his or her choice of mediums in relation to your target markets and your product line. Does the candidate's choice of the marketing mix make sense for your current product offerings? You want to see if this applicant has the experience and knowledge necessary to make intelligent choices in apportioning dollars based on your target markets and existing or new product line.

Product Marketing Manager

 4. *How do you determine which of your product's features are most attractive to your target market?*

Sample Answer: I like to do product testing but only in a few select markets where I know my competitors are planning to launch their own products. It's also helpful to ask distributors and wholesalers what sells well and why. I've found, too, that our salespeople are excellent sources of information because they are in direct contact with our target market and can get immediate feedback on what appeals to these customers.

Advice: The candidate should be able to give you examples of how he or she thoroughly tested products and found the features that most appealed to his or her target market. What steps or methodology did the candidate use to confirm the product's appeal to customers? How did he or she analyze customer preferences in relation to product design and functionality, and what effect did this have on the decision to emphasize certain features over others?

• • •

5. *Tell me about a marketing program that failed. What would you do differently today?*

Sample Answer: I wouldn't call this a failure but rather a missed opportunity. We focused our marketing program for our new explorer game on a television series that we thought was aimed at the preteen market, which was also our market for the product. As it turned out, high school teenagers fell in love with the show and became the dominant audience, but they had no interest in the game. Looking back, I would say that we should have paid more attention to retail promotions.

Advice: To determine the reason a program failed to generate positive results, consider whether the candidate lacked experience, overlooked details, misinterpreted customer data, or failed to anticipate a shift in the market. Hindsight aside, how would the candidate put together a marketing program for your company, and where would he or she place emphasis in terms of overall strategy and dollar allocation? What factors would influence the candidate's thinking and strategy for a new program this time around?

• • •

6. Describe a particularly effective marketing strategy that worked for you.

Sample Answer: With our most recent product introduction aimed at ten-to-thirteen-year-olds, we decided to augment our television ad campaign with a "Family Day" theme at each of the retail outlets that carried the new products. We signed up a popular child actor to appear at several outlets in the Midwest to kick off the campaign, and we encouraged parents to learn more about the safety features built into the product while the kids demoed the product in each outlet.

Advice: Why was the strategy successful, and what specific factors contributed to its success? Did success come after a series of trial-and-error plans, or did the candidate hit a home run the first time out? What elements of the strategy were most effective, and why? Discover the candidate's methods for creating a strategy, including his or her decision-making process for allocating funds to support either a product launch or an existing product.

7. *If your product and your competitor's product are virtually the same, how do you convince the public to buy your product instead of your competitor's?*

Sample Answer: Well, I decided last year that because the features of our new toy line were similar to our competition's, it was important to play up our safety record as a special appeal to parents. This also helped us get an endorsement from the National Safety Board. We then chose a very popular and well-respected child actor as a spokesperson for the product.

Advice: Here you're testing the candidate's creativity in positioning a product and his or her ability to recognize and exploit weaknesses in a competitor's strategy. Is the candidate savvy enough to respond quickly to a competitor's product positioning, and to come up with a new strategy that convinces customers to ignore the competition and focus instead on his or her product? The candidate should go beyond simple price incentives and lay out a strategy that establishes a product more firmly in the consumers' minds.

• • •

 8. *Your competitor has dropped its price on a product that directly competes with yours. How would you counteract that price drop?*

Sample Answer: I would focus on quality and any advantage, big or small, that my product has over the competition. If we decide not to drop our price, we must have compelling reasons for the customer to maintain brand loyalty. One way to do that is to play up features the competition has not thought to include in its product and emphasize strengths that justify our price point and will appeal to our market.

Advice: See if the candidate can forgo a price war and develop a strategy that continually reminds consumers of the product's benefits above and beyond price. Is the candidate creative enough to recognize what buttons to press when persuading consumers to ignore a price differential and focus on benefits and features of the product? What has the candidate done in the past to avoid a price war with a competitor, and what did he or she do specifically to maintain or even gain market share during this time?

• • •

9. *Okay, now suppose your competitor has reached the market with a product that is similar to a product you still have under development. Your estimated test period is three to four months. Would you cut short that period to match your competitor's entrance into the market?*

Sample Answer: My former company believed that focusing on product quality and customer satisfaction was more important than rushing a product to market just to match the competition. However, if testing within the first few weeks yielded positive results in terms of quality and safety, I wouldn't hesitate to ship the product as soon as possible.

Advice: You want to test the candidate's decision-tree capability with respect to weighing time to market against product quality given a competitor's market entrance with a similar product. Does the candidate's ability to analyze this type of situation and choose a course of action seem valid under the circumstances? Is he or she decisive enough and able to take calculated risks to counter a move to market by his or her competitor?

Product Marketing Manager

10. *You're my competitor. Tell me why I should be afraid of you.*

Sample Answer: I've got the financial resources and marketing muscle to double the shelf space for my latest product line, which directly competes with your product at all major retail outlets. In addition, I've just launched a partnering program with a major British toy company to market and sell my new line in western Europe. I've also just completed a major television ad buy in the top ten markets in the U.S. for all of the Saturday morning kids' shows, and movie theaters across the country will be featuring displays of our new line when the movie *Gonzo Comes Home* opens next week.

Advice: The candidate should have in-depth knowledge of your industry and competition and know how to attack the weaknesses in your marketing strategy. Does the candidate's knowledge of your competition combined with his or her marketing savvy add up to a legitimate plan to undermine your best efforts in the marketplace? Are you impressed enough with the candidate's response to give second thoughts to your current marketing strategy?

Publicist

1. *Tell me about a project for which you suggested a truly creative idea.*

Sample Answer: I was working as an intern on a promotion for a local furniture company, wherein the owners were the spokespeople. They were doing a series of appearances for Mother's Day to bring more traffic into the store. Instead of just setting up chairs for appearances, I thought it would be kind of fun to have the audience sit in furniture from the store. The owners thought my idea was great; more people could see and sit in their couches, love seats, and chairs—it looked terrific!

Advice: Get the candidate to describe in depth how the idea came about and what steps he or she took to implement the idea. Do you think the candidate's idea was exceptional? What other examples demonstrate the candidate's creative flair? Ideally, you want to confirm that the candidate consistently develops outstanding solutions to tough problems and has the ability to follow a concept through an entire campaign or product promotion.

• • •

2. *Tell me about your telephone experience.*

Sample Answer: As a publicity assistant for Pendant Publishers, I spent at least half my time each day on the telephone, publicizing new books and authors and booking media tours. I developed good relationships with producers at several national television and radio shows, which I maintain to this day.

Advice: What communication techniques does the candidate use to conduct business effectively on the phone? Determine how comfortable the candidate feels contacting the press on a daily or weekly basis. Does the candidate have other types of phone experience, such as telemarketing for products or services, that have made an immediate impact on his or her phone skills?

3. *How persuasive are you?*

Sample Answer: I find that persuasiveness goes hand in hand with creativity. You can keep calling someone, trying to convince him or her to cover a client, countless times, and that could be very ineffective and sometimes damaging to the business relationship. What you need to do is constantly come up with fresh approaches to the topic. For example, if I was trying to repitch an idea to a producer who had already turned it down, I would say something like, "I remembered you said you didn't like my idea because it didn't have a women's angle. Well, here's a great one that both of us must have missed during our first conversation." One rule I live by is that the more information you gather on a client before you make a pitch—and the more approaches you tailor to each individual you are contacting—the greater your chances of getting the coverage you want.

Advice: Determine the candidate's effectiveness in selling or "pitching" ideas, concepts, or products to a variety of audiences. How persistent is the candidate in going after the press or other people who can be influential in promoting his or her client's product or service? What language or techniques does the candidate believe are most effective in convincing someone to listen to his or her story? Are you convinced that the candidate has what it takes to persuade key individuals in the media, or industry analysts, that your product is worthy of their attention?

4. *What type of writing do you prefer, and how have you honed your writing skills in your other positions?*

Sample Answer: I enjoy writing nonfiction, like newspaper and magazine pieces. I also have a lot of experience writing press releases and advertising copy. I've brought a lot of samples to show you, if you'd like to see them.

Advice: Get the candidate to show you writing samples and discuss why he or she feels comfortable with a particular writing style. Can the candidate meet an aggressive deadline or make late changes to copy on the fly without a loss of quality or creativity? Is the candidate comfortable with adapting his or her style to meet your needs and standards? You should also find out what writing experiences have been most influential on the candidate's current writing style.

• • •

5. *What papers and magazines do you read? What about radio and television?*

Sample Answer: I regularly read *USA Today*, the *New York Times*, the *Chicago Tribune*, the *San Francisco Chronicle*, and the *Washington Post*. I also try to keep up with People magazine, listen to National Public Radio, and tune in to several morning television talk shows. I don't stick just to these sources, though; I'm constantly picking up new magazines and watching whatever shows are considered hot. In fact, I saw your full-page ad for your new line of athletic shoes in the *Times* on Tuesday. It really looked terrific!

Advice: Does the candidate stay current with publications that span a range of interests rather than a narrow niche, such as medical journals or electronics publications? What types of programs does the candidate watch and listen to on a regular basis, and when does he or she listen and watch most often? Ask the candidate to give you specific examples of print publications or radio and TV programs he or she follows.

• • •

6. *What types of events have you planned in the past, and how did they go?*

Sample Answer: I've planned many different types of events, including fund-raising dinners, celebrity benefits, book signings, and radio station contests. The key to making an event a success, I've found, is creative thinking and careful planning. Once when I was working at Pendant Publishers, I was publicizing the autobiography of a major political figure who was, at the time, running for Congress. Because of some canceled speaking engagements, the politician suddenly had some free time to do book signings. I had only two weeks to put together several signings, which are usually scheduled months in advance. It helped that he was a hot figure in the media at the time, but I couldn't have pulled it all off without calling in a few favors. We ended up generating a lot of local publicity, and the signings were a complete sellout.

Advice: You should be looking for not only a variety of experiences in planning events but also the specific role the candidate played in making each event a success. What was the scope of his or her involvement, and what did the candidate learn from the experience? What would he or she do differently, given the chance? What obstacles were overcome, and what challenges faced, when the candidate managed multiple resources and people?

• • •

7. *What kind of contacts have you been able to establish in your previous positions?*

Sample Answer: I have a huge Rolodex of media contacts that I've built up over the years, though I try to focus on cultivating and maintaining relationships with only a few key contacts. For instance, I'm good friends with Linda Smith at the *Lauren Rickey Show*, Bill Jackson at *Wake Up America*, and Jennifer Collins from *90 Minutes*. I also have a lot of newspaper editor friends. In fact, Josie Manning from the *Post* is an old college friend of mine.

Advice: Determine whether the candidate is effective networking among industry PR types, media, and individuals from different companies in different industries. How often does the candidate stay in touch with these people, and under what conditions does he or she usually meet with them (such as lunch, dinner, cocktails, or a ski weekend)? Ask the candidate to describe the first meeting with a contact, and the professional benefits derived from the relationship.

8. *Pretend I'm a member of the media. Make me want to do a story about this career book, the U.S. Jobline Directory.*

Sample Answer: The *U.S. Jobline Directory* features hundreds of toll-free telephone numbers job seekers can call to get job and hiring information from prospective employers. At first glance you can see that this book offers a great service for someone who is job seeking: the opportunity to find great information in almost all cases without cost. The *U.S. Jobline Directory* does all the legwork for a job hunter!—Once I had formulated this pitch, I would have to define my target audience. The first thing to know about any book on job seeking is that there is an extremely wide market. A good publicist would formulate several pitches that could be used for college students, women job seekers, downsized employees, and so on. Next, I would target college publications, women's magazines, lifestyle and business editors at newspapers, and career editors at mainstream publications, as well as at corporate newsletters. I would also pitch the book to local and national television shows and radio business.

Advice: Here you're testing the candidate's selling skills, knowledge of the product, and awareness of the reasons the product would fall into the category of products a media representative would normally review. What issues or "hooks" has the candidate described that would get you to write the story? How did the candidate open the conversation, and what was the first thing that immediately grabbed your attention? Are you convinced that the candidate's plan of attack for promoting this product is strong enough to attract the people who would be most interested in writing or talking about it?

9. ## How do you handle a dissatisfied client?

Sample Answer: I listen empathetically to try to determine why the client is unhappy with the publicity campaign. I assure the client that everything that can be done will be done to his or her satisfaction and acted upon promptly.

Advice: How does the candidate react when a client calls at four p.m. on a Friday afternoon to complain about a lack of publicity for his or her product? Can the candidate remain calm, or does he or she become argumentative or defensive? Does the candidate have experience in handling client issues?

• • •

10. ## What types of jobs have you held other than publicity jobs?

Sample Answer: I'm currently working as an associate producer for WMBR TV's *Good Morning, Cincinnati* program. In addition to organizing all production details for studio tapings, I'm responsible for generating and researching story ideas, and booking guests and panelists. I also coordinate all local publicity, such as running ads in local newspapers. Before that I was a promotional assistant for the University of Washington's theater group. I implemented promotional campaigns for on-campus productions that involved, among other things, writing and designing advertisements and initiating student involvement in the group.

Advice: You want to see if the candidate has a broad range of experiences that have helped shape his or her skills in public relations. What other types of PR or communications positions has the candidate held over the last few years, and which one was his or her favorite? What does the candidate believe to be the most influential experience in sharpening his or her abilities as a PR professional? The candidate's answer should also be an indication of the types of activities he or she prefers on a day-to-day basis.

• • •

11. What was your most difficult assignment?

Sample Answer: I was assigned a promotion project to get customers into a low-traffic mall for Christmas. Research showed that the mall was a favorite with teenagers but not with parents. So to increase the adult traffic, we ran mother/daughter and father/son promotions and contests. In fact, I've brought some of the ads and press releases here in my portfolio. Would you like to see them?

Advice: You want the candidate to demonstrate that no matter how tough the assignment appears, he or she will dive in and make the assignment a success. You should look for the candidate to provide you with concrete examples of a PR campaign, including samples from a portfolio or stories of successful interactions with difficult clients. How did the candidate manage to overcome obstacles, and what did he or she learn from the experience that helped in later troublesome PR projects?

Public Relations Account Executive

1. *What qualifications do you have that will help you as a public relations account executive?*

Sample Answer: I have two years' experience as a company media spokesperson with a $30 million a year company, as well as three years' account experience with a PR firm. I also have a degree in communications from UCLA.

Advice: The candidate should cite skills and accomplishments that address your needs for this public relations opening. Do not settle for job titles. Expect the candidate to have a good grasp of what you are looking for, and to try to match his or her accomplishments with your needs.

• • •

2. *How did you become interested in public relations?*

Sample Answer: My two biggest role models are my parents. My mother has been an editor for the local newspaper for the last twenty years, and my father is a businessman. Since I was a child, I've always wanted to combine their two businesses, and PR does just that.

Advice: Make sure the candidate gives you more than a vanilla response such as, "I really enjoy working with a variety of people," and outlines specific experiences that led him or her to choose a career in public relations. Did an individual, course, or some prior work experience influence the candidate's decision to pursue public relations?

Public Relations Account Executive

3. *Which undergraduate courses do you think really prepared you for a career in public relations?*

Sample Answer: Effective Listening was extremely helpful because we concentrated on identifying barriers to effective communication, as well as analyzing information critically. Understanding Mass Communication was very enlightening because it helped me develop a basic understanding of communication theories and processes.

Advice: Depending upon the candidate's undergraduate degree, you should expect a mixture of courses that focus on writing, speaking, and the social sciences, such as psychology or sociology. What aspects of his or her course work specifically contributed to the candidate's ability to succeed in public relations? If he or she decided to take additional courses today, what would they be, and why would they be essential to continued growth in public relations?

• • •

4. *What writing classes did you take in college?*

Sample Answer: I took Organizational Writing, which emphasized adapting the tone to the audience and the purpose of the message. Professional Writing and The Power of the Written Word sharpened my skills further. I also took a creative writing course that gave me the opportunity to try both prose and verse writing. I think effective writing skills are necessary for success in business, and these classes helped me gain the confidence and the skills needed to address most situations.

Advice: Obviously, writing is a critical skill for success in public relations, and you want to see if the candidate has taken the initiative to improve his or her writing skills through additional courses and seminars beyond freshman writing courses. What types of writing classes appealed to the candidate, and what aspects of his or her writing style needed improvement?

Public Relations Account Executive

5. *How do you think new information technology will affect public relations?*

Sample Answer: I think new technologies are already dramatically affecting the way PR business is conducted. A big component of PR is communication, and you might say all forms of communicating are undergoing a revolution. How clients want information, and how we deliver it to them, are good basic examples.

Advice: You want to go beyond measuring the candidate's computer literacy here and find out if the candidate stays on top of new technologies such as the Internet and understands their value as effective PR vehicles. How will these new technologies impact the way public relations professionals do their jobs, both today and in the future?

• • •

6. *What challenges do you think information technology will present to public relations professionals?*

Sample Answer: I think information technology is creating ever greater challenges for PR professionals. Because of the sheer speed in which information is transferred, as well as the staggering accessibility of information, we must be even more precise in our thinking and writing. However, I think these developments will create new and exciting opportunities.

Advice: Determine if the candidate looks forward to confronting new technology in the workplace. How does he or she see it working to solve client problems? In what areas does the candidate believe new technology will make the biggest impact? How will he or she respond to these challenges and take advantage of advances in technology?

7. ## What do you read on a regular basis?

Sample Answer: I read all of the PR publications, especially *Reputation Management* and *Public Relations Journal*. Beyond PR I like to read the related industry publications, like *Ad Age, Ad Week,* and *Brand Week* because I find it helpful to keep up with what's going on in marketing communications. I also read the journals in my clients' industries, and I make a point of reading the current business trends books. I also think it's important to read the *Wall Street Journal* every day because in PR it's essential to have the big-picture perspective.

Advice: The candidate should display a well-rounded interest in both business and trade publications as well as any business books that he or she finds helpful in gaining knowledge in general and assisting with client problems in particular. You might also want to find out what books or magazines the candidate reads for enjoyment or self-improvement.

• • •

8. ## Do you read any information technology publications?

Sample Answer: I read *Wired* magazine because I consider it to be the guru of information technology publications, so to speak. There are also dozens and dozens of publications covering every aspect of information technology, but *Wired* helps me keep on top of the big picture in a rapidly evolving industry.

Advice: If you are in the technology sector or have clients that are in the high-tech industry, it's imperative that you find out whether the candidate keeps up with new technological developments. What types of high-tech journals or publications does the candidate read on a regular basis? How does he or she use information from these journals to promote products or services for client companies or for his or her own company?

Public Relations Account Executive

9. *What types of public relations projects have you worked on?*

Sample Answer: When I worked in corporate PR, I was the spokesperson who talked to the media about any situation for which comment was needed. I also wrote the quarterly and annual reports, took care of financial communications, and dealt with analyst meetings. Currently, in my agency job, I work on the national and global accounts for both a major sports shoe company and a photographic film company.

Advice: Ideally, you want a candidate whose breadth and depth of experience working on different types of projects for different companies or industries will closely parallel the work in the position for which he or she is applying. What role did the candidate assume in working on these projects, and what did he or she take away from these experiences that would benefit your company? You should test not only the candidate's experience but also the types of projects in which he or she excels in a particular role.

• • •

10. *Do you have experience with identity management consulting?*

Sample Answer: I did a project for a class in college in this area. I chose a large frozen food company that had been aggressively diversifying its business. I created a report that identified a corporate image, and I also developed branding and naming strategies and explored organizational structure issues.

Advice: If identity work will be a key component of the new job, the hiring manager needs to probe carefully the candidate's depth and breadth of experience. This is especially true if the candidate lacks experience; the hiring manager may want to test the candidate's ability by asking hypothetical questions or seeking opinions on repositioning a particular well-known brand.

What has been your most frustrating experience working in public relations?

Sample Answer: I take my client accounts very seriously, but sometimes agencies don't give the attention and resources needed for their clients' accounts. In a big agency things become impersonal, and success is measured solely by the number of account time sheets and expense reports that you sign off. I think it's crucial to stay focused on what's really important, which is creatively growing and servicing the client.

Advice: You want the candidate to assess straightforwardly a project or client that created problems and explain the way he or she overcame obstacles to solve the problems. The answer should give you ample evidence of possible problems that may surface during projects or with clients associated with your current opening. How has the candidate managed to deal with these frustrations and turn them into positives?

• • •

 Do you approach your projects from a task- or a project-oriented position?

Sample Answer: I think being able to work both ways is essential in PR. Project deadlines inevitably are stepped up, and new emergencies can arise at any time. I would say I'm task oriented when I have a stretch of time to compartmentalize and get a project done. When something suddenly comes up, I switch into the project-orientation mode so I can keep several things going at once.

Advice: What you're really asking here is whether the candidate fancies him- or herself someone who enjoys doing task-centric work as opposed to managing an entire project, which would include some detail- or task-oriented work. Does the candidate prefer to dig into a project task by task, or to oversee a project and delegate tasks to others?

Public Relations Account Executive

13. *Are you comfortable with computers?*

Sample Answer: Yes, I'm proficient on both a Macintosh and a PC. I'm also hooked up to the Internet at home. I like to use a project manager software program at the office for maximum efficiency in keeping client projects organized.

Advice: What is the candidate's depth of knowledge regarding computer hardware and software, and how proficient does he or she feel with standard applications such as word processing and spreadsheets? Because technology is playing an increasing role in how companies promote products and services, you must make sure the candidate has the proper attitude toward using computers to enhance publicity efforts for either a client or his or her own company.

• • •

14. *Do you have any experience with budgeting?*

Sample Answer: Yes. In fact, that's a big part of my responsibility with my two major accounts. I work with my clients to develop a budget that we must maintain, which is really a challenge sometimes. But I have a good relationship with my clients, so working together, we're usually able to come up with creative solutions to get everything done efficiently.

Advice: In addition to the candidate's communication skills, the position you're seeking to fill may require the ability to prepare budgets. Does he or she have departmental or project budget experience? What experience does the candidate have with profit and loss statements? What dollar amounts is the candidate used to handling on a regular basis for his or her budget?

15. *What do you think your agency could do better?*

Sample Answer: I think the agency is pretty good at what it does. If anything, I believe the firm should do a little more PR work for itself, perhaps even hire an advertising agency. You can always be bigger and better, and I suspect we'd have even more clients if more businesses knew what we're capable of doing.

Advice: Where does the candidate believe his or her agency has either missed opportunities to attract new business or failed to service clients in an effective manner? What does the candidate think the agency could do to correct any weak areas or improve an existing area that directly impacts the firm's bottom line? This question helps separate the candidate's viewpoint from that of his or her employer.

• • •

16. *Do you prefer to work on your projects individually or with a team?*

Sample Answer: Sometimes it's more efficient to work individually in the interest of advancing a project, but ultimately I think a team gets things done. I really enjoy interacting with colleagues and clients because if I work alone on something for too long, I start to feel isolated.

Advice: What you really want to find out here is if the candidate will fit your agency's style. If your firm works with teams, can the candidate be a team player, or does he or she prefer to work alone and thus might not be compatible with your group or department? Does this candidate need exclusive accolades to be an effective contributor, and can you live with someone who has outstanding credentials but lacks the motivation to work as part of a team?

Public Relations Account Executive

17. Are you accredited?

Sample Answer: Yes, I've been accredited with an APR from the Public Relations Society of America. I'm also accredited with the International Association of Business Communicators.

Advice: Accreditation suggests a certain professional standing within public relations and is an indication that the candidate is serious about the industry and strives for professional excellence.

• • •

18. Do you belong to any other professional associations?

Sample Answer: I belong to the American Marketing Association. I find it helpful because of its marketing publications. I also belong to the associations of my clients' industries.

Advice: What activities does the candidate believe are important with respect to organizations outside the workplace, and what role does he or she assume within these associations? Does the affiliation help the candidate professionally, and if so, in what ways? Does he or she use membership as a networking tool to bolster the number of contacts in a particular industry?

19. *In your opinion, what constitutes a tremendous public relations success?*

Sample Answer: Not the number of column inches of information written in the paper but the ability to truly solve a client's problem. Sound public relations advice doesn't result in articles in the paper. Success is the advice to do the correct thing to avoid difficult situations.

Advice: An important underlying issue here is whether the candidate judges success by the amount of publicity generated, or by the larger purpose of maximizing a client's sales, profitability, positioning, or other objective. What does the candidate believe is his or her most significant accomplishment, and why? How did it impact his or her company, or client's company, and could the candidate duplicate this success for you? You're not looking for numbers here, but, rather, for the way in which publicity generated new business for a client.

• • •

20. *What would you do if a client asked you to stretch the truth in a press release or press conference?*

Sample Answer: I would encourage my client to be creative in coming up with a solution to the problem. Stretching the truth may help in the short run, but it never does in the long haul.

Advice: You're testing the candidate's ethics and integrity against his or her desire to service the client at all costs so as not to lose business for that company. How far will the candidate go to protect a client, and can he or she envision a situation in which going against one's better judgment and manipulating facts to please a client would be an acceptable practice?

Research Associate

1. *When did you first become interested in research as a career?*

Sample Answer: During my freshman year of college as an undergraduate, my economics professor suggested that each of us get a subscription to the *Wall Street Journal. WSJ*'s profiles of corporate financial leaders and their firms got me really excited about this industry.

Advice: When did the candidate realize that this career path was a good choice based on his or her interests and skills, and what aspects of research appealed to the candidate and led to this decision to focus exclusively on this area? You want to make sure that the candidate's interest in the job is based on a continuing interest in progressing as a researcher rather than on a desire to use the position as a stepping stone to another job in a different discipline.

• • •

2. *What are your primary responsibilities as a research associate for your company?*

Sample Answer: As a research associate I have a variety of tasks I must juggle at all times. I develop operational and financial models under the supervision of a senior analyst. I collect data and analyze companies. Most contact with vendors, competitors, and customers comes through me and the other research associates. I also spend a great deal of time preparing marketing materials and client presentations.

Advice: You want to learn about the candidate's level of responsibility, daily tasks, and his or her willingness to tackle a variety of duties associated with the position. How quickly does the candidate take on responsibility for various aspects of a project, and what role does the candidate assume as part of a project team? How does the candidate contribute to the success of a research project?

3. **What experience helps you to be prepared and qualified for this research associate position?**

Sample Answer: I have a B.A. in Economics as well as an M.B.A. I also have three years' work experience as a research assistant. I concentrated on statistics and operations management during my M.B.A. studies.

Advice: The candidate's answer should include both academic work at a college or university and any internships or positions involving full- or part-time research work. You want the candidate to focus on projects in and out of school that relate in some way to the work you have available, and on the ways that these projects are relevant to the job in question.

• • •

 4. **What special licenses do you have that are helpful as a research associate?**

Sample Answer: I have earned a Series 7 license. This makes me a registered financial representative, which means I can give investment advice to the public.

Advice: Licenses or certificates for additional training indicate a willingness on the part of the candidate to pursue a level of proficiency in his or her chosen field of research. Determine what effect the licenses or certificates have had on the candidate's ability to pursue various research opportunities that have enriched his or her knowledge and professional experience.

Research Associate

5. *What has been the greatest challenge in your current research associate position?*

Sample Answer: My greatest challenge has been stepping into an existing marketing program that, up to the point I joined, was not successful. I had to work to maintain the initiative and energy needed to make the marketing program more successful.

Advice: What problem or obstacle did the candidate have to overcome in his or her current position? How did the candidate work through the problem, and what benefits did he or she derive from meeting the challenge and resolving this problem? Does the candidate thrive on challenges, or does he or she prefer to work on only those tasks or problems that are controllable within the scope of the position?

• • •

6. *If you could work with anyone in this industry, whom would you want to work with? Why?*

Sample Answer: There are many bright individuals in this industry, and especially a lot of talented newcomers over the last five years. I would like to work with top management at Smith Associates or Jones, Inc., because of their long-term success. Specifically, working with John Smith, an industry leader, would be extremely beneficial because it would provide an opportunity to learn how he thinks.

Advice: You want to test the candidate's knowledge of your industry and awareness of the most influential figures who are shaping the industry's future. You should also assess the candidate's response to the second part of the question from the standpoint of the qualities and traits that he or she finds impressive, then compare these traits to your own management style.

7. ## What are your career goals for five years from now?

Sample Answer: In five years I'd like to be a senior research analyst for a boutique research firm like this one. I'd like sole responsibility for analyzing the industry and its major companies. I'd like to be in a position where I am making explicit recommendations to clients regarding their investments. I would also like a lot of personal contact with the firm's clients, for whom I have great respect.

Advice: You are not looking for job titles or responsibilities here; rather, you want to see a level of continuing commitment to your company and industry that makes sense given what the candidate has accomplished so far in his or her career. What types of projects or assignments does the candidate envision working on down the road, and what role will the candidate assume within the project?

• • •

8. ## What specific skills have you developed, and what experiences helped you build these skills?

Sample Answer: My strongest skill is my ability to understand my "internal" clients and to prioritize. In my current job I am responsible for managing several studies at once, so I have to give each my full attention at all times, which is, of course, impossible. I have become quite adept at dealing with the most important issue first. This means that I can look at a large number of obligations that are all screaming "Do me first" and instantly realize what needs my attention the most.

Advice: You should expect the candidate to name one or two skills developed in past projects and to tell you how these skills have helped the candidate achieve measurable results in his or her work. Is there one outstanding experience in particular that has enhanced the candidate's skills, and what was it about that experience that positively impacted the candidate's development as a researcher?

• • •

9. If you had extra time to devote to some project, what would that project be?

Sample Answer: I would like to develop an in-depth database of business analyses of all the companies and industries that we cover as a firm. That way all of the research associates could keep fully abreast of each other's work, and the firm as a whole could be stronger.

Advice: You want to see how eager the candidate is to pitch in and help others in the department or organization, and what type of project excites and appeals to the candidate. What would the candidate contribute to the project, and what sacrifices would he or she make to see the project to a successful conclusion?

10. What is your weakness as a research associate?

Sample Answer: I find it sometimes hard to interrupt the firm's senior research staff. They are so busy that I have found it difficult to get time with them when I've needed to. I've developed a "critical memo" system to do this, as needed. I also have a lot of interaction with the other departments in the firm. I've practiced my communication skills on them and now use these with the senior research staff.

Advice: A mature and confident researcher should be able to give you an honest assessment of current skills that need work. Do you consider the candidate's response legitimate, and are you concerned that the candidate's weakness would impair the success of projects at your company?

• • •

11. What opportunities do you see in this industry?

Sample Answer: With the rapid change in technology and product development, the greatest opportunities will be found by discovering where the industry as a whole is going, and then playing a part in creating the new products.

Advice: You want to see if the candidate has kept up with the changes in your industry and can demonstrate some foresight and vision to predict where researchers will be needed and what projects they will be working on in the near future. What products or technologies will develop from research done by individuals like this candidate?

Research Associate

12. What books or publications do you read on a regular basis?

Sample Answer: I have read a lot of books about finance and banking. One that immediately comes to mind is *Understanding Wall Street* by Jeffrey B. Little and Lucien Rhodes. I have also read most of the personal testimonial books, because it never hurts to hear about someone else's experience. Of these, I particularly enjoyed *The Predator's Ball* by Connie Bruck, *Barbarians at the Gate* by Bryan Burrough and John Helyar, and *Liar's Poker* by Michael Lewis.

Advice: Get a feel for the type of reading material the candidate prefers and how it has helped the candidate tackle tough problems on the job. Does the candidate glean inspiring ideas from what he or she reads? How does reading help the candidate to complete a project successfully? Reach a professional goal? Create a personal mission statement?

• • •

13. You've got a great education. Do you think an education is necessary for this research associate job?

Sample Answer: It's necessary but not sufficient. The research analyst job requires lots of technical knowledge best developed in an educational institution. But it's also a game of nerve and wit. You need street smarts as well as book smarts.

Advice: You're testing to see if the candidate will respond by defending his or her educational background, or by focusing on experience or skills that may complement a degree. In what ways does the candidate's professional experience lead to capable research, something that even a great education cannot provide where the daily routine of project research is concerned?

14. ## Would you prefer to work for a full-service or specialty firm?

Sample Answer: I like both but right now want to work for a full-service firm. I want to get broad exposure to all financial markets and opportunities, and a full-service firm offers the best opportunity to do so. If I find an area I'm particularly good at, then I could specialize in a division of a full-service firm, or with a specialty firm.

Advice: Is the candidate flexible and adaptable to different types of projects at different types of companies, and how effective will he or she be as a contributor working in diverse environments? The candidate's answer should give you an indication of the type of firm he or she will work most effectively in.

• • •

15. ## Our analysts work incredibly long hours. Are you used to long hours and lots of stress?

Sample Answer: I thrive on it. On my current job I've often worked fifteen to eighteen hours a day for weeks on end. My spouse is an analyst too, and we both accept the challenge, and support each other. I like to get totally immersed in a project and wrestle it to the ground no matter what it takes.

Advice: How committed is the candidate to completing projects successfully, even at the expense of giving up evenings and weekends to see a project through? Determine whether or not the candidate can take the heat and pound out the long hours, if necessary, to contribute effectively to your project or firm.

Research Technician

1. Do you have any experience writing research or grant proposals?

Sample Answer: Yes, I have helped draft research proposals for the isolation and identification of the bacteria near a known contaminated groundwater source. The company was interested in the effect of the pollution on the type of bacterial populations found in the region.

Advice: You want to see that the candidate has had significant experience not only in writing proposals but also in their preparation and any follow-through necessary to ensure that they have a strong chance of acceptance. What does the candidate believe are the key factors in writing a winning proposal? What obstacles did he or she have to overcome to acquire the skills necessary to become proficient in grant or proposal writing?

• • •

2. Do you have experience lecturing or presenting research material?

Sample Answer: Yes, I recently presented a poster board on a new enzyme isolation technique at the university's molecular biology lecture series. I fielded questions from research colleagues within the university.

Advice: Depending upon the level of experience, you want evidence that the candidate can at least prepare and deliver material or findings to an audience and follow a logical path to reach a conclusion based on the findings. Did the candidate have to put in extra hours to ensure that his or her presentation was sufficient to convey the findings properly? What resources did he or she use that were particularly effective for leading an audience to certain conclusions based on the findings?

Research Technician

 3. *What is the research environment in your present position like? Do you prefer a flexible or regular schedule?*

Sample Answer: The last laboratory I worked in had ten people with about five projects going simultaneously. It wasn't unusual for me to come in at nine in the morning to start an experiment and not leave until ten in the evening. Basically, I'm flexible about my schedule as long as I can get my work finished in a reasonable time period.

Advice: Research facilities often keep unusual hours, so it's not altogether out of the ordinary for candidates to prefer odd working hours. If your company works on a more traditional schedule and the candidate is used to off-peak hours, can he or she reconcile a preferred schedule to your company's environment? Flexibility and adaptability are often important considerations when evaluating this type of candidate, and you need to determine the immediate contribution the candidate can make to your company and weigh it against any quirks in schedules or preferred working conditions.

• • •

4. *Have you ever published an article in a scientific journal?*

Sample Answer: Yes, I was coauthor, with seven other research assistants, of an article published in *Science.* The article was about a new rapid DNA sequencing technique to be used later in the human genome project.

Advice: What was the scope and nature of the article or articles, and how often has the candidate been published in the last couple of years? You will want to determine not only the number and types of articles but also whether the candidate stays on top of current issues in the scientific community and if his or her research and findings are generally regarded as significant in a particular branch of research.

Research Technician

5. *Tell me why this research project interests you.*

Sample Answer: After reading your last two papers on the analysis of the partial crystal structure for this enzyme, I am very interested in the structural studies you and your colleagues at Brookhaven are pursuing. With my background in the structural and functional study of E. coli endonuclease, this enzyme is of definite interest to me.

Advice: Here you're testing the candidate's depth of knowledge and how well he or she has done the necessary homework on your current project. What aspects of the research, in particular, interest the candidate, and what can he or she contribute to your project? You want to be sure that the candidate's interests lie not in personal gratification but in making a significant contribution to the research team. The applicant should complement other team members' skills and abilities, not overshadow them.

• • •

6. *Have you ever had any unexpected or unpredictable results with your research before? If so, what happened, and what did you do to defend your position?*

Sample Answer: As a graduate student getting my master's degree, I was working with a group on analysis of a protein crystal structure, and our analysis disagreed with a popularly held theory on the mechanism of the protein. Our group was grilled by senior researchers in the department. As it turns out, several of the senior professors and researchers were most impressed and surprised. Also, two months later a paper corroborating our theory was published.

Advice: You want to see if the candidate can handle something "out of left field." What does he or she do with the final results—stand firm and refuse to revisit the research, or attempt to apply further tests or hypotheses to confirm the original results? You're looking not only for conviction but also for thoroughness and an ability to spot inconsistencies or to prove logically how results were obtained in the face of the "acid test" of the scientific community.

7. *Tell me about any future plans you might have for schooling or furthering your scientific career.*

Sample Answer: Presently I am enrolled part-time as a graduate student in biology at the local university. I plan to work for several more years while earning my master's degree. Eventually I would like to complete my Ph.D. in neurobiology.

Advice: Determine how active an interest the candidate has in this field and where he or she wants to go beyond this position. It is common for a research assistant to take courses relevant to the work he or she is doing. You need to know if the candidate plans to return to the classroom for an extended stay, or if he or she is interested in teaching full-time, and would be taking your position as a stopgap measure.

• • •

8. *How long do you expect to commit to a position here?*

Sample Answer: Though I have worked within three laboratories over the last several years, my main reason for changing has been the moving of the primary researcher or the loss of grant funding when results weren't as expected for the research project. I have been in my last position for almost three years now. I expect to remain in my next position for at least two more years.

Advice: What is the candidate's level of commitment to research, and what does he or she look forward to once this project is completed? Researchers have a tendency to follow the money, and you want to make sure the candidate has a long-term interest in the types of projects you offer within your department, and will not jump at another project somewhere else or abandon your project for greener pastures.

Retail Buyer

1. Why do you want to be a buyer for this department store?

Sample Answer: I've always shopped at this department store rather than the other two main stores in town. I remember my mother bringing me here to shop when I was a child, and my grandmother always shops here as well. I think the attitude and style of this store, especially because it's a family-owned and -operated business, sets it apart favorably from the other department stores in town.

Advice: Look for the candidate to express a genuine interest in your store operations and specific product lines such as women's or kids' clothing. What experience does the candidate have with stores such as yours, and what excites him or her about buying for your type of retail outlet?

• • •

2. If you could work with anyone in this field, whom would you want to work with, and why?

Sample Answer: Down the road I'd really like to work with Tommy Hilfiger Sportswear. My spouse is a merchandise coordinator for that company and works closely with the stores as a liaison between Mr. Hilfiger and the merchandising people, hosting seminars on the products and other things like that. It's a great company, and it's growing by leaps and bounds. The company also treats its employees well. For now, however, I enjoy doing what I'm doing.

Advice: What retail outlet, chain, or store does the candidate admire most, and what does he or she find particularly attractive about it? Will the candidate sustain an interest in buying for your store or chain for several years, or will he or she likely try to find other opportunities in retail?

3. *What are your primary responsibilities in your current retail buying position?*

Sample Answer: I'm a buyer for boys' better sportswear and collections, so I buy sizes four to seven and eight to twenty in Polo, Levi's, and Girbaud. I'm in charge of selecting merchandise and negotiating prices with vendors. I go to market four times a year to do that. Merchandising clothes collections involves looking at a table and figuring out how it can tell a story, so I make sure everything I buy will coordinate on the sales floor. I'm also in charge of store distribution, inventory control, and markdowns. However, I spend most of my time at my computer, crunching numbers. The department store computer system provides the opportunity to see immediately if something's really selling. That way I can call a vendor right away when I see a product is hot.

Advice: Determine the level of buying authority, types of buying activities, and other responsibilities, including finance and administration that the candidate handles on a regular basis. What does the candidate enjoy most about his or her current position, and what does he or she think is the most important responsibility associated with it? Has the candidate enjoyed increasing responsibility in the position?

• • •

4. *How does taking markdowns work?*

Sample Answer: When you take a markdown, it's going to affect your gross margin, which is what your review as a buyer is based upon. Therefore, you get the vendor to help you make up the difference in the price of the clothing. It's what buyers refer to as vendor money. Many vendors will guarantee your gross margin. If you don't attain that gross margin, they'll kick in money to make sure you get there, but they're not going to give you the money unless you ask for it. It's hard to ask for money, but if they don't give it to you, they'll give it to someone else. They budget out for markdown money, and when it's gone, it's gone.

Advice: Here, you're testing the candidate's knowledge and experience in handling this aspect of retail, and his or her ability to articulate the process clearly. When do markdowns occur, and who is involved in the process? What is the buyer's role in this process, and how does he or she minimize buying mistakes? Also, does the candidate inadvertently mention a buying mistake for which he or she was responsible? How serious a mistake was it?

• • •

5. What has been your greatest challenge as a buyer?

Sample Answer: Growing up, I was fairly shy. Having to come out of my shell has been a big challenge. But in my position I can't be shy, because I have to deal with so many vendors. For instance, when I went to my last market buying, my purchases totaled $2.5 million. In fact, my review is based on whether I have increasing gross margin dollars. In order to increase gross margin dollars, I must be good at negotiating with vendors and convincing them to break prices on certain things and to give me vendor money.

Advice: You should look for one or two examples of how the candidate had to overcome a problem or obstacle to become a more effective buyer. Did the candidate overcome any personal limitations, or lack of industry knowledge, to succeed as a buyer?

6. *What specific personal skill do you think is the most important for a retail buyer to possess?*

Sample Answer: Speaking from experience, I would say my most developed personal skill as a result of being a retail buyer is negotiating. I also think it's the most important skill because buyers must negotiate every day.

Advice: What personal quality does the candidate believe makes a real difference when buying merchandise? Is the skill one that he or she developed on the job, or is it a personality trait that helps the candidate secure what he or she needs from a client? Why is this personal skill so effective for the candidate as a retail buyer? How would this skill work in your business environment?

• • •

7. *What professional retail buying skill do you concentrate the most on improving?*

Sample Answer: Number crunching is my weakness. But 95 percent of my day is spent in front of my computer, so learning the system and understanding why we use the numbers we use is one area I've tried to improve. I was an assistant buyer for only three months, so there are a lot of things I didn't learn, like dealing with stock projection, projecting a 10 percent increase, and things like that. But I'm becoming more and more comfortable with the numbers.

Advice: Can the candidate frankly discuss a weakness that he or she plans to turn into a strength in the future? Has this weakness always been readily apparent to the candidate, or did a particular event or job responsibility expose it? How does the candidate plan to eliminate the weakness?

8. If you had extra time to devote to some project at the buying office, what would that project be?

Sample Answer: I don't have time to work on extra projects at the office, but at home I've been working on a back-to-school promotion, because that's a really big time for us and because Tommy Hilfiger is introducing boys' sizes four to seven. There's a lot of opportunity and growth in that market, so I'm putting together a little packet to send out to all of the store managers and area sales managers, giving them Tommy merchandising and display guidelines and explaining what kinds of deliveries they can expect. I think this project is important in order for us to have a successful back-to-school and a successful introduction of the new Tommy line. I don't think the stores will know what to do without these guidelines.

Advice: Look for examples that show initiative. How has the candidate started a project and brought it to a successful conclusion? The candidate's answer here should also provide insight into his or her favorite activities and the types of skills and abilities the candidate enjoys using in the position of retail buyer. What does the candidate do best, aside from buying activities, and how is his or her current project going to enhance retail skills?

• • •

9. What future opportunities do you envision in retail?

Sample Answer: The biggest opportunity for retail stores is expansion by takeovers. Fortunately, the store I work for is big enough that it's taking over other stores. There's also a lot of opportunity as the chain gets bigger. One example is the potential to gain more business by making department stores more attractive to consumers. Stores such as Eddie Bauer and The Gap

have eaten away at department store business because they carry just the basics, and people like the ease of shopping at those stores for those basics. Department stores can't carry just T-shirts and jeans, so they need to prove to consumers why they're better than the other chains.

Advice: You are tapping not only the candidate's experience but also his or her vision and ability to think strategically when identifying different market segments for your retail store. You should expect the candidate to discuss why these opportunities are more attractive than others and provide details of how a store like yours can take advantage of these opportunities. Do you agree with the candidate's assessment of the potential for new markets opening up to retail?

• • •

 Do you think mail-order catalogs are threatening the business of department stores?

Sample Answer: I don't think they're a big threat because people generally want to touch and feel merchandise before they buy it. However, people have more than one option now, and they'll go with the best value. Because customers have become so price conscious, I think department stores have had to reduce costs to be able to maintain their margins and remain competitive.

Advice: You're not necessarily looking for hard numbers here but for an overall impression of how catalogs fit into the retail picture and how they'll affect store sales in the future. Does the candidate have any thoughts on how retail stores can coexist with mail order and not lose a significant number of sales? What kind of advantages does the candidate think mail order has over retail storefronts, and what can retail stores do to enhance offerings and find new customers to offset any loss to mail order?

Retail Buyer

11. What retail publications do you read?

Sample Answer: I currently read *Kids Fashion*, *Earnshaw's*, and *Children's Wear*. They cover the latest trends and different kids' shows that are coming to New York and Dallas. Also, the buyer I work for has been with our store for twenty years and is very highly thought of. She gave me a textbook, the *Buyer Handbook*, that I keep on my desk.

Advice: Beyond business publications, what types of industry journals does the candidate read on a regular basis, and what information does he or she take away from these publications to become a more effective buyer? Has the candidate discovered any new ideas in these publications that would help your store improve offerings and subsequently attract new business?

• • •

12. What kind of computer skills do you have?

Sample Answer: I'm PC literate. I've worked a bit on the Macintosh as well, but I'm much more fluent on an IBM or IBM-clone machine. I'm also very adaptable in terms of learning new programs. For example, while in a summer corporate retail position during college, I had to learn to use Harvard Graphics and Lotus 1-2-3 for a project I was working on. I found it easy to learn several new programs because I was already so comfortable with an IBM-type computer. I've also used Windows for years.

Advice: Determine the candidate's depth of knowledge regarding computer hardware and software, and his or her proficiency with standard applications such as word processing and spreadsheets. Because technology is playing an increasing role in how companies deliver products and services to customers, make sure the candidate has a proactive attitude toward using computers to enhance his or her skills as a retail buyer.

13. Do you enjoy interacting with people?

Sample Answer: Yes. While working as a sales associate in New York City, I found that interacting with people was probably the most important part of my job. Although it was necessary to be knowledgeable about the product line and to keep my area neat, interacting well with customers was crucial. Generally, we had repeat business from an established clientele, so relationship building and maintaining was also a very big part of the business. After time I continued to work with certain customers, so I kept a notebook of each of my clients, including their clothing preferences and needs. I think the reason I was so successful as an associate at the boutique was because I not only enjoyed our clientele but also was good at interacting with them.

Advice: A retail buyer not only needs a good eye for product but also should have excellent communication ability. In what situations does the candidate prefer to meet and interact with clients and other retail industry individuals? Does he or she feel comfortable meeting clients in social situations, such as for dinner or on the golf course, and can he or she mix business with pleasure? What types of people does the candidate believe he or she gets along with the best, and why?

• • •

14. Do you mind sitting at a desk for long periods of time?

Sample Answer: I think it's difficult for anyone, at least initially, to sit in front of the computer or at a desk for long periods of time, but I find that I accomplish more when I do. Like anything, you get used to it.

Advice: You want to make sure that the candidate has

realistic expectations about the job and is not drawn to this position by glamour or large financial rewards. Determine whether the candidate can handle routine tasks on a daily basis without getting bored or distracted, and whether he or she can stick with one or more tasks for a long period of time without becoming frustrated. This question is particularly appropriate for a candidate seeking to make a transition from store operations to merchandising.

• • •

15. What basic advice would you give an assistant area sales manager for selling your line?

Sample Answer: Don't mix different sale items together on the same rack. For example, don't put 25 percent off and 50 percent off merchandise together on one bunker, because it confuses the customer. Also, when you look at a table, it should tell a story, so use imaginary color palettes when arranging displays. With Tommy Hilfiger, for example, the group color code is on the hang tag with the UPC code, so it's almost like painting by number. Put all the same group codes on a table and make it look good. Straighten and fluff frequently.

Advice: How does the candidate communicate the strengths of his or her product line, and what would the candidate do in a retail outlet to position his or her products for maximum visibility? How would the candidate sell products against the competition, and what in-store promotions or marketing programs would the candidate recommend to encourage increasing sales volume?

Retail Buyer

16. *Describe your last week as a retail buyer.*

Sample Answer: Right now my supervisor and I are concerned because we took some markdowns last month. Because vendors guarantee your bottom line, Girbaud gave us $50,000 worth of merchandise at cost, which is the equivalent of $100,000 at retail, all of which goes directly to my bottom line. That's like another $100,000 in gross margin last month. So we're really pushing this month for that money from Girbaud. Therefore, for the last three or four days I've spent most of my time on the phone negotiating with vendors to guarantee my gross margin. You've got to get in line for vendor money and hope you're at the top of the vendor's list. I'm lucky because I'm with this store and we're fairly big. We've got a lot of buying power and a lot of clout. But the store has seven divisions, and there's a lot of competition between each division. So we're competing against each other for markdown money. The whole buying business gets kind of cutthroat, but I like it.

Advice: You should expect the candidate to relate his or her favorite activities as a retail buyer and try to avoid discussing more mundane tasks or responsibilities associated with the position. Press the candidate to describe a typical day, and dig to see if he or she will reveal any tasks or issues that cause problems and that might be repeated in your opening.

Retail Store Manager

1. Tell me, what excites you about this position?

Sample Answer: I am very attracted to the cooperative team approach of the regional managers and the individual store managers. Knowing that my input will be taken seriously and that my ideas will eventually materialize in the form of store improvements is a motivating factor for me to seek opportunities with your chain.

Advice: You want evidence that the candidate truly feels as though he or she were born to work in retail. The enthusiasm should be tempered with examples of why the candidate finds your position so attractive and interesting. Does the candidate have a good feel for your company and your products or services, and can he or she step in tomorrow and make a difference?

• • •

2. What has been your most positive retail experience, and why?

Sample Answer: I would have to say that my most positive experience was right out of school as a sales trainee with Carter's Stores. I knew from my first day on the job that retail was where I wanted to be because I enjoy customer contact, problem solving, and helping customers find what they need to make their lives more productive. That experience has been confirmed with each position that I have held in retail.

Advice: What elements of the candidate's previous position motivated the candidate to excel and perform beyond expectations? Why has retail been more rewarding than any other career alternative? What, specifically, can the candidate pinpoint as the reason for his or her success in this industry? You want examples of the candidate's favorite day-to-day activities and the skills and talents these activities highlight.

3. *What is the size of the store you are managing and its sales volume?*

Sample Answer: I'm responsible for the clothing department at Walker Stores, which has a total square footage of fifteen thousand square feet. My average yearly sales volume is $2.8 million.

Advice: Look past the numbers to determine if the candidate has the type of retail management experience that would allow him or her to be successful managing one of your outlets. Does the candidate have the ability to manage effectively the resources, people, and customer traffic in your store or chain, given his or her background?

• • •

4. *How do you motivate your sales associates?*

Sample Answer: Keeping turnover low is a priority for me, and one of the best ways to do that is to make associates feel as if they are contributing to overall store management. I have regular meetings where each associate is able to discuss what he or she believes would improve store performance. That includes everything from store displays to the appearance of certain departments, as well as what we can do to better serve the customer. In addition, I have monthly one-on-one meetings with each of my associates to discuss any personal or employment issues that they believe hamper their effectiveness in the store.

Advice: Determine if the candidate has the people and communication skills necessary to get maximum performance from his or her associates. What has the candidate found to be the most challenging aspect of getting sales associates to give top-notch performance day in and day out? Ask for examples of times when the candidate developed creative solutions to motivate his or her employees to go the extra mile and make their jobs more rewarding as a result.

Retail Store Manager

5. *What criteria do you use in evaluating candidates for the position of sales associate?*

Sample Answer: I look for someone who is enthusiastic and hardworking and has genuine people skills. I also want someone who can quickly address a customer's needs so we don't lose a sale because of an indifferent or lazy attitude. I look for candidates who can display patience and listen attentively to the customer no matter how trivial the request or problem.

Advice: How adept is the candidate in pinpointing skills, talents, or abilities in a prospective associate that will translate into success? How does the candidate define those special qualities that separate the average or mediocre performer from someone who will excel as a sales associate in retail?

• • •

6. *When do you decide to add additional people to checkout counters?*

Sample Answer: If more than two people are waiting to purchase items, I move to open another register and assign someone register duty until traffic abates. During the holiday season I often find myself not only helping out at the register but also doing double duty in customer service. My philosophy is to do whatever it takes to satisfy the customers and keep the store operating at peak efficiency.

Advice: This question goes to the heart of the candidate's ability to gauge customer traffic, organize shifts and personnel, and keep the store traffic moving without unnecessary delays. Can the candidate plan shifts and anticipate customer traffic without neglecting his or her other duties or responsibilities? You are testing here the candidate's ability to understand the relationship between strong customer service and effective store operation.

7. *If a customer had a complaint, would you prefer to handle it directly or refer the call to customer service?*

Sample Answer: Because I pride myself on a hands-on approach, I would handle the complaint on the spot. I think it is critical to listen to a customer and respond almost immediately so the customer feels that he or she is being heard and treated with respect. There is no more certain way to lose someone's business than to treat a complaint with an indifferent attitude.

Advice: How proactive is the candidate in dealing with customers, and can he or she take responsibility to resolve a dispute as opposed to dismissing the customer's complaint outright? Does the candidate have the ability to analyze quickly the core of the complaint and devise a solution that will meet the customer's needs while satisfying all store policies? Or does the candidate prefer to avoid confrontations altogether and pass off any problems to customer service?

● ● ●

8. *What was your shrinkage relative to other stores in the chain?*

Sample Answer: For the last two years my shrinkage percentage ranked in the bottom 20 percent of the chain.

Advice: This is a numbers question calling for a numbers response. Anything else indicates an inability to understand and manage a retail store.

9. *A well-known vendor sends a representative to visit one of our stores. She is visibly unhappy with a store display for one of the vendor's new products. How do you turn this negative situation into a positive?*

Sample Answer: I would first ask her to list her objections so that I could get a better understanding of the source of her unhappiness. Because merchandising programs are handled at the corporate level, I would then bring her into my office and call the person responsible for the program. I would carefully go over each point with the corporate merchandising manager and ask him or her for recommendations about how we could improve the display. I would then add my own suggestions to his or her list and work with the representative to improve the display.

Advice: How does the candidate handle an irate representative and take steps to ameliorate the situation to the satisfaction of the representative and his or her supervisor? This is a test of the candidate's ability to think on his or her feet, listen carefully, and accept responsibility, as opposed to shoving blame up the ladder. What specific action did the candidate take to turn a potential disaster into a positive outcome?

• • •

10. *What is it about our retail operation that is most attractive to you?*

Sample Answer: Your stores have always represented top dollar value with a professional attitude and a proactive approach to store management. I also am excited by the breadth of product selection, and the strong emphasis on in-store merchandising that your firm is known for.

Advice: How much does the candidate know about your store's, or chain's, philosophy and mode of operation? You will also want to determine the candidate's overall knowledge and experience in retail and the particular aspects of your store or chain he or she finds impressive. What is it about your store or chain that is more dynamic or attractive than other retail outlets or chains? Does the candidate have personal experience of, or know individuals who work for, your store or chain?

• • •

11. If your corporate office advertised an item in error, should you explain to the customer that it wasn't your fault?

Sample Answer: I don't believe that is a wise move. Store personnel are often on the firing line when operational mistakes occur. However, the customer doesn't distinguish you from the company you work for. To the customer you are the company, and you should apologize and offer an alternative solution.

Advice: This type of question tests the candidate's ability to recognize when it is best to assume responsibility quickly even when not at fault. Further, you should determine if the candidate knows when to walk the fine line of adhering strictly to corporate policy or taking action to satisfy the customer, irrespective of any corporate mistake or oversight.

Salesperson

1. *Tell me about the product you are currently selling.*

Sample Answer: My primary focus is on our flagship product, a fully integrated accounting package for middle-market-sized manufacturing firms. Designed exclusively for such firms, it gives particular focus to cost accounting and inventory control.

Advice: You want more than just product features here; you really should be looking for a "minisell" of the candidate's current product or product line. Test the candidate's key selling strengths. Do you completely understand how the product functions and what benefits it brings to its target market? Does the candidate have a thorough grasp of the advantages of his or her product over competitors' products? Does he or she also have an understanding of the target market for the product?

• • •

2. *How much of your time is spent cold calling new accounts as opposed to servicing existing accounts?*

Sample Answer: At this point I spend about 70 percent of my time working on new accounts. I have trained my assistant to the point where he can handle routine requests and issues concerning existing accounts, although I also keep in touch regularly with the clients by phone and with personal visits.

Advice: You want to cut right to the heart of the matter and determine if the candidate enjoys getting on the phone to prospect for new clients, or supporting existing customers. Make sure the candidate is specific. How many cold calls does the candidate make each week? How many decision makers does he or she talk with? What parts of the week are set aside for cold calling?

3. How many new accounts did you land last year?

Sample Answer: I closed seven new accounts last year and already have commitments for four this year. Out of the total five-person sales force, I ranked second in number of new accounts but first in the dollar volume from new accounts.

Advice: How aggressive is the candidate in going after and closing new business? Does he or she have the qualities to stay focused and consistently meet or exceed quota? What special techniques or methods does the candidate use to convince prospective clients to buy his or her product? How does the candidate go about generating leads for new business? Does he or she prefer to make the first contact via phone or in person? If generating new business is important to you, you need evidence that this applicant has the ability and desire to pursue and close new business on a regular basis.

• • •

4. What is the most common objection you encounter, and how do you overcome it?

Sample Answer: Lack of recognition of the company name makes it challenging to get presentation time at new accounts. Our main competitors have much broader product lines, much larger market shares, and much more visibility. This can also lead to some difficulty in closing sales.

Advice: You not only want to hear the nature of the objection but also an explanation of how the candidate has overcome it and eventually closed the sale. Why does the candidate believe clients bring up this objection, and does he or she have an answer ready to fire, or modify the answer depending upon the client? If you brought up the objection during the interview, how would the candidate overcome it and convince you to continue to listen to his or her pitch?

Salesperson

5. In an ideal job, would you like to spend more or less of your time cold calling?

Sample Answer: Cold calling is my job. I enjoy it, and I'm good at it. But I'd really like the chance to sell for a company like yours that has tremendous recognition.

Advice: This question forces the candidate to confront the strength of his or her desire to call prospective clients and sell them on your product. Although many candidates prefer to spend much of the day calling on existing accounts, they might be willing to cold call more often if other aspects of the job appeal to them. You must determine if a balance exists; an answer that leans toward a preference for calling only existing accounts obviously will not work for you if you need someone to do a lot of cold calling.

• • •

6. What lead sources have you found most productive?

Sample Answer: Although referrals from existing accounts are my best lead source, I also call some accounts whose names I find in industry directories.

Advice: Determine if the candidate is creative and aggressive in compiling sources from which to prospect for potential clients. How does the candidate evaluate his or her sources, and which source does he or she find to be most reliable? You are also measuring here the candidate's ability to build from his or her network to add new clients continually while servicing existing customers.

• • •

7. Tell me about some of the most extreme lengths you have gone to to close sales.

Sample Answer: I spent eighteen months trying to land an automotive parts manufacturer after successfully landing two of the company's competitors. The MIS manager would not even see me, however, because as it turned out, he was friends with the account executive from another software firm. I tried everything, from sending e-mail to calling the company president, to cornering the prospect at trade shows. Finally I looked in my college alumni book and saw that the executive assistant to the MIS manager had been a couple years behind me in school. I arranged to meet him through mutual friends and convinced him of the superior value of our product. He then sold his boss on bringing the software into the company.

Advice: Just how far will this candidate go to close a sale, and what signs or indicators tell the candidate that extreme measures are called for? Do you agree with the candidate's methods, and does this candidate exhibit street-smart selling tactics, or energy that could be channeled into selling other clients? How creative or original was the candidate's final solution to convince a hesitant customer to drop all objections and buy?

• • •

8. How have you performed relative to your goals or quotas?

Sample Answer: Last year I was 27 percent over my sales quota for new accounts—the highest in the firm.

Advice: This question is strictly about numbers and whether the candidate is a consistent performer who does not use excuses to explain poor results. You should also get an idea of how the candidate's goals were set each year to determine if they were realistic for the type of product sold or if the numbers were too inflated or too easy to attain. Do the numbers vary in any way as to raise red flags about the candidate's capabilities?

• • •

9. What about your sales to existing accounts last year?

Sample Answer: Last year my largest existing account made a strategic decision to narrow its supplier base, and we were dropped as an approved vendor. I'm still trying to get back into the account. Sales to my other existing accounts were strong, but because of the shortfall at my largest account, I came in just under my goal.

Advice: Did the candidate experience any drop off or lose any long-standing accounts to the competition? Expect the candidate to focus on how he or she manages to strike a balance between canvassing for new accounts and continuing to support existing accounts. Also be aware of any hints of complacency or a lax attitude toward established clients, as this may be a sign that the candidate takes old accounts too much for granted.

• • •

10. Did you meet your goal last year?

Sample Answer: I was a little under my goal last year, but only one person met her goal, because the product update we were selling had not been carefully debugged and the trade press really panned it. However, I still led the firm in new accounts closed that year.

Advice: If the candidate hesitates or tries to duck the question by making excuses, you obviously should be concerned about hiring this person. However, there could be extenuating circumstances involved in falling short of a goal so you should get the candidate to explain the situation carefully.

• • •

11. What sales handle might you use in selling our product line?

Sample Answer: I would emphasize your leading position, not only in the inventory management software market, but also in manufacturing MIS systems as a whole.

Advice: Here you're testing the candidate's level of familiarity with your product line and determining whether he or she can pick out key features and benefits that sell. You are also looking for certain intangibles such as tone of voice, smile, warmth and friendliness, sincerity, language (including body language), and listening skills. Does the candidate understand your needs and know how this product can fulfill those needs? Raise an objection to see how the candidate reacts to and overcomes it.

• • •

12. *How do you feel about overnight travel?*

Sample Answer: Travel is no problem. I've done a lot of it, and I know it comes with the territory.

Advice: If travel to other parts of the state or country is a large part of this position, you need to determine the level of commitment the candidate has by gauging his or her willingness to spend a good deal of time on the road. In order to continue the interview, candidates may say that travel is no problem when in fact it is. You may have to decide if other attributes the candidate brings to the job outweigh any hesitations about being on the road.

• • •

13. *In comparison to other salespeople, what do you see as your strengths and weaknesses?*

Sample Answer: I'm probably the strongest in person and over the phone. Frankly, I enjoy selling and consulting on new systems or major upgrades more than being a coordinator for service or billing issues; however, in all of my jobs I've done well in working with my assistant or a staff person to coordinate such day-to-day issues.

Advice: Can the candidate accurately describe the key skills and abilities he or she brings to the table and which of these needs improvement? What does the candidate consider his or her greatest selling asset, and which trait would the candidate change to become even more effective at selling?

Systems Analyst

1. *Describe your philosophy of what would be important if you were the senior systems analyst and had to staff your organization with programmers and systems analysts.*

Sample Answer: I would look for the same characteristics that have enabled me to be effective in the past: the ability to conceptualize, think logically, and verbalize easily. If my people had these traits, then I'd know they have the skills to talk to client groups and translate accurately what they've said into meaningful systems design. I'd also want people with programming experience.

Advice: Determine if the candidate has the ability to build an organization from the ground up. What criteria does the candidate use to evaluate engineers and other analysts? Examine the qualifications listed by the candidate to see what he or she considers important for success as a technical or programming specialist. Would you feel comfortable putting this candidate in charge of building up the technical capacity of your company?

• • •

2. *Are there certain personal qualities you believe are uniquely compatible with the information systems profession?*

Sample Answer: I like people who are eager to learn and experiment, because things change very quickly in our business, and we have to be able to keep up with technology. And I'd try very hard to look for integrity, given the potential power that systems analysts have to create viruses and to access information that could cause the company or individuals harm.

Advice: What type of individual does the candidate believe will be successful in a technical position? What, specifically, does it take to succeed? Has the candidate given you, in this answer, a convincing personality profile of him- or herself? Are you comfortable that such an individual will fit within the information systems department of your company based on the characteristics or qualities the candidate describes?

• • •

3. Tell me about your own experience with hardware.

Sample Answer: I've worked with a variety of platforms, including DEC and IBM PC. I've experienced several major systems conversions in my fifteen years' experience— for example, when we moved from mainframes to servers and terminals, then to PC platforms.

Advice: Here you are testing the candidate's knowledge of different hardware platforms as well as his or her observations on what changes will take place in the future of computing hardware. What significant trends does the candidate see taking place over the next year to eighteen months that would affect your company's hardware purchasing decisions? How informed does the candidate appear to be on the new platforms that are likely to dominate, and on how they might help your company improve productivity or operational efficiency?

• • •

4. What software are you familiar with?

Sample Answer: I've worked with a variety of applications. Actually, one thing that has been very helpful to me in working for a hospital management company is the background in insurance claims I got by working for my two previous employers, both insurance companies.

Understanding that process, which has a big impact on how we do business as a health care provider, has helped me design tracking reports and create models for various patient scenarios with associated costs of care.

Advice: What has been the candidate's experience with software platforms, applications, and development tools, and which does he or she believe are most effective for specific projects, such as client-server development? What level of expertise does the candidate offer to your company on these different software platforms, and what tools would he or she recommend for your internal projects? You are testing the candidate here for skill level and awareness of new tools, or tools due to come on the market, that could deliver improved or faster application development.

• • •

 5. *In your early programming experiences, what did you have to be able to do well?*

Sample Answer: I had to be able to solve problems and write good code. I also learned other skills, like how to do more thorough research on the front end, including interviewing people and getting them to reveal what kind of information they really need as opposed to what they say they want out of an automated system.

Advice: This question forces the candidate to recall his or her first few programming assignments and the skills or abilities needed then on a daily basis to develop applications successfully. Did the skill involve actual building or testing of the product, or did it have more to do with the end user and the way the candidate managed to translate user requirements into interface design and other front-end components? How did the candidate build on those early experiences and develop new skills?

6. Is it sometimes difficult to get clients to reveal what they are thinking in terms of information output?

Sample Answer: I think that definitely can happen if you rush people. Then I also think there are the type A personalities who immediately think they can tell you how to do the design analysis. Since I know the dangers of rushing the front end of a project, I've learned how to move a conversation along and get that type of person to give more complete and thoughtful background information instead of their own conclusions. One thing that really helped me deal with those types of personalities was to read the book *Seven Habits of Highly Effective People.*

Advice: Determine how effective the candidate's analytical techniques are when they include assessing what a client actually needs for a product or functionality. What steps does the candidate take to get the client to provide enough detail so that it can be effectively translated into a final product that delivers the information in a form suitable for the client?

• • •

7. Describe the process you went through to develop one of the systems at your current company.

Sample Answer: An example is an integration project we did, in which many hospital departments had to share patient information. We wanted to replace the manual process of moving pieces of paper from floor to floor or having patients constantly repeat their names, addresses, and social security numbers as they moved from department to department. We interfaced the patient information from the business office system with patient information from the radiology and lab systems and made it available to the nursing computer system. In doing the initial work we included the director of nursing and all medical department heads and offered them various design alternatives. The goal was to get them to buy in by making a choice.

Advice: Here you are testing the candidate's methodology and logic in developing applications or proprietary systems. Does the candidate visualize how the system will take shape, or does he or she have to use a decision tree or some other analytical device or method to arrive at a solution? What is at the core of the candidate's thought process, and does it make sense to you, given your internal projects?

• • •

8. How would you describe the internal reputation of the information systems department where you worked recently?

Sample Answer: In general, people have always considered my company an excellent place to work. We're known as a cost-driven company, which means our systems group is critical in terms of accurate data collection. I think that the goals of my job and the goals of the company are well connected—we want to save the company money. My department eliminates duplications and automates things so people don't have to key in information manually, which is both time-consuming and error prone. One way my group has earned its reputation is by involving users in our designs so that user needs, as I mentioned before, are the beginning point and end point.

Advice: Can the candidate objectively evaluate the merits of his or her department and the contributions the department made to the overall development of the company? What are the department's strong suits, and how do they reflect the candidate's own ability to contribute to your department? If you called someone from the candidate's department, would that person say things similar to what the candidate has said?

Systems Analyst

9. How would you describe the realities of a systems analyst job?

Sample Answer: I have always understood that it isn't an eight-to-five job. There are a lot of project deadlines to juggle around troubleshooting. I've been awakened at home at midnight because someone's system has locked up, and I understand that. I also understand that to each client group, its project is number one. I've always been able to relieve some of the inevitable pressure because I'm a good time manager.

Advice: Get the candidate to outline his or her expectations of what a systems analyst should accomplish on a daily basis and what he or she has actually experienced as a systems analyst. What differences between the job description and the actual job surprised or disappointed the candidate, and what does the candidate believe this type of position offers that is not ordinarily found in the job description? Would the candidate still choose to be a systems analyst, if given a chance to make the choice again?

• • •

10. Why do you want to continue to work in systems design?

Sample Answer: I'm certainly ready for more managerial responsibility; in addition to on-the-job training, I've also completed an executive M.B.A. program to build my management skills. In terms of why systems work continues to appeal to me, there's never a dull moment. The job requires left- and right-brain thinking and a lot of intelligence as well as creativity. I remember my initial interest in learning data processing. After college I was a reservation sales analyst, which was my first introduction to computers. Although that wasn't a challenging enough job for me to stay interested in a career there, I liked having all that information at my fingertips. I decided it would be interesting to be the person behind what's inside the computer. That's why I left the job to go back to school and get another degree—this time to learn systems. And I know I want to stay in this field. Whether the company is downsizing or fighting inflation, the MIS department will provide a critical skill.

Advice: What is the source of the candidate's passion for systems work, and why does he or she believe it will hold his or her interest for the long haul? What specific duties or responsibilities in systems design are attractive to the candidate, and what other aspects of systems design offer learning and growth opportunities that will expand the candidate's background and technical acumen?

• • •

11. *Where do you see real opportunity to use management information in a new way in this industry?*

Sample Answer: Except for true acute care, which will stay in the hospitals, the industry will have to have a realistic handle on costs. The primary health care transition will be the capitation model, in which physicians are paid on a per patient basis and have to figure out how to make a profit out of that within an HMO plan. Accounting and finance departments will have to allocate certain dollars to specific specialists and make them operate profitably. Individuals will pay a hospital group, which subcontracts work out to different specialists. Within health care and hospitals specifically, no one can tell exactly what a patient day costs. If you could come up with a realistic model for different patient scenarios, you could really decrease the instances of abuse in the system, ranging from insurance and claims processing to scheduling. The goal is to minimize cost and maximize value.

Advice: Can the candidate think strategically and devise new opportunities for information to be packaged for other departments within the company or within the industry? What, specifically, does the candidate consider new uses for management information systems, and how can these systems hold value over a period of time? What would the short-term versus long-term benefits be for the industry?

• • •

12. *What do you think are critical skills for an information project manager?*

Sample Answer: You have to be able to speak well with MIS management at the client site. You also have to know when to answer questions and when to bring in a specialist. So good problem solving and quick evaluation or diagnostic skills are really important. Technical people aren't necessarily good at some of these things.

Advice: What does the candidate think he or she needs to step up to the next level and manage a project from start to delivery? Look for the candidate to outline what he or she believes separates the followers from the leaders, and to define the skills necessary to manage people and resources while envisioning the outcome of the project and managing the details along the way.

Systems Analyst

 13. *How do you get people to embrace a new software product?*

Sample Answer: I demo it so they can see it hands on. Then I get their ideas about what type of output they will need—reports, data, and so forth. I demonstrate how that will be presented by using sample screens before I actually develop the product. This way I avoid miscommunication.

Advice: What specific techniques does the candidate enjoy using to get others to see the value in a product? How persuasive is the candidate in selling you on the merits of his or her latest product? Does the candidate effectively combine a review of features with functionality and qualitative benefits, such as improved efficiency and productivity? You should assess not only technical expertise here, but also the creative ability to convince others, who may be at a different technical level, of the merits of the product.

• • •

14. *What have you learned about training users after a system implementation?*

Sample Answer: I've learned to get them involved at the front end. For example, getting a user who has just worked on terminals to use a mouse, even with a game of solitaire, is a good way to make the person comfortable with a new machine. That way you avoid information overload, because the user won't be hit with the new software and with learning how to use a mouse at the same time.

Advice: You want to gauge how effective the candidate's methods are for training end users once a product has been implemented. What steps, including documentation, does the candidate believe are necessary to ensure that the user's experience is enhanced by the training and not a waste of time? How does the candidate go about getting the user to "buy into" the product, as opposed to casually accepting it, or worse, totally disregarding the candidate's training efforts?

15. *Describe a new system that was a great success in terms of ease of implementation.*

Sample Answer: At my current company we designed our benefit management software product on the front end, knowing it would be used in divergent businesses. We set up parameters to be table driven, so when doing implementation, our project managers can set up tailored products for different businesses without having to recode the product. So a key to a good product is to have a market niche or vertical market approach so that your project managers know the business; our niche is selling insurance application products. Our document imaging-based operations management product provides customer service and problem resolution for health insurance companies and managed care companies.

Advice: You are trying to determine not only the candidate's ability to build systems that are easy to implement, but also the methodology and approach the candidate takes in building the system from scratch to ensure easy implementation. Does the candidate break down the design phase and testing to ensure that the implementation will go smoothly? How involved are the end users in this process? Does the candidate believe that he or she can bring this methodology or approach to your projects with similar results, and if so, why?

• • •

16. *When you integrate several types of systems, what problems do you typically run into?*

Sample Answer: At my current company we have a client-server product on Intel servers. If customers have a mainframe product we have to interact with, we must write files in a format to pass them back and forth in batch mode. Very little of it is real time. The way we've gotten around that is to use DDE, or dynamic data exchange, links to be able to bring it up into the mainframe Windows environment. That way we avoid entering data into two systems.

Systems Analyst

Advice: Look for the candidate's ability to predict, based on his or her experience, situations that will arise when multiple systems are integrated. This skill goes beyond troubleshooting: can the candidate break a problem down, or at least identify the trouble spots within a system, to start creating a workaround or a solution that will maintain a high level of system performance?

• • •

17. What new technology do you think will be most significant over the next few years?

Sample Answer: The real trend is downsizing and going to client-server products. We still need to run applications on multiple platforms simultaneously. Specifically in the health insurance environment, we need to run historical patient information on mainframes for speed. Although that information is centrally located on the mainframe, many different people, such as specialists in an HMO plan, must be able to access the current patient record and add to it, using a client-server system. Right now, in most organizations, there isn't a central file with a total patient record, so a specialist relies on patient memory. Once multiple platforms access that primary file, the specialist can get a complete picture.

Advice: Encourage the candidate to give you a frank assessment of what technologies and platforms will dominate over the next few years and what impact that will have on your industry. Test the candidate's knowledge and desire to stay abreast of new technologies: Is he or she interested in pursuing these technologies? What benefits does the candidate think will result from using these new tools?

18. *Data security has come into the spotlight more and more. What are your views?*

Sample Answer: It hasn't been a big problem for my current company because insurance companies—the payers—have kept patient records all under one roof. Where it will be significant is in cost capitation, because groups will have to share patient information to control the cost. The number one thing that can make the health care system more effective is the sharing of information, so when someone is referred to a specialist in an HMO structure, that doctor is relying on clinical records and actual lab values rather than sketchy information from the patient. Duplication of tests is also avoided. The way to accomplish all this is to have systems that can talk to each other so specialists and subspecialists can talk to each other. In other words, information must become patient centered as opposed to specialist centered.

Advice: This subject is always sensitive for technical people because of the number of systems that have been prone to weaknesses in data integrity. You need to determine what the candidate thinks are the best options for protecting data, who should have access, and how it should be built into a particular system. Ironclad, failsafe methods don't exist, but the candidate should be aware of security problems that exist in various operating systems and ways to build gatekeepers to avoid data loss.

• • •

19. *When do you believe client-server architecture is better than hierarchical systems?*

Sample Answer: Client-server is lower cost, but you give up security, speed, and data integrity. Hierarchical provides a simple structure to link things together—accounts payable/receivable, financial information, project control, and so on.

Advice: Does the candidate know enough about various information systems requirements in different corporate environments to recommend a particular system implementation that is more appropriate than others? What type of needs analysis is required to determine the type of system that is most beneficial, both from an information standpoint and from the end user's point of view?

• • •

20. As more and more people set up home offices and use notebook computers, how is systems use impacted?

Sample Answer: In my last company our customers were handling the processing of twenty thousand or more documents per day. When the Clean Air Act in New York required people to work at home, data entry of claims at home proliferated using ISDN lines— three-channel phone lines with high bandwidth allowing you to designate point-to-point voice and data communication. In a case like that the employee can be more productive, with less interruption, at home.

Advice: Is the candidate aware of changing workplace trends that necessitate the use of mobile technologies within a corporate management information system? What tools does the candidate believe are most effective in allowing mobile users to work on the road or from home? What sort of training and maintenance are required to make sure users are able to access information quickly and effectively with minimal downtime?

Technical Support Specialist

1. Tell me about your most recent technical support experience.

Sample Answer: At my last company we had eighteen specialists supporting three different products. It was a challenge to get up to speed on each of the products, but I thoroughly enjoy helping customers resolve product problems and eagerly look forward to additional training on new products that we develop so I can continue to provide a high level of service.

Advice: You want to find out what types of daily activities the candidate enjoys, how he or she interacts with other reps, and why technical support is so attractive to the candidate as a career option. If you hear anything that suggests indifference or a less than enthusiastic response to helping customers solve problems, you should probably be concerned. What does the candidate do to impact a company in a positive manner through his or her efforts?

• • •

2. What was your most difficult support experience?

Sample Answer: When I joined my last company, it was introducing a software product on a platform that I wasn't familiar with. It took longer that I thought to learn the product, so I had difficulty for a while handling questions about it. But I found those few days to be a great learning experience, and I believe that being technically challenged like that only served to make me a better specialist.

Advice: You want the candidate to be frank about a support experience in which he or she was less than prepared to deal with the customer's problem. What steps did the candidate take to try to solve the problem, and when did the candidate realize he or she might be dealing with a situation that was, at least temporarily, overwhelming? You want to see how resourceful the candidate is in trying to solve this kind of problem, as well as how creative he or she can be when faced with a challenging technical question.

Technical Support Specialist

3.

What do you believe are the three most important skills that a technical support specialist should possess?

Sample Answer: I believe first and foremost that you have to love helping people solve their problems. If you don't, you're not going to be a good support specialist. Second, I think you need patience to be able to get the customer to articulate his or her problem clearly so that you can make a good decision in helping to solve it. Finally, you have to be part salesperson, because, obviously, the customer is distressed about some problem with the product, and you want to make sure he or she leaves with a good feeling about both the product and the company. The customer needs to believe that it was worth the time it took to make a phone call seeking support.

Advice: You should already have a certain set of skills in mind when you ask this question; then try to get a sense of what the candidate believes makes him or her a top-notch specialist. In the process the candidate should mention not only technical capability but also qualitative skills such as good listening and coaching ability, and the ability to get the customer to outline the problem clearly and see the rationale behind the solution.

• • •

4.

Why do you think people with good communication skills fail as tech support specialists?

Sample Answer: Well, having those skills doesn't necessarily make you a good tech support specialist. You have to be able to think through a problem logically and sequentially, and understand a customer's thought pattern. The job involves more than just listening to a customer yell and scream about the problem; you have to be able to pull apart the problem piece by piece and then put it together to find the solution.

Advice: You want to hear about more than the obvious technical acumen here; you should be looking for the candidate to touch upon areas like an in-depth understanding of the product, aggressiveness in searching for a solution, an ability to pick apart the details, and a tendency to see the "big picture" and how the problem might affect other aspects of product development for the company.

• • •

5. *Why do you think it's important for a company to have an in-house technical support department?*

Sample Answer: As a tech support specialist for my last company, I learned a lot about the products and the company at the same time I was solving customers' problems. Therefore, I could almost act as a sales rep in that I could really trumpet the strengths of the products, and the benefits they could produce for the customer.

Advice: How well does the candidate understand the tech support function within his or her company, and what specific benefits, other than the obvious troubleshooting, can an in-house department bring to the company? Although tech support departments are generally not considered revenue centers for a company, how can tech support help the company grow and expand? You want to see if the candidate is creative enough to think of ways that information gathered through tech support calls can be utilized in other parts of the company.

Technical Support Specialist

6. *What do you think is the most challenging product to support?*

Sample Answer: Probably the most difficult product that I've encountered is one that runs over a computer network, because in that case, you're dealing with different computers, different configurations, and different platforms. Not only do you have to work with the product and try to figure out something that might be wrong with it, but you also have to deal with the network configuration.

Advice: Here you want to gauge the candidate's confidence in his or her technical skills, intelligence, and ability to solve problems. This should be an opportunity for the candidate to demonstrate a real aptitude for problem solving at its highest level.

• • •

7. *At what point do you bring a customer's problem to your boss's attention?*

Sample Answer: I would make every attempt to resolve the problem over the phone with the customer, in the hopes that I could bring it to a satisfactory conclusion. I do realize, however, that a customer may be difficult or obstinate, or will simply refuse to accept what I'm trying to do to help. At that point I know, if there's a resolution in sight, I need to get my manager's assistance to solve the problem.

Advice: You want to test the candidate's judgment on whether and when a problem requires the attention of the department supervisor, as opposed to the candidate's staying with the customer until a satisfactory resolution is achieved. Evaluate the candidate's maturity, problem-solving skills, and ability to recognize when a problem is beyond the scope of his or her ability to resolve it. Does the candidate look for help right away, or is he or she willing to stay with a problem to try to work out a solution?

8. *Have you ever had a situation in which you were unable to resolve a customer's problem?*

Sample Answer: I recall a time when a customer called in with a problem that was so unusual, we hadn't run across it (and we do keep a running log of problems and issues). Rather than say "I give up" or "I don't know," I told the customer that I would make a good-faith attempt to resolve the problem, but I would need to consult with our engineers and get back to the customer within twenty-four hours.

Advice: This is a judgment question for the candidate: Does he or she have the maturity and intelligence to resolve a customer's problem? What does the candidate do to ensure that the customer will not hang up angry or dissatisfied? Some candidates may believe that asking for help is a sign of weakness or technical incompetence rather than of keeping the customer's best interests on the forefront and making sure that a resolution is well within reach.

• • •

9. *Do you ever find yourself burning out from being on the phone so much?*

Sample Answer: I love being on the phone; I really enjoy talking to customers, listening to their concerns, and helping them solve their problems. Phone work to me is really very enjoyable and a great way to help a company support and sell products.

Advice: Expect the candidate to go to great lengths describing how enjoyable it is supporting customers on the phone. Dig a bit deeper, though, and try to get the candidate to describe exactly why he or she thinks being on the phone eight hours a day is a perfect job. Some candidates may try to dodge this question by not disclosing true feelings about phone work, so it's imperative that you watch for signs of hesitation or nervousness in the candidate's response to this question.

Technical Support Specialist

10. What are your goals beyond being a tech support specialist?

Sample Answer: Right now I'm totally focused on improving my technical support skills and helping my company provide top-notch support. Beyond that I would like to continue to grow and develop my career in technical support.

Advice: You want to see how ambitious this candidate is and what he or she wants to do in the short term. Ultimately, you need to find out if the candidate is using this position as a brief stopover to some other position in your company presumably more glamorous or exciting. What is the candidate's commitment to furthering his or her career in technical support, and what steps will he or she take to get there?

• • •

11. Do you feel comfortable sharing information with other tech support specialists?

Sample Answer: At my last company I got a call from a customer who was having problems with a product that I had only recently become familiar with and that another rep in the department had supported before it was assigned to me. I wasn't totally familiar with the product at the time of the call, but I did know a little bit about what was going on. I helped the customer as best as I could, then went to the other tech support specialist to get more information about how to solve the problem. I was able to return the favor a few weeks later when that same tech support person asked me for advice about a customer problem of his own.

Advice: You want to see if the candidate is the type of individual who likes to have personal control over a product and every customer's problem with the product. At what point does the candidate believe it becomes necessary to consult with other representatives to solve a customer problem? You want to make sure you are getting a team player who puts the company first and his or her own personal agenda second.

• • •

 12. *If you got a call from a customer with a problem that you knew you couldn't resolve within thirty seconds, what would you do?*

Sample Answer: I'd be honest with the customer from the start, admitting that I couldn't solve the problem, but I would assure the person that I would make every effort to come up with an answer within twenty-four hours. If I couldn't, I'd refer the customer to an appropriate resource that could provide both immediate assistance and an answer that would be satisfactory to the customer.

Advice: How persistent is the candidate in trying to help a customer, even if he or she knows the answer is not within reach? You should be looking for creative solutions from the candidate, and an ability to think and react quickly to satisfy the customer. How does the candidate turn this situation into a positive for the company?

Technical Support Specialist

13. *If a customer verbally abused you, how would you handle it?*

Sample Answer: I would remain calm and professional at all times, and I'd never let my personal feelings enter into a tech support situation. I wouldn't respond to any abuse; I'd just make a note of it in my log and continue to help the customer as best I could. If the situation continued, I'd politely ask him or her to call back and ask for my manager, because at that point I think it would be pretty clear I could not resolve the problem.

Advice: You want to find out what kind of personality the candidate has and how the candidate handles a stressful situation like a customer losing control on the phone. Can the candidate remain calm and professional, even under such adverse circumstances? What does he or she do to stay on top of the situation, perhaps even turning it around to where the customer sees the candidate's point of view?

THE PYRAMID HIRING TECHNIQUE

You've just created a job description for a new position, and now you face the unenviable task of looking for the best candidate available to fill the position. You dread having to go through the process, How can you make it as fast and effective as possible?

The key is to take a systematic approach. This approach is based on winnowing out weaker candidates as quickly as possible. However, you should take as much time as you need to very carefully weigh the subtle differences between the stronger candidates.

The Pyramid Hiring Technique

The caliber of people who work for your company will arguably have more impact on the sucess of your company than any other factor. The easiest way to create a terrific work force is to hire terrific people in the first place. Although you may never seem to have the time to hire people carefully, we suggest you do whatever it takes, even if you skimp on time spent on your other pressing chores, to make sure you give hiring the effort it deserves.

Receiving Resumes

1. You should start the screening process with a good quantity of candidates. Ideally you should have at least twelve applicants that meet the basic qualifications. Often, when conducting a through search for an important position, you may examine several hundred resumes. The more resumes you start your hiring process with, the better the chance you will have of finding the right candidate for the job.

At this point the hiring process may be thought of as the base of the pyramid because you have more potential candidates now than you will at any other time during the hiring process.

First Resume Sort

2. You should begin sorting through resumes immediately. Sort them from weakest potential to strongest. Your first pass at sorting resumes should be effective but shouldn't take up an inordinate amount of your time.

To proceed successfully through the pyramid hiring process, you need to spend minimal time eliminating weaker candidates and invest more time weighing the subtle differences between stronger candidates.

Completeing the first resume sort places you higher on the pyramid and closer to offering the position to a qualified candidate.

Second Resume Sort

3. Take a second look at your candidates from the first sort. Again, quickly elimate the weak candidates and focus on developing a list of strong candidates.

The "pyramid" hiring process

The Pyramid Hiring Technique

4. *Phoners*

When you call the candidates from your second resume sort, conduct a brief phone interview in order to determine whether or not to arrange an in-person interview.

Phone interviews are great timesavers. You don't have to tell the candidate how long the phone interview will last. If you decide two minutes into the interview that the person isn't suitable for the position, there isn't any need to pretend an interest for some promised time.

Go to the heart of the matter quickly. Even if a salary range was clearly stated in any position advertisements, confirm with candidate that the pay scale is acceptable to him or her. If it isn't, say thank you and good-bye. Neither your time nor the time of the potential candidate has been wasted.

The next set of questions might revolve around any concerns you have about the candidate's qualifications based on his or her resume. If the interview goes well, you could possibly spend an hour or more on the phone with the candidate. If it goes unusually well, invite the candidate in for an interview. If it goes only pretty well, wait until you finish conducting all of your phone interviews before deciding whether or not to see the candidate in person.

5. *In-Person interviews*

In-person interviews are invariably time-consuming. Be cautious about how many candidates you invite in even for first interviews. Three to six candidates is generally a good number. If the position isn't very demanding or doesn't require extensive skills or vast experience, you may be able to select the candidate you will offer the position to from your first in-person interviews. If not, narrow the field down to those few people you'd like to invite in for a second interview.

6. *Additional Interviews*

For most professional positions you will conduct two rounds of interviews. Be even more selective about who gets invited back for a second interview than you were in choosing the candidates for the first in-person interviews. Usually two people make it to the second interview stage. Sometimes only one person is invited for a second interview—the person the job is generally offered to.

Usually it is during the second interviewing round that additional people are called to interview the candidate or candidates. These are often people who would most likely interact closely with the applicant, should he or she be hired.

The Pyramid Hiring Technique

Final Word

7. Remember that you want to spend as little time as possible eliminating the weakest candidates. More time should be expended on discerning the subtle differences between your strong candidates—looking for those special experiences or skills that can make one qualified candidate really stand out from another qualified candidate.

"You want to spend minimal time screening out the weakest candidates and maximum time comparing the more subtle differences between the strongest candidates."

Second interviews

Conduct at least two interviews with a candidate before hiring him or her, especially if the position is very important. Candidates often relax and let their guard down somewhat during a second interview. This will give you a chance to "meet" the real person. It is entirely possible that you will get a different impression of a candidate during a second interview. Sometimes a candidate will even respond differently to the same questions asked at the first interview!

ACCOUNTING MANAGER

Growing auto repair shop seeking top-flight Accountant with aggressive, hands-on accounting management skills including AP/AR. Knowledge of auto repair industry and Quick-books a +. Fax resume and salary requirements to 508

Accountant: Accounts Receivable

National automobile rental agency seeks organized, detail-oriented entry level individual to coordinate accounting for credit card transactions and associated receivables related to business in its busy Hartford aeroplex office. Motivated individual with demonstrated ability to juggle multi-tasks must have BA in accounting. Interested applicants are invited to submit resumes to Car-4-A-Day, 120 Airport Way, West Hartford, CT 06107.

BANK TELLERS
IMMEDIATE OPENINGS!

Immediate openings in all branches of AtlantaBank for experienced Bank Tellers. Growth potential for the motivated. Fax resume to Business Resources at 404-555-6778.

BOOKKEEPING/ ACCOUNTING

Small medical office requires the services of savvy bookkeeping/ accounting professional to oversee financial responsibilities for two busy family practice physicians. Experienced required in receivables, payables, and aggressive, but gracious, bill collections. 5+ years experience necessary with medical office background a definite +. Qualified applicants should fax resume and salary requirements to 514-555-3467.

Computer Technician

Chicago's largest electronic imaging service bureau is expanding rapidly with new branches opening in seven metro locations. Full-time experienced graphics output wiz with hands-on laser printer, digital printer, Iris Imaging, flatbed and drum scanning, Linotronic, Macintosh, and PC troubleshooting capabilities sought immediately to travel locations as required to keep us up and running and number one. Fax resume to 312-555-9999.

CUSTOMER SERVICE REPRESENTATIVE

Residential Interior Decorator pursuing creative individual with an avid interest in home decor to assist interior designers in servicing clientele. A background in design or demonstrated applied arts skills required. If you are also energetic, intuitive, wild about color and texture, eager to learn the trade, and flow with the trends, send us your resume today. TrendSetter Interiors, P.O. Box 950, Miami, FL 03111.

Electrical Engineer

Westerlund Ambitronics is searching for an electrical engineer with ten+ years in the home lighting system design and installation field. Excellent communication skills required to work closely with owners, architects and building contractors, management and marketing skills a definite plus. Excellent salary, company car and great benefits package. Please forward resume and salary expectations to N.K. Westerlund. Westerlund Ambitronics, 151 Razor Back Road, Rutland, Vermont 05701.

EVENT DIRECTOR

Centre Dome North desperately seeking a energetic, organized, multi-talented events coordinator to oversee planning and execution of sports, convention, trade show, fund-raising, and other events held at the dome. Must be able to prepare and target budgets, source and contract vendors, and manage time schedules. Outgoing, diplomatic personality required for close work with clients. Ten years experience corporate or facility events planning experience a must. Business background or education a +. Fax or send resume and salary requirements to Human Resources. Dept. C, Centre Dome North, 1045 Highland Street, Redlands, CA 00000, Fax: 804-555-5566. Equal Opportunity Employer

Field Recruiter

Fast paced personnel placement agency seeks well organized, charismatic communicator with strong networking skills to recruit and place professionals in high level positions at prestigious firms. Travel required. Fax resume to 617-555-8989.

Graphic Designer

Highly creative graphic designer sought to develop business communication, presentation, internet presence, and direct mail pieces for American Crafter's Catalogue Company..We represent internationally recognized artisans and require collateral and multimedia materials that reflect elegance and quality. The ideal candidate will be skilled in QuarkXpress, Director, Photoshop and Illustrator. He or she will have a minimum of five years retail/direct marketing design experience; will be capable of producing CD-ROM and Web Site graphics. If your portfolio is exceptional, your attitude dedicated, your imagination beyond limits—send three non-returnable samples, your resume and salary requirements to ACCC, P.O. Box 45, Charlotte, NC 28201. All submittals will be acknowledged. ACCC is an equal opportunity employer.

IMPORT CLERK

International freight forwarder has immediate opening for Ocean Import Clerk. One year experience required. Full time position with excellent benefits. EOE. Please call 212-555-5656 for appointment.

Legal Secretary

Part time legal secretary sought for busy law firm. Flexible hours—mother's, evenings, weekends OK with potential for full time in the future. Excellent Word Perfect 5.2 skills and experience required. Fax resume to 617-555-8900. EOE. .

LEGAL SECRETARY

Experienced legal secretary sought by Waltham firm. Top pay for top skills and credentials. Mr. Walters 617-555-9350..

Marketing Coordinator

Leading construction management company seeking organized, motivated individual with excellent administrative, interpersonal and communication skills to support marketing management team. Work includes PR implementation, media contact, event and presentation coordination and database management. WP and ACT! required. Writing and design skills a definite plus. Excellent entry position with advancement potential. Degree preferred. Fax resume 518-555-9900.

MARKETING DIRECTOR

West Coast Gourmet Coffee purveyor with chain of trendy coffee bars and catalog mail order service conducting a search for a savvy, proven marketing director to position our company for success along the Northeast Corridor—Maine to Florida. This is a start-up opportunity integrating West Coast marketing resources with your own team development. Your resume must demonstrate extensive knowledge of the gourmet food industry, proven market development and penetration skills and fast track results. If you think you can place our name on the public's palette in six months—you're 'the key player we're looking for. Forward resume in confidence to Dept. G, The Daily Hemisphere, P.O. Box 780, 99 Planet Drive, Portland, OR 97201.

Medical Receptionist/Secretary

Full time medical receptionist/secretary sought for busy four physician office in Troy. Knowledge of managed care procedures, familiarity with national and local medical plans, computer billing using MediBill 3.1, appointment scheduling, and diplomatic, caring attitude all necessary. References required. Salary negotiable dependent upon experience. Benefits. Equal Opportunity Employer. Send resume to 45 East Main Street, Troy, NY 12180.

NURSING SUPERVISOR
Psychiatric Home Care

Home care organization seeks Master's prepared psychiatric nurse with seven years acute experience and a minimum of two years home care experience. Demonstrated management skills required to schedule and oversee activities of ten visiting nurses and associated staff. Must have excellent communication and organizational abilities. Full benefits package. Send resume in confidence to HCS, Department PY, Code 3456, P.O. Box 78, Omaha, NB 68112.

SUNDAY CLASSIFIEDS GET RESULTS!

More regional companies, large and small rely on the Sunday Sphere Classifieds to attract the top candidates for their job openings than any other search vehicle. Searching for the right applicant? Have your query in by Wednesday.

WORKSHOPS
BEFORE INTERVIEWING

INTERVIEWING THE CANDIDATE

AFTER THE INTERVIEW

Very few, if any, of today's managers are thoroughly grounded in the hiring process from start to finish. To help you understand the intricacies of what it means to find and hire top performers, we have divided this chapter into smaller sections that describe various stages of the hiring process. There are three overall sections. The first one covers what you need to do to find and interview the best candidates. The second section discusses what you need to look for in the actual interview to select the best candidate. The last section covers subjects such as checking references, negotiating salary, and making the offer. Although finding and hiring top performers is never easy, these workshops will provide you with valuable tips and suggestions about what you should focus on at each stage of the hiring process.

The Interviewing Process

1. Stages of Interviewing

It is not unusual for a company to have as many as six to eight rounds of interviews with a candidate for a professional position; normally, companies do at least two and sometimes three rounds of interviews before deciding to hire someone. The first interview is the screening interview, during which you ensure that the candidate meets your basic minimum requirements in two categories. The first category includes qualifications, skills, knowledge, and experience, and the second includes personal qualities such as leadership, communication, teamwork, motivation, and style.

The initial interview should be no longer than an hour and no shorter than a half hour. It can be conducted on-site or at a location determined by both parties. After this first interview there should be a decision to reject or to pursue the candidate's qualifications further. In the second interview you want to gather the managers involved for a full or a half day of interviewing. In this interview scenario you determine the suitability of the candidate for the position. It is your responsibility to be thorough and complete in evaluating the candidate's compatibility with your organization and his or her qualifications.

2. Categories/Requirements

You measure the first category—qualifications, skills, knowledge, and experience—with a direct line of questions relating to the resume. This process includes reviewing work samples and transcripts and checking references. The second category, which involves personal qualities such as leadership, communication, teamwork, motivation, and style, is a little more difficult because you must probe, analyze, and assess the responses and come to a conclusion about whether the candidate measures up as a leader, a team player, and a communicator.

Phone Interviews

1. Screening Candidates

Phone interviews are being used more and more as a tool for evaluating candidates prior to bringing them into the company. Many hiring managers do not have the time to spare to clear their schedule for an in-person interview at the first meeting.

2. Setting an Agenda

Before you call a prospective candidate, make sure you have a clear agenda with a series of questions in several areas that you want to cover regarding the candidate's background and interest in your company. As a courtesy to the candidate, you should schedule a time for the phone interview rather than assuming that the candidate can talk to you on the spot. Of course, if the candidate is ready and willing to talk, all the better!

3. Second-Round Interview

Phone interviews can be used for a secondary round of interviews if a key executive is not in the office on the day of the in-person interview. If you schedule a phone interview for the executive, make sure you prepare a set of questions and a summary of what has been determined, so he or she does not cover ground that has been reviewed already by the other hiring managers.

4. Personal Interaction

The biggest disadvantage of a phone interview is the lack of personal contact with the interviewee. You have no way of reading body language, eye contact, and enthusiasm. Especially important is the number of times and the way in which the candidate smiles and reacts physically to your gestures.

Who Should Interview

1. First Interviewer

Ideally, the person who does the screening, or initial, interview is an individual who has held the position you're trying to fill, has been with the company for a minimum of three years, and has moved through that job and now holds a higher position. This person is usually the most qualified to give information about the job, sell the job, and assess whether the candidate has what it takes to do the job.

2. Team Interviewing

For the second round, higher-level managers, including immediate supervisors, should become involved in the process. This round of interviews will be a team effort. It should include recent hires, who have joined the company in the past six months to a year, because they will want to know what it is like to work with the candidate. Virtually everyone has a vote in this process. Anyone who does interview should have received some basic interview training and should have an understanding of state and federal employment laws that govern the use of legal and illegal questions.

Two Interviewers

Just when you think you've been doing pretty well at hiring people, you make a big hiring mistake that, in retrospect, you should have realized in advance. It happens to everyone. Hiring is not a perfect process. It is highly subjective and based on a good deal of soft information. So, whenever possible, have at least one other person carefully interview the final candidates for a position. You may be surprised with a fresh perspective.

Attracting Candidates

1. World Wide Web

More and more often jobs are being found through electronic job banks such as Adams CareerCity, which you can access through the World Wide Web at www.careercity.com. At this time companies may place ads for professional openings at no charge. Call 617-767-8100 for more information, or fax us your classified ad at 617-767-0994.

Electronic job banks such as Adams CareerCity are particularly effective for filling technical and career-oriented professional positions.

2. Newspapers

Regional newspapers are the most traditional way to attract job applicants. Particularly for major metropolitan newspapers, even small ads can be fairly expensive.

3. Trade Publications

In some industries you may want to try a trade publication that targets your industry or a specific niche in that industry.

4. Professional Groups

You may want to try sending a one-page job description to all professional groups and associations you belong to that publish newsletters or regularly post openings either on-line or at the association's headquarters.

5. Networking

Use the phone to network among colleagues in the industry and your peers in competing organizations; ask them for ideas to use when locating candidates for your openings.

Before Interviewing

Inexperienced Interviewers

1. Training Your Interviewers

Inexperienced interviewers can cause problems if they are brought into a high-level interviewing situation. Anyone conducting interviews should have at least a half day of training, including instruction on the equal opportunity employment guidelines and legal and illegal questions.

2. Offering Guidance and Direction

In addition, the interviewer should know the job description inside and out and be able to determine how a candidate will function in the job. Inexperienced interviewers very often do not understand the guts of the job and must be trained or at least offered guidance on what to ask and look for in a job candidate. You do not want to bring an inexperienced interviewer into a situation well into the interview process where he or she must interview a senior manager.

Structured Versus Unstructured Interviews

1. Structured Interview

Structured interviews are those in which you ask the same questions to all of the job candidates, so that you can compare answers later. Structured interviews are used in an attempt to be fair and objective, because results are quantified. With a structured interview the conversation tends to be forced and rigid, and people tend to give responses that are guarded and cautious. As such, the candidate is less likely to reveal much information about him- or herself. The job applicant may think it is important to be conservative and tight-lipped and may not relax and show his or her true character. You want the candidate to talk from the gut and to tell you what he or she believes is important and why the job seems desirable.

Before Interviewing

Unstructured Interview

2. Unstructured interviews are free-flowing conversations with no set agendas or specific list of questions. Within this free-flowing environment you should ask certain of technical questions as well as a couple technical or case questions. The value of an unstructured interview is that you can take it in a direction that flows naturally rather than having to guide the interview. Very often, using this method, you will uncover a number of skills or attributes not apparent on the resume. The disadvantage is that it is more difficult to compare responses when you ask different questions of the candidates.

The Best Choice

3. An interview needs to be as natural as possible. You are looking to reach some form of agreement. The more conversational and the more unstructured the interview, the more likely it is that you will gather quality information about the candidate and make a more informed choice for the position.

Before the Interview

Reviewing Interview Guidelines

1. Review the job description and the classified ad before the interview. Have any information handy that the candidate might ask for, such as a copy of the job description, recruitment brochures, annual reports, 10Ks, marketing literature, and benefits checklists.

Know the time frame for completion of the search: How many candidates will you interview? Are there any internal candidates who qualify for the opening? When is your starting date for this position?

Interview Logistics

2. Make sure you alert other company managers to the possibility that you might ask them to interview the candidate.

Have a few opening questions ready. Also, plan how to open the interview: What initial comments will you use to relax the candidate and get him or her to open up to you?

Decide on the structure of the interview, and have at least five or six points in mind that you want to cover during the interview.

Writing a Job Description

1. Key People

There are three key people who should be involved in writing the job description—the immediate supervisor, the department head, and, depending on the size of your company, a human resources specialist in charge of job classifications.

2. Job Description Content

The job description should be reality based and should focus on educational requirements, work experience, special skills, responsibilities, the reporting manager, objectives (such as sales quotas), compensation, hours (if applicable), and the location where resumes should be sent. You want to write the description to reflect accurately what the candidate will be doing on a day-to-day basis. Do not inflate it so that it looks like a description for a more senior position.

If you have standard job descriptions already prepared, it is important that you include specific information relating to the position and containing a hiring profile of the ideal candidate.

Evaluating Candidates

1. Screening Resumes

Gather as many resumes as possible. At this point you will be doing a rough screening of the applications that were sent in response to advertisements, internal posting systems, or your professional network. Try to be objective and consistent with the job description.

Evaluate education and experience before you proceed to accomplishments and other information that accompanies the resume.

2. Choosing Your Top Ten

You need to whittle the list of candidates to at least ten applicants you want to interview. You may want to conduct a phone screening with several possible candidates in order to determine your strongest three to five applicants and prioritize whom you want to see in person.

3. Comparing and Contrasting

After you prioritize the candidates, look at their backgrounds more closely to note similarities and differences, as well as any supporting material they may have included, like graphic designs, writing samples, product samples, or other relevant material.

Differentiating Similar Candidates

1. Whom Do You Like?

When you are interviewing several candidates who have backgrounds that closely resemble each other, you should explore how comfortable you feel with each candidate. Who do you think will respond to your direction and be the most productive? Assess whether the candidate exhibits enthusiasm and a genuine interest in the people and environment rather than just in the job.

2. Determining Compatibility

Determine the strength of the candidate's interpersonal skills. Will he or she be compatible, in terms of personality and temperament, with your department and company culture? Find out what type of work environment the candidate prefers. Is it consistent with your particular environment?

3. Work Environment

What type of work style does the candidate prefer? Is he or she more comfortable in stressful situations, or in a laid-back environment? Compare the style of the individual with that of your company.

4. Who Stands Out?

Is there anything that one candidate has produced that makes him or her stand out from the other applicants? Even with similar backgrounds, certain candidates may produce particularly eye-catching work, such as unusual brochures or technically challenging products, that indicates strong creative instincts. If necessary, give your finalists a small test that measures their skills or ability to handle a key aspect of the job.

Diversifying the Pool of Applicants

1. Investigating Multiple Sources

To ensure that you attract applicants from different walks of life, you should tap into different sources—such as groups and associations that serve minority candidates, the handicapped, homemakers, midlife career changers, and professionals over the age of forty-five.

Do not overlook technical schools, colleges, and professional institutions that often help identify alumni who represent different minority groups.

2. Association Postings

Most associations publish newsletters, or sponsor events where you can leave your business card and job postings. You can post advertisements in these newsletters or at association offices, announcing an open house at your company or some off-site location.

Posting Job Openings Internally

1. The First Step

The internal posting of job openings should be the first step in the recruitment process. You must notify employees in your company of any potential openings by using a standard job description format that is consistent with other forms of internal written communication.

2. Using E-mail

If your company has an internal e-mail system that is used to announce company events or general information about the organization, you can use this system to post job openings.

Make sure you provide the correct e-mail address of the hiring manager as well as any information required to apply on-line or in person.

3. Accessibility

You must ensure that all employees are encouraged to apply for any positions you post. The postings should be in a location accessible to all employees. You do not want an employee coming up to you, after you fill a position, wondering why he or she wasn't considered, or worse, wondering why he or she did not even know the position was available.

Internal Referral Program

1. Employee Referrals

Internal referral programs have proved to be very successful for companies that have thought through ways to reward employees for referring potential candidates. One of the main reasons to set up a program of this kind is that your employees are the best salespeople for your company. They can promote the benefits of working for your company to their friends or colleagues in the industry. They are also good sources for finding potential candidates to fill your openings.

Gift Ideas

You do not need to offer fancy gifts as rewards—a gift certificate to a nice restaurant or department store will suffice. If you want to be creative, you might offer a weekend getaway to a resort location, or a ski weekend at a popular mountain lodge. If your company is located in a major metropolitan area, think about offering tickets to the theater or a sporting event.

Avoiding Monetary Gifts

Avoid offering a lot of money. Gifts such as $1,000 or more simply encourage employees to refer people, regardless of their qualifications, for the sake of the cash bonus. Greed does not work in this case!

Networking to Find the Right Candidate

Where to Look

Similar to a job candidate who uses networking, you should also use your network to notify contacts that you have an opening and are looking for a particular candidate. Do not hesitate to call friends, family members, and members of your church or community group who might know someone who can help you. Give as many details as you can about the type of person you are looking for, the skills and background necessary to do the job, and the salary.

Focusing Your Networking

Networking, from a hiring manager's perspective, is largely word of mouth. You want to network in circles where you have the best chance of finding the right candidate. Always document how the candidate found you. Make sure you know someone in the network who knows the candidate.

External Versus Internal Candidates

1. Handling Internal Candidates

Internal candidates have to be handled very carefully because there is an underlying assumption that they are valued employees and are considered important to the long-term success of the company. If internal candidates are considered but are not qualified, you must be careful how you inform them of this.

2. Internal Hiring Process

How much do you want to encourage internal candidates to apply for openings? If they are qualified, they should receive first consideration for the opening. You need not go through the traditional screening process with these candidates because they have already established a track record with your company. What you want to consider is how well they meet the qualifications of this new position. Do they want to make the sacrifices necessary to do the job?

3. A Fair and Equal Process

If you decide to hire an outside candidate who is less qualified than an internal candidate, you face a possible legal action at the worst and, at the least, a disgruntled employee who may be valuable to you and may decide to leave, forcing you to go through another hiring process.

To ensure that the process is fair and equal for all potential candidates, get as many managers, including human resources associates, involved in the process at the start. You will avoid potentially embarrassing situations and arrive at the best decision for all concerned.

Interviewing the Candidate

Selling the Candidate on the Job

1. Selling the Candidate

Continually and subtly sell the candidate on the job and the company as you gather information about the candidate. Assessing the candidate's suitability for the job should be an ongoing process as you simultaneously promote the company culture and the dynamics of the job. Reassure the individual that he or she is a valued contender and meets the job requirements as you have outlined them.

2. Encouraging Feedback

Near the end of the interview invite the candidate to give an opinion about whether he or she is suited for the position. Does the applicant see him- or herself blending in easily with your department, and if so, why? If the candidate has some reservations about the company or the job, you should reemphasize, without going overboard, the strong points of the job and the company.

3. Closing Tips

When you close the interview, assure the candidate that he or she is right for the job, even though you can't commit to making an offer at that time. Relocation may also be an issue, so you may have to sell the town or city as well, not just to the candidate but also to his or her family, especially in a dual-career situation.

Dealing with Concerns

1. Building Trust

You must establish enough of a rapport to get the candidate to open up and cordially express his or her thoughts. Work on building trust so that the candidate is willing to reveal any hidden anxieties regarding job responsibilities. For instance, does the candidate fully understand his or her daily routine and job performance expectations? Does the candidate have "quality of life" concerns—in other words, is he or she worried about balancing work with outside commitments?

2. Questions to Ask

Some questions you might want to ask include the following: "What was the most frustrating aspect of your last position?" or "If you could change one aspect of your last job, what would it be?" These and similar questions will help you determine if the candidate has a good understanding of the realities of the job, if his or her concerns are legitimate, and whether he or she is well suited to the job. You should make an effort to draw the candidate out and be sure that you have answered his or her concerns as thoroughly as possible.

Objective Interviewing

1. Relating Questions to the Job

You want to ask questions that are directly related to the job or the company. Avoid personal or emotional issues that have nothing to do with the specific responsibilities of the job. Everything you ask or discuss should be related to the job description.

An effective tool to use to ensure an objective interview is the technique of "patterning"—in other words, you want to ask each candidate a set pattern of questions so you can interpret the results and compare responses among the candidates.

2. Focusing on Company Issues

With respect to the company, you may discuss the work environment only as it pertains to the job—in other words, the day-to-day activities of the job within a plant or office. You may also ask questions that focus on the candidate's understanding of the industry, your company culture, and specific responsibilities.

3. Probing the Candidate's Background

Try to discover the reasons why the candidate left previous jobs, what changes or contributions he or she would have made if given the opportunity, and the pluses or minuses of each job he or she has held. Responses to this type of inquiry will provide a good deal of objective information that should help you make good hiring decisions.

Questions for Different Levels of Hires

1. High-Level Candidates

For high-level positions, such as chief financial officer or vice president of marketing, you want to measure the impact the candidate had on the bottom line of the department he or she worked in. In other words, did the candidate have profit and loss responsibility? Did he or she increase market share, cut costs, or raise sales by some significant amount? How was the candidate's success achieved? Encourage the candidate to give you specific examples that indicate how he or she can contribute in much the same way to your company.

2. Mid-level Candidates

For mid-level hires you want to probe the candidate's effectiveness in increasing productivity within his or her department. Did the candidate show enough initiative to take charge of projects and add to the growth of the department? You are not necessarily looking for quantifiable or even measurable results—just some indication of the candidate's ability to contribute to the growth of the company.

3. Entry-Level Candidates

For entry-level hires your questions should encourage the candidate to discuss his or her experiences in school and to share some accomplishments that have great personal meaning. These accomplishments can be from academia, volunteer work, internships, part-time employment, or summer jobs.

Questions for Different Industries

1. Understanding Your Industry

When you interview candidates who are coming to your company from various industries, make sure you are convinced that each has a good grasp of your field. Does the candidate understand how products or services are purchased and sold? If you are in manufacturing, does the candidate have an understanding of the processes you use to make your products? How familiar is the candidate with recent trends and developments in the field? Does he or she know what your competition is up to?

Probing the Candidate's Strategy

Ask the candidate to talk about his or her job search strategy and to discuss different companies he or she is interviewing with. Make sure the candidate is consistent and realistic as far as job expectations are concerned while pursuing new opportunities in new industries.

Evaluating the Candidate's Technical Ability

You also want to make sure the candidate is knowledgeable about current technologies that you employ in your company. Does he or she belong to an industry association; attend meetings, seminars, or classes; and demonstrate a willingness to learn and improve his or her skills to fit the demands of your industry? Can the candidate adjust and adapt to the pace in your company and be an effective contributor? Make sure you ask for examples of how the candidate believes he or she can make the adjustments necessary to contribute to your organization immediately.

Clarifying the Candidate's Experience

Study the Resume Carefully

Any resume can look flashy and impressive, but you must get to the core of the candidate's accomplishments and evaluate them closely. Make sure the candidate gives examples of what he or she did to contribute to a company's success, and ask for details or steps that illustrate accomplishments. Separate fluff from substance.

Set questions

Although it will take a time investment, you should have a strong list of questions ready before you begin interviewing a candidate. When interviewing multiple candidates for the same position, ask the same questions of each prospect in exactly the same manner. This will allow you to compare candidate responses fairly.

2. Determine Depth of Experience

You must determine whether the candidate has repeated one year of work experience several times, or whether he or she has grown professionally and gradually acquired wisdom and know-how over the years. If the candidate has done the same thing repeatedly over a span of, say, ten years, this demonstrates a lack of growth with no cumulative building of skills and knowledge.

Taking Notes During an Interview

1. Don't Overdo It

Candidates often will ask you if they can take notes during an interview. You, too, should take notes on the candidate's answers as the interview unfolds. Take care not to overdo the note taking, though. If you are furiously trying to capture every word during the interview, the candidate may become guarded or too cautious or, even worse, may give short, nondescript answers. Take only enough notes to enable you to recall significant facts.

2. Avoid Controversial Issues

When you take notes, make sure you jot down only key words or phrases that pertain to the job. Be mindful of equal opportunity employment laws, as anything you write down will become part of an employment file and can be requested in the future by the Equal Opportunity Employment Commission or state agencies. Avoid political discussions or religious references when writing your notes or when asking questions. You may jot down notes in the margin of the candidate's resume, but make sure you have a clean copy to give to other people in the organization who will also be conducting interviews and taking notes. You don't want your notes to bias them unnecessarily one way or the other.

After the Interview

Checking References

1. When to Check

Checking references is usually done at or near the end of the interview process. Too often it is not done well or thoroughly enough. When you have reached the stage in which you are close to making a decision on a candidate, ask him or her to supply up to five references, at least one reference from every job that he or she has held. In addition to professional references, the candidate may offer a reference letter from a former professor or colleague.

References

Be leery of putting too much weight on positive references. Virtually everyone has some positive references. Sometimes people even give positive references for people they have fired because they fear legal action, want to get them off unemployment because their company is indirectly paying for it, or just want to "help out" the candidate.

2. Who Does It

If your company is large enough to have a professional human resources specialist, he or she should do the reference checking. By the final stage, you, the hiring manager, should call at least one reference if you are the direct supervisor.

Reference checking should not be done in writing; you will get little in the way of verification. All you probably will get is name, rank, and serial number. Because of the potential liability, most companies are reluctant to put anything in writing.

3. Checking by Phone

When you call a reference, prepare to spend some time on the phone. Build rapport, and get him or her to feel comfortable with you. Assure the person that everything will be held in the strictest confidence and that you want to make sure you are doing right by the candidate and your company.

Negotiating Salary and Benefits

1. The Candidate's Expectations

Before you extend an offer to a candidate, make sure you have a concrete idea of his or her expectations, in terms of both salary and benefits. Also, is the candidate looking for a bonus structure that is consistent with your company's or department's plan? If you are interviewing for a sales position, keep in mind that the candidate's idea of a commission plan may differ from what you have to offer. It is a good idea to get this out on the table as soon as possible.

2. Being Fair and Reasonable

Lead with an offer that is both fair and reasonable. "Fair and reasonable" in this case means you do not want to get someone too cheaply, or he or she will most likely bolt at the next best offer. You also do not want to overpay and disrupt your salary scale as it exists in your department. The offer should be in a range that makes sense for both you and the candidate.

3. Avoiding Confrontations

If the candidate balks at your offer, hear him or her out. Do not become confrontational or emotional—it is better to listen to the reasons why the candidate feels he or she is worth more than your offer and consider the reasons before passing judgment.

1. Confirming Your Offer

Always negotiate in good faith. Stand by your offer, and confirm it in writing. You may decide to give a time limit as to when the offer expires, but make sure the candidate understands the time limit and knows when he or she must respond to the offer.

Making the Offer

1. How to Make the Offer

The actual offer, whenever extended, should be made in person. If distance is an issue, a phone or videoconferencing offer can substitute.

2. Who Does It?

The ideal person to make the offer is the immediate supervisor. There are occasions, due to company policy, in which a human resources specialist or manager may make the offer. It is important for the immediate supervisor to make the offer because there will likely be some negotiating between the candidate and the supervisor. Negotiating an offer can involve discussing compensation, benefits, starting date, date of first review, relocation, and other such issues. Because the candidate and the immediate supervisor will be working together, they should get used to talking to one another; therefore, it would be more prudent for them to do the negotiating rather than for a human resources associate to negotiate with a potential employee.

3. Preparing the Offer Letter

After extending an offer, prepare an offer letter, make two copies, and send one to the prospective hire. The offer letter should be as brief as possible—no more than a page or a page and a half in length. Include the important facts, such as starting date, job title, compensation, and conditions or expected duties of the position. Benefits should be summarized, and a benefits brochure should be attached. The candidate should be invited to talk to a benefits specialist if he or she has any questions. The time limit on the offer letter can vary. For midlevel executives it will be about two weeks. You should give a maximum deadline for starting work, to allow the candidate ample time to give notice at his or her old job.

ACCOUNTING MANAGER

Growing auto repair shop seeking top-flight Accountant with aggressive, hands-on accounting management skills including AP/AR. Knowledge of auto repair industry and Quick-books a +. Fax resume and salary requirements to 508

Accountant: Accounts Receivable

National automobile rental agency seeks organized, detail-oriented entry level individual to coordinate accounting for credit card transactions and associated receivables related to business in its busy Hartford aeroplex office. Motivated individual with demonstrated ability to juggle multi-tasks must have BA in accounting. Interested applicants are invited to submit resumes to Car-4-A-Day, 120 Airport Way, West Hartford, CT 06107.

BANK TELLERS

IMMEDIATE OPENINGS!

Immediate openings in all branches of AtlantaBank for experienced Bank Tellers. Growth potential for the motivated. Fax resume to Business Resources at 404-555-6778.

BOOKKEEPING/ ACCOUNTING

Small medical office requires the services of savvy bookkeeping/ accounting professional to oversee financial responsibilities for two busy family practice physicians. Experienced required in receivables, payables, and aggressive, but gracious, bill collections. 5+ years experience necessary with medical office background a definite +. Qualified applicants should fax resume and salary requirements to 514-555-3467.

Computer Technician

Chicago's largest electronic imaging service bureau is expanding rapidly with new branches opening in seven metro locations. Full-time experienced graphics output wiz with hands-on laser printer, digital printer, Iris Imaging, flatbed and drum scanning, Linotronic, Macintosh, and PC troubleshooting capabilities sought immediately to travel locations as required to keep us up and running and number one. Fax resume to 312-555-9999.

CUSTOMER SERVICE REPRESENTATIVE

Residential Interior Decorator pursuing creative individual with an avid interest in home decor to assist interior designers in servicing clientele. A background in design or demonstrated applied arts skills required. If you are also energetic, intuitive, wild about color and texture, eager to learn the trade, and flow with the trends, send us your resume today. TrendSetter Interiors, P.O. Box 950, Miami, FL 03111.

Electrical Engineer

Westerlund Ambitronics is searching for an electrical engineer with ten+ years in the home lighting system design and installation field. Excellent communication skills required to work closely with owners, architects and building contractors, management and marketing skills a definite plus. Excellent salary, company car and great benefits package. Please forward resume and salary expectations to N.K. Westerlund, Westerlund Ambitronics, 151 Razor Back Road, Rutland, Vermont 05701.

EVENT DIRECTOR

Centre Dome North desperately seeking a energetic, organized, multi-talented events coordinator to oversee planning and execution of sports, convention, trade show, fund-raising, and other events held at the dome. Must be able to prepare and target budgets, source and contract vendors, and manage time schedules. Outgoing, diplomatic personality required for close work with clients. Ten years experience corporate or facility events planning experience a must. Business background or education a +. Fax or send resume and salary requirements to Human Resources, Dept. C, Centre Dome North, 1045 Highland Street, Redlands, CA 00000. Fax: 804-555-5566. Equal Opportunity Employer

Field Recruiter

Fast paced personnel placement agency seeks well organized, charismatic communicator with strong networking skills to recruit and place professionals in high level positions at prestigious firms. Travel required. Fax resume to 617-555-8989.

Graphic Designer

Highly creative graphic designer sought to develop business communication, presentation, internet presence, and direct mail pieces for American Crafter's Catalogue Company..We represent internationally recognized artisans and require collateral and multimedia materials that reflect elegance and quality. The ideal candidate will be skilled in QuarkXpress, Director, Photoshop and Illustrator. He or she will have a minimum of five years retail/direct marketing design experience; will be capable of producing CD-ROM and Web Site graphics. If your portfolio is exceptional, your attitude dedicated, your imagination beyond limits—send three non-returnable samples, your resume and salary requirements to ACCC, P.O. Box 45, Charlotte, NC 28201. All submittals will be acknowledged. ACCC is an equal opportunity employer.

IMPORT CLERK

International freight forwarder has immediate opening for Ocean Import Clerk. One year experience required. Full time position with excellent benefits. EOE. Please call 212-555-5656 for appointment.

Legal Secretary

Part time legal secretary sought for busy law firm. Flexible hours—mother's, evenings, weekends OK with potential for full time in the future. Excellent Word Perfect 5.2 skills and experience required. Fax resume to 617-555-8900. EOE. .

LEGAL SECRETARY

Experienced legal secretary sought by Waltham firm. Top pay for top skills and credentials. Mr. Walters 617-555-9350..

Marketing Coordinator

Leading construction management company seeking organized, motivated individual with excellent administrative, interpersonal and communication skills to support marketing management team. Work includes PR implementation, media contact, event and presentation coordination and database management. WP and ACT! required. Writing and design skills a definite plus. Excellent entry position with advancement potential. Degree preferred. Fax resume 518-555-9900.

MARKETING DIRECTOR

West Coast Gourmet Coffee purveyor with chain of trendy coffee bars and catalog mail order service conducting a search for a savvy, proven marketing director to position our company for success along the Northeast Corridor—Maine to Florida. This is a start-up opportunity integrating West Coast marketing resources with your own team development. Your resume must demonstrate extensive knowledge of the gourmet food industry, proven market development and penetration skills and fast track results. If you think you can place our name on the public's palette in six months—you're the key player we're looking for. Forward resume in confidence to Dept. G, The Daily Hemisphere, P.O. Box 780, 99 Planet Drive, Portland, OR 97201

Medical Receptionist/Secretary

Full time medical receptionist/secretary sought for busy four physician office in Troy. Knowledge of managed care procedures, familiarity with national and local medical plans, computer billing using Medi-Bill 3.1, appointment scheduling, and diplomatic, caring attitude all necessary. References required. Salary negotiable dependent upon experience. Benefits. Equal Opportunity Employer. Send resume to 45 East Main Street, Troy, NY 12180.

NURSING SUPERVISOR Psychiatric Home Care

Home care organization seeks Master's prepared psychiatric nurse with seven years acute experience and a minimum of two years home care experience. Demonstrated management skills required to schedule and oversee activities of ten visiting nurses and associated staff. Must have excellent communication and organizational abilities. Full benefits package. Send resume in confidence to HCS, Department PY, Code 3456, P.O. Box 78, Omaha, NB 68112.

SUNDAY CLASSIFIEDS GET RESULTS!

More regional companies, large and small rely on the Sunday Sphere Classifieds to attract the top candidates for their job openings than any other search vehicle. Searching for the right applicant? Have your query in by Wednesday.

LEGAL ISSUES

Because the hiring process is so time-consuming, it is often easy for today's managers to overlook the legalities of the hiring process. In this chapter we give you an overview of the federal laws that cover discrimination against job candidates, and list some (but not all) of the questions that are considered illegal and should not be asked at any time during an interview. Remember that by no means is this a complete list of questions, and you need to be aware of the fact that your company can be held liable if even one of your managers asks an illegal question during an interview, with or without your knowledge. This is an extremely critical area of the hiring process and, depending upon where you live, remember that juries, judges, and prosecutors tend to be more sympathetic to workers than to corporations.

Keep Hiring Legal

If you think common sense is a good enough rule of thumb for keeping hiring legal, think again! All hiring managers need to have a basic understanding of the legalities of hiring. And some of the legal issues are probably not as straightforward as you may think. This applies not just to those making a final hiring decision, but to every single person interviewing a job candidate. Although this section addresses the legalities of hiring in general in the United States, remember that every hiring situation has its own unique legal concerns. Futhermore, employment law changes quickly with new court decisions. When in doubt, don't be penny wise and pound foolish— consult with an expert employment attorney before you get into trouble.

In the United States federal law prohibits employers from discriminating against job candidates on the basis of race, color, national origin, religion, sex, physical handicap, or age. In some states or localities additional characteristics, such as sexual orientation, may also be prohibited from entering into the hiring equation.

Although the actual law seems straightforward, court interpretations have more narrowly defined what constitutes discriminatory hiring practices. Even questions that negatively affect a protected class of applicants may be, and often have been, deemed illegal.

As a rule of thumb, job interview questions should focus specifically on the applicant's ability to successfully perform the duties inherent to the position being applied for.

Remember, as a business owner you are responsible for all of the hiring practices of all of your managers. You need to make sure that they understand the law, are careful to write nondiscriminatory help-wanted ads, don't ask illegal questions during the interview, and give full and fair consideration to all candidates.

These questions are examples of the most commonly asked illegal questions. Other questions of the same type may also have been deemed illegal, but because of the broad interpretations of the courts, it would be impossible to list all questions that might be considered illegal.

Just don't ask:

1. Are you married?
Many questions that relate to the sex of the applicant are illegal, including any question about marital status.

2. Do you have children?
It is illegal to ask an applicant any questions about children, primarily because such questions can lead to discrimination against women.

3. How old are you?
It is illegal to ask an applicant his or her age. This law is designed to protect applicants over the age of forty. You may ask the applicant if he or she is over the age of eighteen—if the applicant is not, you may need to know the applicant's age to ascertain the applicability of federal, state, and local child labor laws.

4. Did you graduate from high school or college?
An educational degree should not be a job requirement and should not be asked about in an interview unless the employer can demonstrate that successful performance on this job requires a specific level of education. Otherwise, this requirement and line of questioning can be construed as discriminatory because some minorities have less educational background than nonminorities.

5. Have you ever been arrested?
You should not ask an applicant if he or she has been arrested. You are generally well advised not even to ask about felony convictions, unless such a conviction would be unusually relevant to the position being sought. These questions can be discriminatory, because some minority groups have, on average, higher records of arrest and convictions than nonminorities.

6. How much do you weigh?

All questions about physical appearance are illegal because they tend to discriminate against women and some minorities.

7. What country are you from?

This question is clearly illegal because it discriminates on the basis of national origin.

8. Are you a U.S. citizen?

This question is illegal because it may be used to discriminate against people who have legally immigrated to the United States but have not become citizens.

9. What is your native language?

This question discriminates on the basis of national origin.

10. Are you handicapped?

You cannot ask about an individual's possible handicaps. Furthermore, employers are generally required to make special accommodations for physically challenged applicants.

Procedures

1. Help-wanted ads

Advertising for job openings must be clearly nondiscriminatory. For example, an ad reading "Strong warehouseman able to lift one-hundred-pound boxes all day long" is blatantly discriminatory against women who may be able to carry out the warehousing function described. An ad that reads "College students sought for summer house painting work" is illegal because there is no reason why a person needs to be a college student to paint a house.

2. Keeping records

You must keep applications for all positions on file for a period of one year if you have solicited these applications. You should also keep records of the criteria you used to select candidates and the reason why rejected candidates were not offered the position.

ACCOUNTING MANAGER

Growing auto repair shop seeking top-flight Accountant with aggressive, hands-on accounting management skills including AP/AR. Knowledge of auto repair industry and Quick-books a +. Fax resume and salary requirements to 508

Accountant: Accounts Receivable

National automobile rental agency seeks organized, detail-oriented entry level individual to coordinate accounting for credit card transactions and associated receivables related to business in its busy Hartford aeroplex office. Motivated individual with demonstrated ability to juggle multi-tasks must have BA in accounting. Interested applicants are invited to submit resumes to Car-4-A-Day, 120 Airport Way, West Hartford, CT 06107.

BANK TELLERS

IMMEDIATE OPENINGS!

Immediate openings in all branches of AtlantaBank for experienced Bank Tellers. Growth potential for the motivated. Fax resume to Business Resources at 404-555-6778.

BOOKKEEPING/ ACCOUNTING

Small medical office requires the services of savvy bookkeeping/ accounting professional to oversee financial responsibilities for two busy family practice physicians. Experienced required in receivables, payables, and aggressive, but gracious, bill collections. 5+ years experience necessary with medical office background a definite +. Qualified applicants should fax resume and salary requirements to 514-555-3467.

Computer Technician

Chicago's largest electronic imaging service bureau is expanding rapidly with new branches opening in seven metro locations. Full-time experienced graphics output wiz with hands-on laser printer, digital printer, Iris Imaging, flatbed and drum scanning, Linotronic, Macintosh, and PC troubleshooting capabilities sought immediately to travel locations as required to keep us up and running and number one. Fax resume to 312-555-9999.

CUSTOMER SERVICE REPRESENTATIVE

Residential Interior Decorator pursuing creative individual with an avid interest in home decor to assist interior designers in servicing clientele. A background in design or demonstrated applied arts skills required. If you are also energetic, intuitive, wild about color and texture, eager to learn the trade, and flow with the trends, send us your resume today. TrendSetter Interiors, P.O. Box 950, Miami, FL 03111.

Electrical Engineer

Westerlund Ambitronics is searching for an electrical engineer with ten+ years in the home lighting system design and installation field. Excellent communication skills required to work closely with owners, architects and building contractors. management and marketing skills a definite plus. Excellent salary, company car and great benefits package. Please forward resume and salary expectations to N.K. Westerlund, Westerlund Ambitronics, 151 Razor Back Road, Rutland, Vermont 05701.

EVENT DIRECTOR

Centre Dome North desperately seeking a energetic, organized, multi-talented events coordinator to oversee planning and execution of sports, convention, trade show, fund-raising, and other events held at the dome. Must be able to prepare and target budgets, source and contract vendors, and manage time schedules. Outgoing, diplomatic personality required for close work with clients. Ten years experience corporate or facility events planning experience a must. Business background or education a +. Fax or send resume and salary requirements to Human Resources, Dept. C, Centre Dome North, 1045 Highland Street, Redlands, CA 00000, Fax: 804-555-5566. Equal Opportunity Employer

Field Recruiter

Fast paced personnel placement agency seeks well organized, charismatic communicator with strong networking skills to recruit and place professionals in high level positions at prestigious firms. Travel required. Fax resume to 617-555-8989.

Graphic Designer

Highly creative graphic designer sought to develop business communication, presentation, internet presence, and direct mail pieces for American Crafter's Catalogue Company..We represent internationally recognized artisans and require collateral and multimedia materials that reflect elegance and quality. The ideal candidate will be skilled in QuarkXpress, Director, Photoshop and Illustrator. He or she will have a minimum of five years retail/direct marketing design experience; will be capable of producing CD-ROM and Web Site graphics. If your portfolio is exceptional, your attitude dedicated, your imagination beyond limits—send three non-returnable samples, your resume and salary requirements to ACCC, P.O. Box 45, Charlotte, NC 28201. All submittals will be acknowledged. ACCC is an equal opportunity employer.

IMPORT CLERK

International freight forwarder has immediate opening for Ocean Import Clerk. One year experience required. Full time position with excellent benefits. EOE. Please call 212-555-5656 for appointment.

Legal Secretary

Part time legal secretary sought for busy law firm. Flexible hours— mother's, evenings, weekends OK with potential for full time in the future. Excellent Word Perfect 5.2 skills and experience required. Fax resume to 617-555-8900. EOE. .

LEGAL SECRETARY

Experienced legal secretary sought by Waltham firm. Top pay for top skills and credentials. Mr. Walters 617-555-9350..

Marketing Coordinator

Leading construction management company seeking organized, motivated individual with excellent administrative, interpersonal and communication skills to support marketing management team. Work includes PR implementation, media contact, event and presentation coordination and database management. WP and ACT! required. Writing and design skills a definite plus. Excellent entry position with advancement potential. Degree preferred. Fax resume 518-555-9900.

MARKETING DIRECTOR

West Coast Gourmet Coffee purveyor with chain of trendy coffee bars and catalog mail order service conducting a search for a savvy, proven marketing director to position our company for success along the Northeast Corridor—Maine to Florida. This is a start-up opportunity integrating West Coast marketing resources with your own team development. Your resume must demonstrate extensive knowledge of the gourmet food industry, proven market development and penetration skills and fast track results. If you think you can place our name on the public's palette in six months—you're the key player we're looking for. Forward resume in confidence to Dept. G, The Daily Hemisphere, P.O. Box 780, 99 Planet Drive, Portland, OR 97201

Medical Receptionist/Secretary

Full time medical receptionist/secretary sought for busy four physician office in Troy. Knowledge of managed care procedures, familiarity with national and local medical plans, computer billing using Medi-Bill 3.1, appointment scheduling, and diplomatic, caring attitude all necessary. References required. Salary negotiable dependent upon experience. Benefits. Equal Opportunity Employer. Send resume to 45 East Main Street, Troy, NY 12180.

NURSING SUPERVISOR Psychiatric Home Care

Home care organization seeks Master's prepared psychiatric nurse with seven years acute experience and a minimum of two years home care experience. Demonstrated management skills required to schedule and oversee activities of ten visiting nurses and associated staff. Must have excellent communication and organizational abilities. Full benefits package. Send resume in confidence to HCS, Department PY, Code 3456, P.O. Box 78, Omaha, NB 68112.

SUNDAY CLASSIFIEDS GET RESULTS!

More regional companies, large and small rely on the Sunday Sphere Classifieds to attract the top candidates for their job openings than any other search vehicle. Searching for the right applicant? Have your query in by Wednesday.

CREATING JOB ADS FOR NEWSPAPERS AND ONLINE SERVICES

One aspect of the hiring process that managers sometimes take for granted is placing a help-wanted classified ad. In Chapter 5 we discussed various avenues that hiring managers can pursue to post openings and attract qualified applicants. Here we will focus on two popular forms of classified advertising—newspapers and on-line. We'll give you an easy format with a step-by-step approach to creating on-line and newspaper ads for any type of professional opening. For purposes of illustration we will use Adams Media's Web site (www.careercity.com) as a source for posting on-line job advertisements.

Newspaper Classified Advertisement

*B*uilding a newspaper classified job ad is relatively straightforward once you establish the number of categories you want to use for the ad.

Start with a very specific job title, include the industry classification or business, a brief job description specifying duties and responsibilities as you understand them, the years of experience you are looking for in the ideal candidate, and the degree or licenses required. The bottom of the ad should include company contact information and specify an individual who is responsible for collecting the resumes. You may want to list a company phone, fax, or e-mail address if you wish applicants to contact you directly at any point during the hiring process.

Following is an example of a completed newspaper help-wanted advertisement.

Newspaper Classified Advertisement

① Job title is important
A job title alone can produce responses. Choose one that reflects the most important overall responsibility of the position.

② Be specific
Avoid generalizations when you create classified job advertisements, or you may attract resumes that don't match your hiring needs.

③ Key job requirements
Focus on two or three key responsibilities and summarize them in one short sentence.

④ Concise background
Knowledge, skill, and experience requirements should be carefully thought out and conveyed precisely to discourage unqualified applicants from applying.

⑤ Use bullets
If you have a sizable list of responsibilities or background requirements, use bullets to make your job description easier to read. Bullets can also make your classified ad more noticeable.

⑥ Use words sparingly
Be concise. Ads can cost a lot of money. They should contain no more than three short sentences, including the company name, address, and fax number.

⑦ Include company contact information
The end of the ad should include the information necessary for the candidate to make contact with you—whether to a department or specific person; whether by mail, phone, fax, or e-mail.

OFFICE MANAGER ◄ ①

Consulting Firm seeks Office Manager to manage accounting, inventory, and purchasing support. ◄ ③
Good salary and potential in rapidly growing company. Send resume to: HSS, 289 Spring Road, First Floor, Parkton, MD 44925

DESKTOP PUBLISHING

Moonscape Design, Inc. has a full-time opening in their Graphic Communications Department. ◄ ②
Experience required in
- Windows & DOS
- QuarkXpress
- Ventura Publisher ◄ ⑤
- Corel Draw
- F3 ProDesigner
- Business forms
- Complex paste-ups

Great benefits. Send resume and salary requirements to RS34 Lemon Lane, Fogtown, VT 02222

MANUFACTURING ENGINEER

CaveTronics has an opening for a hands-on, methodical individual to design and modify manufacturing processes and tooling for sub-sea-level shop. Two to four years manufacturing engineering and electronics experience required. ◄ ④
Mail resume to : CaveTronics, 601 Underhill Way, Thornrock, NM 12345

⑦

Creating an on-line ad is not much different from creating a newspaper classified ad, with a few exceptions.

You'll first want to include the date when the ad was posted for the benefit of users scrolling through a list of on-line job postings. You should make sure to include a job title, the state where the job is located, whether the position is full-time or part-time, and a brief description with qualifications and benefits.

You may also want to include a miscellaneous section for information that would not ordinarily fall into the other categories but that you feel would help potential job seekers applying for the position.

The rest of the ad should encompass the standard information found in job classifieds: namely, a degree, if required; salary (optional); location; the date you want the candidate to start; and the closing date for resumes to be submitted to the company.

Here is an example of a finished on-line ad.

J o b s

EMERSON CONSULTING (CA)

Posted on; 11/31/96
When responding to this post, please include Job Code: CCity 4346094

Job Title: PROJECT ASSISTANT FINANCIAL CONTROLLER

Job Location: San Diego, CA

Job Description: Emerson Consulting, a leading global management and technology organization, is seeking professionals with experience in a variety of technical roles to join our outsourcing practice. The following position is based in the San Diego, California area and requires no travel. Duties include tracking project financials, processing payables, and preparing project budgets and status reports.

Qualifications: Requires college degree in Finance or Accounting and 2+ years in project-based accounting or related experience. Must have solid analytical and organizational skills, as well as proficiency with personal computers and Lotus. Consideration is also given to candidates with skills in Client/Server security, e-mail administration, configuration management, asset management, service-level management, and software distribution. Also requires strong analytical/problem-solving skills and solid organization and documentation abilities.

Benefits: We offer a salary commensurate with experience and excellent benefits.
Miscellaneous: For more information, please visit our Web site at http://www.emerson.com. Emerson Consulting is an Equal Opportunity Employer.

When contacting this company, please mention that you saw this listing on CareerCity. Invest in your job hunt with
Adams JobBankTM Fast Resume Suite Software.

{ Job Search Engine } { Home }

*T*he Adams Media World Wide Web site (www.careercity.com) offers employers the opportunity to upload their job listings to attract qualified applicants.

The site includes up-to-date career information along with an area for employers to post job listings. As of the publication date of this book, you can post an unlimited number of listings free of charge and tell us how long you want the listings to appear on our site. All job listings once received will be posted in two business days. Employers can now search our growing resume database. The site will also include mailing information for over twenty thousand companies found in our Adams JobBank™ Fast Resume Suite™.

You can post listings on our Web site quickly and easily by one of a couple of methods. You can buy our CD-ROM package, Hiring Top Performers, and use the software to connect to our site. (We have included a Web browser if you don't have one currently installed on your computer.) Once on our site, you will find information leading you to the section of the site where you can place your listings.

Or, if you prefer, you can use the Adbuilder module in our software to create an on-line ad as a text file, which you can then attach to an e-mail message and send to us at the following address: **jobs@careercity.com.**

Regardless of which method you choose, you can always use your favorite e-mail program to send job listings to us at any time via the Internet at **jobs@careercity.com**. By using CareerCity as a method of attracting applicants, you will be tapping into a broad yet highly qualified pool of candidates from many different industries, backgrounds, and disciplines. If you follow our on-line format for placing job postings, you will find that the candidates who respond to your posting will more than meet your minimum requirements for that opening.

www.careercity.com

FREE JOB LISTINGS ON THE WORLD WIDE WEB

CALL (617) 767-8100, EXT. 324

Yes, you read that right!

Direct employers can post unlimited professional job listings at no charge on CareerCity.

(While there is no charge at the time this book went to press, this policy is subject to change and is not applicable to employment agencies. Only Equal Opportunity Employers may post listings.)

http://www.careercity.com

A bit about us:

Adams Media Corporation is the leader in the career guide publishing field. We have dominated best-seller lists for more than ten years and are now working to create synergies between our successful books and new cutting-edge technologies. Our Web site, CareerCity, is a complete job-hunting web site, containing a diverse amount of career information. It is one of the newest ways for us to help you target the professional talent you need.

Here are the facts:

1. E-mail us through the Internet at jobs@careercity.com, or send us a Windows or Macintosh disk.
2. When a position is filled, just call us at (617) 767-8100, ext. 224 or e-mail us at jobs@careercity.com and we will remove your listing for you.
3. Any position can be advertised that is a professional position.
4. Your listings will stay on the service for as long as the position is open.

Details, Details, Details:

1. Job listings are unlimited.
2. The following should be included, in this order: Date of posting, job title, company address, job code, contact name, contact's phone number, contact's fax number, contact's e-mail address, position description, qualifications required, benefits information, status (full-time/part-time), salary, location, job category (computer; finance/accounting/consulting; general; management; medical/health care; office/administration; sales/marketing/PR; education/social work; and technical noncomputer), starting date for position, and closing date for resumes.

ADAMS MEDIA CORPORATION
260 CENTER STREET
HOLBROOK, MA 02343
TEL: (617)767-8100, EXT. 324

ACCOUNTING MANAGER

Growing auto repair shop seeking top-flight Accountant with aggressive, hands-on accounting management skills including AP/AR. Knowledge of auto repair industry and Quick-books a +. Fax resume and salary requirements to 508

Accountant: Accounts Receivable

National automobile rental agency seeks organized, detail-oriented entry level individual to coordinate accounting for credit card transactions and associated receivables related to business in its busy Hartford aeroplex office. Motivated individual with demonstrated ability to juggle multi-tasks must have BA in accounting. Interested applicants are invited to submit resumes to Car-4-A-Day, 120 Airport Way, West Hartford, CT 06107.

BANK TELLERS

IMMEDIATE OPENINGS!

Immediate openings in all branches of AtlantaBank for experienced Bank Tellers. Growth potential. for the motivated. Fax resume to Business Resources at 404-555-6778.

BOOKKEEPING/ ACCOUNTING

Small medical office requires the services of savvy bookkeeping/ accounting professional to oversee financial responsibilities for two busy family practice physicians. Experienced required in receivables, payables, and aggressive, but gracious, bill collections. 5+ years experience necessary with medical office background a definite +. Qualified applicants should fax resume and salary requirements to 514-555-3467.

Computer Technician

Chicago's largest electronic imaging service bureau is expanding rapidly with new branches opening in seven metro locations. Full-time experienced graphics output wiz with hands-on laser printer, digital printer, Iris Imaging, flatbed and drum scanning, Linotronic, Macintosh, and PC troubleshooting capabilities sought immediately to travel locations as required to keep us up and running and number one. Fax resume to 312-555-9999.

CUSTOMER SERVICE REPRESENTATIVE

Residential Interior Decorator pursuing creative individual with an avid interest in home decor to assist interior designers in servicing clientele. A background in design or demonstrated applied arts skills required. If you are also energetic, intuitive, wild about color and texture, eager to learn the trade, and flow with the trends, send us your resume today. TrendSetter Interiors, P.O. Box 950, Miami, FL 03111.

Electrical Engineer

Westerlund Ambitronics is searching for an electrical engineer with ten+ years in the home lighting system design and installation field. Excellent communication skills required to work closely with owners, architects and building contractors. management and marketing skills a definite plus. Excellent salary, company car and great benefits package. Please forward resume and salary expectations to N.K. Westerlund, Westerlund Ambitronics, 151 Razor Back Road, Rutland, Vermont 05701.

EVENT DIRECTOR

Centre Dome North desperately seeking a energetic, organized, multi-talented events coordinator to oversee planning and execution of sports, convention, trade show, fund-raising, and other events held at the dome. Must be able to prepare and target budgets, source and contract vendors, and manage time schedules. Outgoing, diplomatic personality required for close work with clients. Ten years experience corporate or facility events planning experience a must. Business background or education a +. Fax or send resume and salary requirements to Human Resources, Dept. C, Centre Dome North, 1045 Highland Street, Redlands, CA 00000, Fax: 804-555-5566. Equal Opportunity Employer

Field Recruiter

Fast paced personnel placement agency seeks well organized, charismatic communicator with strong networking skills to recruit and place professionals in high level positions at prestigious firms. Travel required. Fax resume to 617-555-8989.

Graphic Designer

Highly creative graphic designer sought to develop business communication, presentation, internet presence, and direct mail pieces for American Crafter's Catalogue Company..We represent internationally recognized artisans and require collateral and multimedia materials that reflect elegance and quality. The ideal candidate will be skilled in QuarkXpress, Director, Photoshop and Illustrator. He or she will have a minimum of five years retail/direct marketing design experience; will be capable of producing CD-ROM and Web Site graphics. If your portfolio is exceptional, your attitude dedicated, your imagination beyond limits—send three non-returnable samples, your resume and salary requirements to ACCC, P.O. Box 45, Charlotte, NC 28201. All submittals will be acknowledged. ACCC is an equal opportunity employer.

IMPORT CLERK

International freight forwarder has immediate opening for Ocean Import Clerk. One year experience required. Full time position with excellent benefits. EOE. Please call 212-555-5656 for appointment.

Legal Secretary

Part time legal secretary sought for busy law firm. Flexible hours—mother's, evenings, weekends OK with potential for full time in the future. Excellent Word Perfect 5.2 skills and experience required. Fax resume to 617-555-8900. EOE. .

LEGAL SECRETARY

Experienced legal secretary sought by Waltham firm. Top pay for top skills and credentials. Mr. Walters 617-555-9350..

Marketing Coordinator

Leading construction management company seeking organized, motivated individual with excellent administrative, interpersonal and communication skills to support marketing management team. Work includes PR implementation, media contact, event and presentation coordination and database management. WP and ACT! required. Writing and design skills a definite plus. Excellent entry position with advancement potential. Degree preferred. Fax resume 518-555-9900.

MARKETING DIRECTOR

West Coast Gourmet Coffee purveyor with chain of trendy coffee bars and catalog mail order service conducting a search for a savvy, proven marketing director to position our company for success along the Northeast Corridor—Maine to Florida. This is a start-up opportunity integrating West Coast marketing resources with your own team development. Your resume must demonstrate extensive knowledge of the gourmet food industry, proven market development and penetration skills and fast track results. If you think you can place our name on the public's palette in six months—you're the key player we're looking for. Forward resume in confidence to Dept. G, The Daily Hemisphere, P.O. Box 780, 99 Planet Drive, Portland, OR 97201

Medical Receptionist/Secretary

Full time medical receptionist/secretary sought for busy four physician office in Troy. Knowledge of managed care procedures, familiarity with national and local medical plans, computer billing using Medi-Bill 3.1, appointment scheduling, and diplomatic, caring attitude all necessary. References required. Salary negotiable dependent upon experience. Benefits. Equal Opportunity Employer. Send resume to 45 East Main Street, Troy, NY 12180.

NURSING SUPERVISOR Psychiatric Home Care

Home care organization seeks Master's prepared psychiatric nurse with seven years acute experience and a minimum of two years home care experience. Demonstrated management skills required to schedule and oversee activities of ten visiting nurses and associated staff. Must have excellent communication and organizational abilities. Full benefits package. Send resume in confidence to HCS, Department PY, Code 3456, P.O. Box 78, Omaha, NB 68112.

SUNDAY CLASSIFIEDS GET RESULTS!

More regional companies, large and small rely on the Sunday Sphere Classifieds to attract the top candidates for their job openings than any other search vehicle. Searching for the right applicant? Have your query in by Wednesday.

Rejection Letter

Rejection Letter, Without an Interview

XYZ Corporation • 345 Sidewinder Place • Suite 431 • Boise, Idaho, 87554

January 4, 1997

Ms. Jane Smith
345 Holly Lane
Anywhere, USA

Dear Jane:

Thank you very much for your interest and application to XYZ Corporation for the position of Account Manager.

After carefully reviewing your credentials, we are unable to find a suitable match between your background and experience and openings at our company.

We wish you luck in your search and, again, thank you for your interest in XYZ Corporation.

Regards,

John Doe

John Doe
Human Resources Manager

Rejection Letter, After an Interview

XYZ Corporation • 345 Sidewinder Place • Suite 431 • Boise, Idaho, 87554

January 4, 1997

Ms. Jane Smith
345 Holly Lane
Anywhere, USA

Dear Jane:

Thank you very much for your interest and application to XYZ Corporation for the position of Account Manager.

Although your background and credentials are impressive, we have decided to pursue another direction and therefore cannot offer you employment at this time. We will keep your resume in our active file for a period of one year.

Thank you again for your interest in XYZ Corporation.

Sincerely,

John Doe

John Doe
Human Resources Manager

LETTERS 8

*D*epending upon where you are in the hiring process, you will need to contact your candidates either by phone or, in most cases, by mail. The letters in this section cover everything from responding to a potential candidate's inquiry about job openings, to a job offer letter. Remember that in some cases these letters are going to job applicants who have had no previous contact with the company, so the language in these letters reflects a polite but concise style that avoids any misleading inferences about possible employment.

Job Offer Letter

XYZ • **XYZ Corporation** • 345 Sidewinder Place • Suite 431 • Boise, Idaho, 87554

January 4, 1997

Mr. John Smith
123 Anywhere Lane
Boise, Idaho, 87554

Dear Mr. Smith:

We hereby extend to you an offer of full-time employment as a Senior Project Manager here at the XYZ Corporation. Your first date of employment will be February 1.

Your compensation will be $2,543.67 payable every two weeks in arrears. Paychecks are distributed on alternate Thursdays for the two-week period ending on the preceding Sunday.

Your first salary review will take place on January 1, 19xx. Pay increases are based on merit as well as on the financial situation of the company at the time of the performance review.

The first ninety days of your employment will be regarded as an initial employment period. After successful completion of this period, you will be eligible for sick days, which accrue at the rate of 1 half day per month.

The company offers medical insurance, group life insurance, short- and long-term disability, as well as two weeks paid vacation per year. You will be eligible for the company's 401k plan and bonus plan after you complete your initial period of employment.

Please sign and return this agreement. This offer will remain in force for a period not to exceed fourteen days.

John Smith   John Smith

Jane Jones   Jane Jones
                      Human Resources Manager

Resume Received

Resume Received, No Openings

XYZ Corporation • 345 Sidewinder Place • Suite 431 • Boise, Idaho, 87554

January 4, 1997

Mr. Chris Smith
123 Hollybrook Lane
Anywhere, USA

Dear Mr. Smith:

Thank you for forwarding your resume and your interest in XYZ Corporation.

At this time we have no openings that match your background and experience, but we will keep your resume in our active file for a period of one year and contact you should a position open up that is a suitable match for your qualifications.

Again, thank you for your interest in XYZ Corporation.

Regards,

John Doe

John Doe
Human Resources Manager

Resume Received, Will Be Considered

XYZ Corporation • 345 Sidewinder Place • Suite 431 • Boise, Idaho, 87554

January 4, 1997

Mr. Chris Smith
123 Hollybrook Lane
Anywhere, USA

Dear Mr. Smith:

Thank you for submitting your resume to XYZ Corporation.

We are currently reviewing your resume to see if there is a match between your background and our current openings. If a suitable match is found, we will contact you as soon as possible.

Again, thank you for your interest in XYZ Corporation.

Regards,

John Doe

John Doe
Human Resources Manager

ACCOUNTING MANAGER

Growing auto repair shop seeking top-flight Accountant with aggressive. hands-on accounting management skills including AP/AR. Knowledge of auto repair industry and Quick-books a +. Fax resume and salary requirements to 508

Accountant: Accounts Receivable

National automobile rental agency seeks organized, detail-oriented entry level individual to coordinate accounting for credit card transactions and associated receivables related to business in its busy Hartford aeroplex office. Motivated individual with demonstrated ability to juggle multi-tasks must have BA in accounting. Interested applicants are invited to submit resumes to Car-4-A-Day, 120 Airport Way, West Hartford, CT 06107.

BANK TELLERS

IMMEDIATE OPENINGS!

Immediate openings in all branches of AtlantaBank for experienced Bank Tellers. Growth potential. for the motivated. Fax resume to Business Resources at 404-555-6778.

BOOKKEEPING/ ACCOUNTING

Small medical office requires the services of savvy bookkeeping/ accounting professional to oversee financial responsibilities for two busy family practice physicians. Experienced required in receivables, payables, and aggressive, but gracious, bill collections. 5+ years experience necessary with medical office background a definite +. Qualified applicants should fax resume and salary requirements to 514-555-3467.

Computer Technician

Chicago's largest electronic imaging service bureau is expanding rapidly with new branches opening in seven metro locations. Full-time experienced graphics output wiz with hands-on laser printer, digital printer, Iris Imaging, flatbed and drum scanning, Linotronic, Macintosh, and PC troubleshooting capabilities sought immediately to travel locations as required to keep us up and running and number one. Fax resume to 312-555-9999.

CUSTOMER SERVICE REPRESENTATIVE

Residential Interior Decorator pursuing creative individual with an avid interest in home decor to assist interior designers in servicing clientele. A background in design or demonstrated applied arts skills required. If you are also energetic, intuitive, wild about color and texture, eager to learn the trade, and flow with the trends, send us your resume today. TrendSetter Interiors, P.O. Box 950, Miami, FL 03111.

Electrical Engineer

Westerlund Ambitronics is searching for an electrical engineer with ten+ years in the home lighting system design and installation field. Excellent communication skills required to work closely with owners, architects and building contractors. management and marketing skills a definite plus. Excellent salary, company car and great benefits package. Please forward resume and salary expectations to N.K. Westerlund, Westerlund Ambitronics, 151 Razor Back Road, Rutland, Vermont 05701.

EVENT DIRECTOR

Centre Dome North desperately seeking a energetic, organized, multi-talented events coordinator to oversee planning and execution of sports, convention, trade show, fund-raising, and other events held at the dome. Must be able to prepare and target budgets, source and contract vendors, and manage time schedules. Outgoing, diplomatic personality required for close work with clients. Ten years experience corporate or facility events planning experience a must. Business background or education a +. Fax or send resume and salary requirements to Human Resources, Dept. C, Centre Dome North, 1045 Highland Street, Redlands. CA 00000, Fax: 804-555-5566. Equal Opportunity Employer

Field Recruiter

Fast paced personnel placement agency seeks well organized, charismatic communicator with strong networking skills to recruit and place professionals in high level positions at prestigious firms. Travel required. Fax resume to 617-555-8989.

Graphic Designer

Highly creative graphic designer sought to develop business communication, presentation, internet presence, and direct mail pieces for American Crafter's Catalogue Company..We represent internationally recognized artisans and require collateral and multimedia materials that reflect elegance and quality. The ideal candidate will be skilled in QuarkXpress, Director, Photoshop and Illustrator. He or she will have a minimum of five years retail/direct marketing design experience; will be capable of producing CD-ROM and Web Site graphics. If your portfolio is exceptional, your attitude dedicated, your imagination beyond limits—send three non-returnable samples, your resume and salary requirements to ACCC, P.O. Box 45, Charlotte, NC 28201. All submittals will be acknowledged. ACCC is an equal opportunity employer.

IMPORT CLERK

International freight forwarder has immediate opening for Ocean Import Clerk. One year experience required. Full time position with excellent benefits. EOE. Please call 212-555-5656 for appointment.

Legal Secretary

Part time legal secretary sought for busy law firm. Flexible hours—mother's, evenings, weekends OK with potential for full time in the future. Excellent Word Perfect 5.2 skills and experience required. Fax resume to 617-555-8900. EOE. .

LEGAL SECRETARY

Experienced legal secretary sought by Waltham firm. Top pay for top skills and credentials. Mr. Walters 617-555-9350..

Marketing Coordinator

Leading construction management company seeking organized, motivated individual with excellent administrative, interpersonal and communication skills to support marketing management team. Work includes PR implementation, media contact, event and presentation coordination and database management. WP and ACT! required. Writing and design skills a definite plus. Excellent entry position with advancement potential. Degree preferred. Fax resume 518-555-9900.

MARKETING DIRECTOR

West Coast Gourmet Coffee purveyor with chain of trendy coffee bars and catalog mail order service conducting a search for a savvy, proven marketing director to position our company for success along the Northeast Corridor—Maine to Florida. This is a start-up opportunity integrating West Coast marketing resources with your own team development. Your resume must demonstrate extensive knowledge of the gourmet food industry, proven market development and penetration skills and fast track results. If you think you can place our name on the public's palette in six months—you're the key player we're looking for. Forward resume in confidence to Dept. G, The Daily Hemisphere, P.O. Box 780, 99 Planet Drive, Portland, OR 97201

Medical Receptionist/Secretary

Full time medical receptionist/secretary sought for busy four physician office in Troy. Knowledge of managed care procedures, familiarity with national and local medical plans, computer billing using Medi-Bill 3.1, appointment scheduling, and diplomatic. caring attitude all necessary. References required. Salary negotiable dependent upon experience. Benefits. Equal Opportunity Employer. Send resume to 45 East Main Street, Troy, NY 12180.

NURSING SUPERVISOR Psychiatric Home Care

Home care organization seeks Master's prepared psychiatric nurse with seven years acute experience and a minimum of two years home care experience. Demonstrated management skills required to schedule and oversee activities of ten visiting nurses and associated staff. Must have excellent communication and organizational abilities. Full benefits package. Send resume in confidence to HCS, Department PY, Code 3456, P.O. Box 78, Omaha. NB 68112.

SUNDAY CLASSIFIEDS GET RESULTS!

More regional companies, large and small rely on the Sunday Sphere Classifieds to attract the top candidates for their job openings than any other search vehicle. Searching for the right applicant? Have your query in by Wednesday.

QUESTIONS AND ANSWERS ABOUT HIRING

No matter what size your business, you will probably be making a hiring decision at some point during the year. Although you naturally must focus on and pay attention to the details of running your business on a daily basis, hiring top performers takes time and energy that, if well invested, will pay big dividends in the future.

If you own a small business, remember that hiring even one superproductive employee a year can have a big impact on how your company grows and develops. The time spent finding and hiring that employee can pay off in new ideas, increased productivity, and other significant contributions that will positively influence your company's growth for several years.

LETTERS

Depending upon where you are in the hiring process, you will need to contact your candidates either by phone or, in most cases, by mail. The letters in this section cover everything from responding to a potential candidate's inquiry about job openings, to a job offer letter. Remember that in some cases these letters are going to job applicants who have had no previous contact with the company, so the language in these letters reflects a polite but concise style that avoids any misleading inferences about possible employment.

XYZ Corporation • 345 Sidewinder Place • Suite 431 • Boise, Idaho, 87554

January 4, 1997

Mr. John Smith
123 Anywhere Lane
Boise, Idaho, 87554

Dear Mr. Smith:

We hereby extend to you an offer of full-time employment as a Senior Project Manager here at the XYZ Corporation. Your first date of employment will be February 1.

Your compensation will be $2,543.67 payable every two weeks in arrears. Paychecks are distributed on alternate Thursdays for the two-week period ending on the preceding Sunday.

Your first salary review will take place on January 1, 19xx. Pay increases are based on merit as well as on the financial situation of the company at the time of the performance review.

The first ninety days of your employment will be regarded as an initial employment period. After successful completion of this period, you will be eligible for sick days, which accrue at the rate of 1 half day per month.

The company offers medical insurance, group life insurance, short- and long-term disability, as well as two weeks paid vacation per year. You will be eligible for the company's 401k plan and bonus plan after you complete your initial period of employment.

Please sign and return this agreement. This offer will remain in force for a period not to exceed fourteen days.

John Smith
John Smith

Jane Jones
Jane Jones
Human Resources Manager

Rejection Letter

Rejection Letter, Without an Interview

XYZ Corporation • 345 Sidewinder Place • Suite 431 • Boise, Idaho, 87554

January 4, 1997

Ms. Jane Smith
345 Holly Lane
Anywhere, USA

Dear Jane:

Thank you very much for your interest and application to XYZ Corporation for the position of Account Manager.

After carefully reviewing your credentials, we are unable to find a suitable match between your background and experience and openings at our company.

We wish you luck in your search and, again, thank you for your interest in XYZ Corporation.

Regards,

John Doe

John Doe
Human Resources Manager

Rejection Letter, After an Interview

XYZ Corporation • 345 Sidewinder Place • Suite 431 • Boise, Idaho, 87554

January 4, 1997

Ms. Jane Smith
345 Holly Lane
Anywhere, USA

Dear Jane:

Thank you very much for your interest and application to XYZ Corporation for the position of Account Manager.

Although your background and credentials are impressive, we have decided to pursue another direction and therefore cannot offer you employment at this time. We will keep your resume in our active file for a period of one year.

Thank you again for your interest in XYZ Corporation.

Sincerely,

John Doe

John Doe
Human Resources Manager

Resume Received

Resume Received, No Openings

XYZ Corporation • 345 Sidewinder Place • Suite 431 • Boise, Idaho, 87554

January 4, 1997

Mr. Chris Smith
123 Hollybrook Lane
Anywhere, USA

Dear Mr. Smith:

Thank you for forwarding your resume and your interest in XYZ Corporation.

At this time we have no openings that match your background and experience, but we will keep your resume in our active file for a period of one year and contact you should a position open up that is a suitable match for your qualifications.

Again, thank you for your interest in XYZ Corporation.

Regards,

John Doe

John Doe
Human Resources Manager

Resume Received, Will Be Considered

XYZ Corporation • 345 Sidewinder Place • Suite 431 • Boise, Idaho, 87554

January 4, 1997

Mr. Chris Smith
123 Hollybrook Lane
Anywhere, USA

Dear Mr. Smith:

Thank you for submitting your resume to XYZ Corporation.

We are currently reviewing your resume to see if there is a match between your background and our current openings. If a suitable match is found, we will contact you as soon as possible.

Again, thank you for your interest in XYZ Corporation.

Regards,

John Doe

John Doe
Human Resources Manager

ACCOUNTING MANAGER

Growing auto repair shop seeking top-flight Accountant with aggressive, hands-on accounting management skills including AP/AR. Knowledge of auto repair industry and Quick-books a +. Fax resume and salary requirements to 508

Accountant: Accounts Receivable

National automobile rental agency seeks organized, detail-oriented entry level individual to coordinate accounting for credit card transactions and associated receivables related to business in its busy Hartford aeroplex office. Motivated individual with demonstrated ability to juggle multi-tasks must have BA in accounting. Interested applicants are invited to submit resumes to Car-4-A-Day, 120 Airport Way, West Hartford, CT 06107.

BANK TELLERS

IMMEDIATE OPENINGS!

Immediate openings in all branches of AtlantaBank for experienced Bank Tellers. Growth potential. for the motivated. Fax resume to Business Resources at 404-555-6778.

BOOKKEEPING/ ACCOUNTING

Small medical office requires the services of savvy bookkeeping/ accounting professional to oversee financial responsibilities for two busy family practice physicians. Experienced required in receivables, payables, bill collections. 5+ years experience necessary with medical office background a definite +. Qualified applicants should fax resume and salary requirements to 514-555-3467.

Computer Technician

Chicago's largest electronic imaging service bureau is expanding rapidly with new branches opening in seven metro locations. Full-time experienced graphics output wiz with hands-on laser printer, digital printer, Iris Imaging, flatbed and drum scanning, Linotronic, Macintosh, and PC troubleshooting capabilities sought immediately to travel locations as required to keep us up and running and number one. Fax resume to 312-555-9999.

CUSTOMER SERVICE REPRESENTATIVE

Residential Interior Decorator pursuing creative individual with an avid interest in home decor to assist interior designers in servicing clientele. A background in design or demonstrated applied arts skills required. If you are also energetic, intuitive, wild about color and texture, eager to learn the trade, and flow with the trends, send us your resume today. TrendSetter Interiors, P.O. Box 950, Miami, FL 03111.

Electrical Engineer

Westerlund Ambitronics is searching for an electrical engineer with ten+ years in the home lighting system design and installation field. Excellent communication skills required to work closely with owners, architects and building contractors. management and marketing skills a definite plus. Excellent salary, company car and great benefits package. Please forward resume and salary expectations to N.K. Westerlund, Westerlund Ambitronics, 151 Razor Back Road, Rutland, Vermont 05701.

EVENT DIRECTOR

Centre Dome North desperately seeking a energetic, organized, multi-talented events coordinator to oversee planning and execution of sports, convention, trade show, fund-raising, and other events held at the dome. Must be able to prepare and target budgets, source and contract vendors, and manage time schedules. Outgoing, diplomatic personality required for close work with clients. Ten years experience corporate or facility events planning experience a must. Business background or education a +. Fax or send resume and salary requirements to Human Resources, Dept. C, Centre Dome North, 1045 Highland Street, Redlands, CA 00000, Fax: 804-555-5566. Equal Opportunity Employer

Field Recruiter

Fast paced personnel placement agency seeks well organized, charismatic communicator with strong networking skills to recruit and place professionals in high level positions at prestigious firms. Travel required. Fax resume to 617-555-8989.

Graphic Designer

Highly creative graphic designer sought to develop business communication, presentation, internet presence, and direct mail pieces for American Crafter's Catalogue Company..We represent internationally recognized artisans and require collateral and multimedia materials that reflect elegance and quality. The ideal candidate will be skilled in QuarkXpress, Director, Photoshop and Illustrator. He or she will have a minimum of five years retail/direct marketing design experience; will be capable of producing CD-ROM and Web Site graphics. If your portfolio is exceptional, your attitude dedicated, your imagination beyond limits—send three non-returnable samples, your resume and salary requirements to ACCC, P.O. Box 45, Charlotte, NC 28201. All submittals will be acknowledged. ACCC is an equal opportunity employer.

IMPORT CLERK

International freight forwarder has immediate opening for Ocean Import Clerk. One year experience required. Full time position with excellent benefits. EOE. Please call 212-555-5656 for appointment.

Legal Secretary

Part time legal secretary sought for busy law firm. Flexible hours—mother's, evenings, weekends OK with potential for full time in the future. Excellent Word Perfect 5.2 skills and experience required. Fax resume to 617-555-8900. EOE. .

LEGAL SECRETARY

Experienced legal secretary sought by Waltham firm. Top pay for top skills and credentials. Mr. Walters 617-555-9350..

Marketing Coordinator

Leading construction management company seeking organized, motivated individual with excellent administrative, interpersonal and communication skills to support marketing management team. Work includes PR implementation, media contact, event and presentation coordination and database management. WP and ACT! required. Writing and design skills a definite plus. Excellent entry position with advancement potential. Degree preferred. Fax resume 518-555-9900.

MARKETING DIRECTOR

West Coast Gourmet Coffee purveyor with chain of trendy coffee bars and catalog mail order service conducting a search for a savvy, proven marketing director to position our company for success along the Northeast Corridor—Maine to Florida. This is a start-up opportunity integrating West Coast marketing resources with your own team development. Your resume must demonstrate extensive knowledge of the gourmet food industry, proven market development and penetration skills and fast track results. If you think you can place our name on the public's palette in six months—you're the key player we're looking for. Forward resume in confidence to Dept. G, The Daily Hemisphere, P.O. Box 780, 99 Planet Drive, Portland, OR 97201

Medical Receptionist/Secretary

Full time medical receptionist/secretary sought for busy four physician office in Troy. Knowledge of managed care procedures, familiarity with national and local medical plans, computer billing using Medi-Bill 3.1, appointment scheduling, and diplomatic, caring attitude all necessary. References required. Salary negotiable dependent upon experience. Benefits. Equal Opportunity Employer. Send resume to 45 East Main Street, Troy, NY 12180.

NURSING SUPERVISOR Psychiatric Home Care

Home care organization seeks Master's prepared psychiatric nurse with seven years acute experience and a minimum of two years home care experience. Demonstrated management skills required to schedule and oversee activities of ten visiting nurses and associated staff. Must have excellent communication and organizational abilities. Full benefits package. Send resume in confidence to HCS, Department PY, Code 3456, P.O. Box 78, Omaha, NB 68112.

SUNDAY CLASSIFIEDS GET RESULTS!

More regional companies, large and small rely on the Sunday Sphere Classifieds to attract the top candidates for their job openings than any other search vehicle. Searching for the right applicant? Have your query in by Wednesday.

QUESTIONS AND ANSWERS ABOUT HIRING

9

No matter what size your business, you will probably be making a hiring decision at some point during the year. Although you naturally must focus on and pay attention to the details of running your business on a daily basis, hiring top performers takes time and energy that, if well invested, will pay big dividends in the future.

If you own a small business, remember that hiring even one superproductive employee a year can have a big impact on how your company grows and develops. The time spent finding and hiring that employee can pay off in new ideas, increased productivity, and other significant contributions that will positively influence your company's growth for several years.

Questions and Answers about Hiring

How much do hiring policies differ from one company to the next?

Dramatically! Whether or not you have previous hiring experience, you need to familiarize yourself with and follow the hiring policies of your current employer. Even at similarly sized firms within the same industry, hiring policies often differ dramatically. In fact, hiring policies sometimes differ even among subsidiaries or divisions of the same firm. Although you may want to adopt the hiring practices that you have learned are effective elsewhere, every firm needs to have consistent hiring practices to be fair and to minimize potential legal problems.

How do you know when you have hired the _right person_?

There is never any one right person for a position. Instead, there are a number of people, almost always many people, who could perform the position

satisfactorily. Your job in the hiring process is to quickly rule out candidates who could not perform the job in a satisfactory manner and then try to determine who is the strongest candidate of the remaining applicants.

How hard is it to master the hiring process?

Learning the basics such as the fundamental legal issues, how to attract quality candidates, and how to make the initial sort of qualified versus unqualified candidates will take little time. And once you have filled a half dozen positions, you should feel fairly comfortable with the process. But hiring is more of an art than a science, and the more people you hire the better you will get at the process.

What success rate should a good hiring manager expect?

Anyone who has a perfect hiring record hasn't hired a lot of people. Even the

best hiring managers make mistakes. But a good hiring manager will hire only a very small percentage of people who don't work out, whereas a weak hiring manager could hire a much larger percentage of people who don't work out. The difficulty of the hiring process underscores why you need to devote a lot of energy and time toward hiring the best candidate.

How much should I rely on intuition versus facts?

Try to stick to the facts, but don't completely discount your intuition. Try to clarify and articulate with everyone involved in the hiring process the key issues of filling a particular position and also the major concerns about or benefits of each candidate. Sometimes you might have only a vague feeling that a particular candidate is stronger or weaker in a certain aspect of the position. You should not ignore your intuition, but do be careful that your intuition does not lead you to reject people just because they are not like you. Discriminatory hiring decisions, even unconscious ones, can land you in court, so do be careful.

Any special issues concerning hiring from within the organization?

While most company's have proactive policies on promoting from within, hiring from within can be like walking in a minefield, especially when you have more than one internal applicant. You need to be extremely careful in evaluating even marginally qualified internal candidates. You also need to go out of your way to extend them every courtesy during the interview process, while at the same time being careful not to raise their hopes of landing the position until it has actually been offered. Also, any internal candidate who is not offered the position should be given this news in person, ideally in a private meeting with either the hiring manager or their super-

visor. Check your company's policy on this procedure.

Should I pay significantly more than allocated for a top candidate?

No. You should decide how much you are going to pay for a position before you start talking with candidates, and then stick with it. Don't pay a candidate a lot more than you allocated because they appear to be extremely talented. Often, less experienced hiring managers decide to pay more than was allocated to candidates with a huge amount of experience. Don't woo overqualified candidates with huge salaries. Apart from spending more money, you run the risk of your new hire finding the position less than challenging and leaving for a more appropriate position at another firm.

When should I bring up salary?

For hourly positions and for and entry-level professional

positions, you should state the salary in the help-wanted ad. However, even if the salary is stated in the ad, you need to be sure to review it again with each candidate before you have them in for an interview. A lot of people respond to help-wanted ads without considering the salary at first. They may also assume that the stated salary is only a starting point for negotiations.

Even for the most senior positions, try to discuss salary in the very first phone call. Try to get an idea of the salary range they are seeking. Don't volunteer information about the salary range yourself. Too often, a candidate says that a salary range is fine, but then later turns down the job because the salary range was not fine, and they had incorrectly assumed that once they were actually offered a position they could negotiate the salary upward.

A lot of candidates will tell you that they will only discuss salary in a face-to-face interview. If this happens, state that your company policy requires you to get an indication of their salary range before you have them in for an interview. If the candidate is still hesitant about discussing money, you might as well move on to the next candidate.

How do I negotiate benefits?

Don't negotiate benefits. If you really want to start making exceptions for a particularly strong candidate, pay them more than you had planned before creating a special benefit package for them. One of the quickest way to create animosity among your employees is to give a new hire a better benefit package.

What's the best way to tell if the candidate can handle the job?

There is nothing like the real thing! The best way is to hire the person first for a fixed period of time. This is one reason why larger companies hire students during vacation periods. But this option is often not realistic for most positions or when you need to hire someone immediately.

For many positions, you should offer tests or scenarios that duplicate as closely as possible the actual work the person will be doing. If the candidate will be doing data entry in accounting, consider testing them on a data entry machine for an hour. If the candidate will be doing editing, give them a poorly written passage to edit. If the candidate will be selling, role-play with them, with you in the role of the customer and the candidate trying to sell you goods or a service. If they are applying for a management position, ask them what decisions they would make in hypothetical situations.

Should I hire someone who has been fired?

First, try to ascertain if they were fired (or forced to resign) because of their personal performance, or if they were laid off because of a company-wide downsizing.

If the candidate was fired because of their performance, try to determine the likelihood of any problems reoccurring if you were to hire them. However, companies are much quicker to fire people today, despite additional legal considerations, than they were some years ago, so don't rule out a candidate simply because they were fired.

On the other hand, if you have to choose between two candidates with roughly similar qualifications, and one was fired from their last position and the other wasn't, you should probably go with the one who was not fired. It is often difficult to get the real reasons why someone is fired. Previous managers are reluctant to divulge information, especially negative information. And often even the job candidate doesn't even comprehend exactly why they were fired. One reason for this is that many people find it difficult to admit to even themselves that their performance was unsatisfactory. Sometime people who have been fired explain to others that the firing was due to a personality conflict, when in fact the only personality conflict was over a very different opinion about the employee's performance: the employee's opinion and the supervisor's opinion.

How can I get references talking?

If you call a reference and simply ask an open-ended question like "tell me about their performance," you will probably get a short answer that doesn't tell you much. Instead, ask a bunch of leading questions zeroing in on the specific concerns you have about a candidate. For example: "Joe seems to have good technical skills, but I'm a little concerned about his lack of management experience. How well did he motivate the two people who reported to him at your firm?"

A more general question that is often effective in getting people to open up is "If we were to hire Joe, what advice would you give us to help him succeed in his next position?"

How can I weigh such discrete issues as experience versus "fit"?

These are issues that need to be considered separately for each company and for each position. For example, if the norm at your firm is to work seventy-hour weeks and the norm at most other firms in the industry is forty-hour weeks, then a candidate's willingness to work longer hours is major issue. On the other hand, if the corporate culture of your firm is highly similar to most others in your industry and you are seeking a highly technical person, then experience may be more of an issue. In short, you need to know what the most important dimensions of comparing candidates are likely to be before you run that first help-wanted ad.

Should I be concerned if a candidate is late for the job interview?

It is amazing how many people are late to job interviews. A lot of people simply underestimate how long it will takes them to get to a new address. If a job candidate is a few minutes late to a first interview, make a note of it, but don't attach too much significance to the fact. However, if a candidate is late to subsequent interviews, you should be more concerned. Not only might the candidate might have a tardiness problem, but they might very well be a difficult employee to manage as well.

Do I need to pay travel expenses for an out-of-town job candidate?

In a word: yes. If you request an employee to come in for an interview from beyond a commutable distance, the candidate may very well assume that you are going to pick up travel costs. It is proper business etiquette to do so.

Questions and Answers about Hiring

If you have not budgeted funds for interview expenses you need to make this very clear to the candidate, preferably in writing. Sometimes creative job candidates will arrange to have one or more employers in a distant city split the costs of traveling for interviews.

What can I do when a candidate gives an evasive answer?

You want to avoid being at all confrontational, because then the candidate will become even more guarded in his or her responses. Instead, restate the question, inferring that you may not have clearly stated your question. For instance you could say, "Very interesting, but what I really meant to ask was why did you change jobs last year?" If you still don't get the type of response you are looking for, you could even offer sample answers yourself. For example: "Did you receive an offer you just couldn't refuse? Were you fired? Tell me what happened."

How can I get candidates to give longer, more insightful answers?

To get a candidate to open up, you need to make them feel relaxed and confident right at the beginning of the interview. Before the interview begins, engage in some small talk, answer any questions they may have, and begin the interview with some easy questions. Then try to begin your questions with phrases such as "Tell me about your last job," rather than "Did you like your last job?" Also ask follow-up questions, such as, "Tell me more about some of things you liked and disliked about your last job."

Should I cut off responses that are too long-winded?

Yes, but do so carefully so as not to offend the applicant. You need to stay in control of the interview and cover all the issues and concerns on your agenda. Signal to the applicant that you're ready to ask the next question with positive phrases like, "Fine, I understand what you're saying. Now let me ask you..."

Should I rule out a candidate who is very negative about a previous boss?

Many applicants have read the books on job interviewing that instruct them not to say anything negative about former supervisors. However, don't rule out the occasional candidate who does say negative things. Just proceed cautiously. Is this a candidate with an honest gripe or are they likely to resent anyone who manages them? Ideally, if you have a likely candidate who has negative things to say about a previous supervisor, try to substantiate the negative information. At other points during the interview, try to get his or her opinion of former other supervisors. If he or she has extremely negative things to say about more than one boss, then you should be much more concerned.

How much time should I spend talking during the interview?

As much as possible, you want the candidate to do the talking! But you do need to talk enough to make the candidate feel comfortable, to stay in control of the direction of the interview, and to make the interview flow smoothly. As a ballpark percentage, you might want to talk 25 percent of the time, and listen to the applicant the rest of the time.

Should I carefully prepare for an interview, or just wing it?

No matter how experienced an interviewer you are, you should always carefully prepare for each interview. For every position you need to determine what the crucial skills are for the position, and what skills are not crucial but would be nice for

an applicant to possess. You also have to prepare for each interview with each applicant for the position. After studying his or her resume and cover letter, or perhaps notes from a previous interview, determine what potential weaknesses or strengths of this candidate you want to further explore.

Should I take notes during an interview?

You need to take some brief notes during the interview, or you'll find it difficult to remember the exact nature of the candidate's response on crucial issues. But if you busily take notes throughout the entire interview, you run the risk of the candidate becoming more guarded in his or her responses. Keeping a list of questions, with space below each questions you plan on asking handy can help you take notes in half the time, because you don't have to write out each question.

How can I tell if the candidate will behave on the job the same way they behave during the interview?

It's impossible to tell for sure, but here are some ways to help you find out. First you should check every reference you can. Also, try to have the candidate back for follow-up interviews. Candidates often act much more naturally during second and third interviews. You might also try to get another manager's opinion. Sometimes it is useful for another manager to ask similar questions and to compare the consistency of the candidate's responses.

How much time should I allocate for an interview?

Even if you immediately decide not to hire a candidate, you owe them the courtesy of a full-length interview lasting at least thirty minutes. One hour is a good length for a first interview when you feel more positive about the candidate. Second interviews are often even longer. At the second interview stage, you may schedule multiple managers to interview a candidate. If you expect any interview to last two hours or longer, it is only courteous to let the candidate know in advance, both so they can plan their schedule and so they will be mentally ready for a longer session.

Suppose the candidate is not dressed appropriately for the interview?

Appropriate dress is less important when you are seeing applicants for entry-level professional or for nonprofessional positions. Simply tell these candidates to dress more appropriately for the next round of interviewing. Do not, however, discount sloppiness in dress, and expect experienced professional applicants to dress appropriately for all interviews.

How much should I weight the interview versus the resume?

Assuming that the candidate has the basic skills to perform the position, you should put more weight on the interview. Pay particular attention to the candidate's attitude about their job. Do they really seem like they are going to give their work their all? Do they have a positive attitude? Also, you need to be sure that the candidate will be a "good fit" with your organization. A recent survey showed that being a "good fit" for the job is increasingly a top concern of corporate recruiters.

Should I tell a candidate at the end of the interview how well the interview went?

No. Do not signal to the candidate in any way how well you feel the interview went. If you tell the candidate the interview went poorly, you put yourself in a very awkward and potentially volatile situation. If you

say the interview went well, you increase your chances of being hit with a discrimination suit if you don't make an offer to the candidate. You could respond by saying something like, "You are one of several candidates that we are interviewing for this position. I'll be in touch with you shortly."

How leery should I be of hiring a manager who worked for an industry laggard?

Unless you're filling a CEO slot, the relative overall success of the applicant's past company isn't going to be a strong indicator of how well they are going to perform for you.

In large corporations in particular, very few managers are going to be in a position to influence the overall direction of the company they worked for. Furthermore, in any large organization some divisions or individual departments may have been less successfully or better managed than others.

Also available as a software product!

Microsoft Windows 95   **CD-ROM**   **3.5" DISK**

Designed for Windows®3.1 and Windows®95

Prepare your interview in minutes!

Choose from over 600 questions to quickly create a customized job interview for any professional opening, at any level, in any industry. Then print out the interview questions along with advice on what to look for in each answer.

Choose from questions that will probe the job applicant's motivation, job fit, accomplishments, personality, management style, skills, creativity, career goals, personal interests, and problem-solving ability. Plus there are questions for special situations, including changing careers, frequent job changes, single-company career, layoffs, and returning to the work force. In addition, there are hundreds of questions for specific careers.

You can also use the 25 workshops to help you find the best people. With over hundreds of multimedia clips, the workshops show you how to increase your pool of qualified applicants, conduct effective phone interviews, check references, sell your top applicants on the job, negotiate salary and benefits, and much more! You can also sharpen you interview skills by knowing what to look for in each answer and how to develop an interview strategy.

Hiring Top Performers also includes AdBuilder™ which creates your classified ad in minutes. Just select the type of ad you want (newspaper or online), choose among pre-written phrases, fill in the blanks, print your ad, and you're done!

SPECIFICATIONS

CD-ROM (Multimedia) Version: Double-speed or higher CD-ROM drive
3.5" Disk (Lite) Version: 3.5" disk drive

Windows: Windows 3.1 or higher, Windows NT, or Windows 95
● 386 PC (486 or Pentium recommended) ●
Sound Blaster or compatible audio ● 4 MB RAM (8
recommended) ● 5 MB free hard disk space

Also available at software retailers nationwide:

How to order: If you cannot find this software at your favorite retail outlet, you may order it directly from the publisher. Call for price information. BY PHONE: Call 1-800-872-5627 (in Massachusetts 781-767-8100). We accept Visa, Mastercard, and American Express. $5.95 will be added to your total order for shipping and handling. BY MAIL: Write out the full title of the software you'd like to order and send payment, including $5.95 for shipping and handling to: Adams Media Corporation, 260 Center Street, Holbrook, MA 02343. 30-day money-back guarantee.

Visit our exciting job and career site at http://www.careercity.com

ABOUT THE AUTHORS

Peter Veruki is Director of Career Planning and Placement at the Owen Graduate School of Management, Vanderbilt University. In addition to serving on the College Placement Council Board of Governors for six years, Mr. Veruki was chairman of CPC's Professional Training and Development Committee, where he helped design and conduct interview training programs. He has held senior level posts in corporate human resources with Chemical Bank and Bethlehem Steel Corporation. He holds a B.S. from Lafayette College and an MBA from Lehigh University.

Bob Adams has started and operated many small businesses—some successful and some not so successful. Throughout his career he has had many opportunities to make hiring decisions and those decisions have impacted his success. He is currently president of Adams Media Corporation, a $10 million a year enterprise. Mr. Adams is a 1980 graduate of the Harvard Business School, where he received first-year honors. He earned his B.A. from Carleton College and his streetwise training in the real world of business and "the school of hard knocks."